HANDBOOK OF QUALITATIVE RESEARCH METHODS ON HUMAN RESOURCE MANAGEMENT

HANDBOOK OF QUALITATIVE RESEARCH METHODS ON HUMAN RESOURCE MANAGEMENT

Editor

Vonda Minett

Socialy
PRESS
AN IMPRINT OF SCITUS ACADEMICS

Handbook of Qualitative Research Methods on Human Resource Management

Edited by **Vonda Minett**

This Book is Printed on Acid-Free Paper. ♾

ISBN: 978-1-68117-739-7

Library of Congress Control Number: 2017938597

Socialy Press

(An Imprint of Scitus Academics),

616, Corporate Way, Suite 2, 4766,

Valley Cottage, NY 10989

www.scitusacademics.com

Notice

Printed in United States of America.

Preface

The importance of human resources has received much attention in recent years. At a macro level, endogenous growth theories suggest that the accumulation of human capital constitutes the main engine of macro-economic growth. At a micro level, resource-based theory points to the human capital of employees as a major source for sustained competitive advantage for individual firms. As a result of the increasing importance of human capital, which to a large extent is related to developments in information and communication technologies. During the last decade, the focus of HRM research has shifted from conceptual studies about the nature of HRM to studies that examine the impact of HRM on organizational performance. In this context, human resources are the most important asset of statistical offices. Appropriate and skilled human resources are essential to ensure the production of high quality statistics and to implement more efficient and effective production processes based on new technologies. Proactive human resources management is essential to achieve the abovementioned change and to allow firms to meet the challenges today and in future. Early approach to research in industrial and organizational (I/O) psychology was oriented towards quantitative techniques as a result of influences from the social sciences. As the focus of I/O psychology expands from psychological test development to other personnel functions, there has been an inclusion of qualitative methods in I/O psychology practice.

The present compilation, Handbook of Research Methods in Human Resource Management, therefore examines how qualitative methods like observation, interviews, ethnography, focus group discussion, nominal group technique, Delphi method, and projective techniques can be used in human resources studies. It is believed that knowledge gained on the applications of these qualitative methods would enhance understanding of workers' behaviors in organizations and facilitate management decisions. Empirical studies are also presented, on how these qualitative methods have successfully been used in organizations.

This Handbook is intended to provide a practical information to managers and policy makers, to enable them to recognise and initiate measures that will make the workplace experience a more pleasant one for workers, and so weaken employees' intent to leave.

Table of Contents

1

CHAPTER

A Qualitative Investigation of the Human Resources Management Practices in Small Businesses

Christopher Collins[1], Jeff Ericksen, Matthew Allen

Cornell University

ABSTRACT

This report provides a summary of our findings from the first phase of our study on human resource practices in small businesses based on qualitative interviews with top managers and owners of small businesses. Below we include a brief description of the sample and an explanation of the hurdle that we experienced when using the terms human resource management practices. On the following pages, we report the main findings of the qualitative phase of our study. The findings are organized into three main sections around the areas of management philosophies, employee management practices, and key employee outcomes that link management practices to firm performance. The overall findings from this first report are summarized in a research model depicted in Figure 1. Funding for this research was provided by the Center for Advanced Human Resource Studies at Cornell University and Gevity, is a provider of comprehensive human capital management solutions to small and medium-sized businesses.

Keywords qualitative investigation, business, practice, human, management, manager, owner, company, employee

SECTION I: OVERVIEW OF THE SAMPLE FOR THE QUALITATIVE STUDY

The Cornell research team completed a total of 54 interviews conducted with small business owners and managers based on a list of contacts provided by Gevity. Of this total, 39 of the interviews were conducted with a contact other than the owner or top manager of the company and 15 of the interviews were conducted with the owner or top manager of the company. Interviews with non-owner contacts were used to collect information regarding the employee management practices of the company and to get a sense of the business conditions and important employee outcomes that affect the performance of the company. Interviews with the owners were used to collect information regarding management philosophies, business conditions, and employee outcomes that affect the performance of the firm. Interviews lasted from 10-25 minutes, were conducted by phone, and were based on questions from a general interview protocol (see attached protocol document – Appendix A).

Problem Using the Terms Human Resource Management Practices

We began this phase of the study by trying to understand the extent to which small businesses were implementing specific types of human resource practices and systems of practices. We found early on through our interviews that the contacts were not extremely familiar with many HR terms. In fact, most of the contacts did not feel comfortable talking about HR practices as they were not sure what if any HR practices their company used. With a good deal of prompting and explanation, our research team found that most of the companies did use HR practices, but the HR practice label was not how they would describe the practices that they had in place. We found that the contacts were more comfortable when we described these practices as how they managed their people. Therefore, we turned from exploring HR practices to trying to understand how these small companies managed employees and people issues.

After changing our protocol to prompt contacts about managing employees, we were able to identify some broad trends across the small companies (see details in following section).

SECTION II: PHILOSOPHIES REGARDING MANAGING PEOPLE

Based on previous research and our interviews, we have identified several dimensions of management philosophy on which small businesses seem to differ. Our analysis of the qualitative interviews that we conducted confirmed the results of Baron and colleagues (Baron & Hannan, 2002; Baron, Hannan, & Burton, 1999; Baron, Hannan, & Burton, 2001). Although Baron and colleagues found five different philosophies, we found evidence for only three basic models/philosophies regarding how small companies manage their employees. Below we define and describe each of the three models that we found from our interviews.

1) Autocracy Model. In this model, the owner or top manager retains tight, hands-on control of most activities and operates as the sole visionary of the firm. This model is characterized by hiring and keeping only those employees that have the skills and abilities to successfully perform a specific job, motivating and retaining employees based strictly on money, and closely monitoring and controlling even the day-to-day activities of all employees.

2) High-commitment Model: In this model, the owner or top manager believes that employee and company performance is best when the company has created a family-like environment in which each employee feels highly valued and an important part of the company. This model is characterized by hiring employees based on their fit to the culture and values of the company, creating a team-oriented environment in which peers are asked to help and provide feedback to one another, and a high degree of investment in employees.

3) Professional Model: In this model, the owner or top manager believes that employees achieve their best performance when treated like professionals. This model is characterized by hiring and

retaining employees that have the skills and abilities to successfully perform a specific job, providing the employees with interesting work opportunities and the chance to develop new skills and knowledge, and providing a specific set of projects or tasks to work on but allowing the employees a large degree of discretion in how to complete those responsibilities.

SECTION III: HUMAN RESOURCE/EMPLOYEE MANAGEMENT PRACTICES

Based on previous research and our interviews, we have identified several dimensions of management philosophy on which small businesses seem to differ. The qualitative interviews confirmed that small businesses do think about and implement specific human resource practices to manage their organization and to guide the actions and behaviors of their employees. As with the management philosophies, our interview results mirrored the findings of Baron and colleagues (Baron & Hannan, 2002; Baron et al, 1999, 2001). There appear to be three recurring dimensions along which small businesses think about organizing and managing employees: (1) finding new employees, (2) retention, and (3) managing employee performance.

1. Finding New Employees describes the practices used by the company and its managers/owner regarding for recruiting and selecting employees to the company. Overall, companies appear to follow one of three generic approaches to staffing:

a) Ensure fit to current job – companies that follow this model primarily look to recruit and hire new employees based on their ability to perform the tasks and duties of the current opening and the ability of the applicants to perform at a high level from the start of employment. The screening/selection practices focus only on testing for the specific set of skills and knowledge necessary for the current job opening.

b) Ensure fit to company – companies that follow this model primarily seek to recruit and select new employees based on how well they will fit with others in the company and the culture of the organization. These companies tend to believe that individuals can be trained on specific job duties and they expect that the individuals hired will be able to grow into other roles than the current positions to which they were hired; therefore, tend to focus on recruiting from the same sources as they used for past hires and selection practices focus on testing for the attitudes, personality traits, values that are reflective of the company and its current employees.

c) Finding exceptional talent – companies that follow this model primarily seek to recruit and hire elite or exceptional individuals success of the organization. These companies look for individuals with great skills and knowledge based on the belief that these types of recruits will help to shape the future direction and competitive advantage of the company. These companies tend to recruit only from elite sources and focus their selection around testing for future potential. These companies may hire a really talented individual even if there is not a current need or opening to which the person fits. This set of practices tends to only be used in technology companies and professional service firms (law offices, consulting firms, etc.). that have long-term potential to affect the

2. Retention describes management practices that companies use to increase retention and employees commitment to the organization. Overall, companies appear to follow one of the three generic approaches to attachment:

a) Fair Compensation – companies that follow this model believe that the employee relationship is based on exchange of labor for money; therefore, they tend to focus primarily on compensation. These companies tend to be market leaders in base pay for employees and look to link bonuses, merit raises, and rewards to individual performance. These companies primarily use performance appraisals to determine merit raises.

b) Interesting and Rewarding Jobs – companies that follow this model believe that the best way to retain highly valuable employees is by providing employees with and environment that is challenging and helps them to grow and develop. These companies offer opportunities for employees to learn new skills through job rotation, training opportunities, internal promotions. Further, these companies structure the work to provide employees with new challenges. These companies use performance appraisals as a way to help employees identify areas for future skill/knowledge development.

c) Creating a Family-like Community – companies that follow this model believe that the best way to increase the chances of retaining highly valuable employees by creating a family-like feeling and strong emotional bond. These companies focus on building a strong sense of community in which employees feel like they are part of a family and would not want to leave the company because this is where all of their friends work. This type of atmosphere is built by openly sharing information with employees, having company-wide meetings, hosting social events and outside activities that bring employees together, and putting all new employees through a comprehensive orientation program.

3. Managing Employee Performance describes the philosophy held by management and owners regarding how to manage employees on a day to day basis to make sure that the employees complete their work at an acceptable level of quality. Companies appear to follow one of four general approaches to coordinating and controlling the performance of individual employees:

a) Direct monitoring – companies that follow this model believe that the only way to ensure that employees perform as expected is by continually monitoring their actions. Companies in this model tend to have a large ratio of managers and supervisors to employees, use technology to monitor employees, allow employees little discretion, and have managers and supervisors in close proximity to employees so that they can continually monitor employee actions.

b) Cultural and Peer Pressure – companies that follow this model believe that peer pressure will keep employees on task and working toward important outcomes, necessitates socializing employees so they understand what is important to the company. These companies encourage employees to provide feedback to one another, ask for co-worker input on employee performance appraisals, and design work based around teams.

c) Professional Standards – companies that follow this model believe that individuals are motivated to perform at high levels and do excellent work because of their professional socialization. These companies focus on hiring individuals that have been socialized to a profession, provide a high degree of discretion to employee judgment.

d) Processes, Rules, and Procedures – companies that follow this model believe that individuals will perform to expectations if the company clearly lays out expectations through formalized policies, rules, procedures, etc. Companies in this model have detailed job descriptions and explicit work rules for employees to follow, have detailed organizational charts so employees understand reporting lines, and have a formal process of performance appraisals and regularly scheduled meeting to provide performance feedback to employees.

SECTION IV: EMPLOYEE OUTCOMES THAT AFFECT FIRM PERFORMANCE

Based on our interviews with both the owner and the non-owner contacts, we identified an array of employee outcomes that may possibly mediate the relationships between the employee management practices and company performance. The data from the interviews suggested that managers and owners of small companies are aware of and can identify the employee outcomes that affect the ability of their company to compete and succeed in their marketplace. Further, a number of the interview participants suggested that they attempt to use management practices to shape and affect these employee outcomes; while 90% of the interview participants noted that they wish they better understood how to affect these employee outcomes. Overall, the interviews supported the notion that the extent to which the company has done a good job of choosing the employee management practices that are appropriate for their company (based on management philosophy, business strategy and conditions, size of the company, etc.) should positively affect these employee outcomes. In turn, these employee outcomes are likely to have strong, positive effects on the performance of the company. Below we briefly outline the employee outcomes that were identified by two or more of the interview participants.

(1) Commitment to the Company. Several of the interview participants noted that they actively attempt to increase the commitment of employees to the organization. Participants noted that when employees are more committed to the organization, then they are likely to stay with the company and to work harder in their job. Thus, there is a belief that higher commitment may lead to lower labor costs because employees with more tenure will be more productive as will employees who work harder. In effect, these companies might be able to accomplish the same amount work as other companies with fewer

employees, because their employees will be better able and more motivated to complete their tasks.

(2) Job Involvement. Many of the interview participants noted that they often had limited resources because they were either a fairly new company or because of the small size of their company. Their employees must be willing to go above and beyond the basic tasks and responsibilities of their jobs if these companies are going to successfully complete given the limitations of their resources. Job involvement is defined as the willingness of employees to exert extra effort that goes above and beyond the requirements of their job. Several of the participants noted that the survival of the firm was really dependent upon the willingness of employees to always exert extra effort, work longer than scheduled hours, and contribute beyond what might normally be expected of employees at other companies.

(3) Adaptability. Several of the interview participants noted that their companies face rapidly changing environments in terms of technology and customer needs; therefore, they needed a workforce that is able to adapt quickly to this changing environment. They noted that the most important factor in the success of their company is the ability and willingness of their employees to continue to learn new skills and knowledge and their willingness to take on new tasks and roles.

(4) Helping Behaviors. Several of the interview participants noted that they are either in an industry characterized by high turnover or the design of the workflow leads to uneven distribution of work. Managers at both types of companies noted that one key the success of their firm is employees' willingness to help one another. In the firms with high turnover, the helping behaviors often come in the form of the willingness of experienced employees to help and mentor new employees. In the firms with an uneven distribution of work, helping behaviors come in the form of employees with idle time helping employees who were swamped with more work than they could handle by themselves.

(5) Customer Orientation. Multiple interview participants noted that their key to success was providing a level of customer service or a service experience that was greater than that provided by competitors. These companies rely on their front line employees to deliver this high level of service every day to every customer. Therefore, the employees of these companies must have a high level of customer orientation if these firms are going to be able to continue to follow their strategy of differentiation based on customer service.

(6) Knowledge Sharing. Several professional service firms noted that one of the keys to success is the ability to share and disseminate best practice knowledge to all of their key employees. This distribution of knowledge allows these companies to always offer their clients the newest solutions or up-to-date information. These participants noted that professionals are not always willing to share their personal knowledge with one another; therefore, it is a priority of the top management to facilitate the exchange of knowledge and information between their key employees.

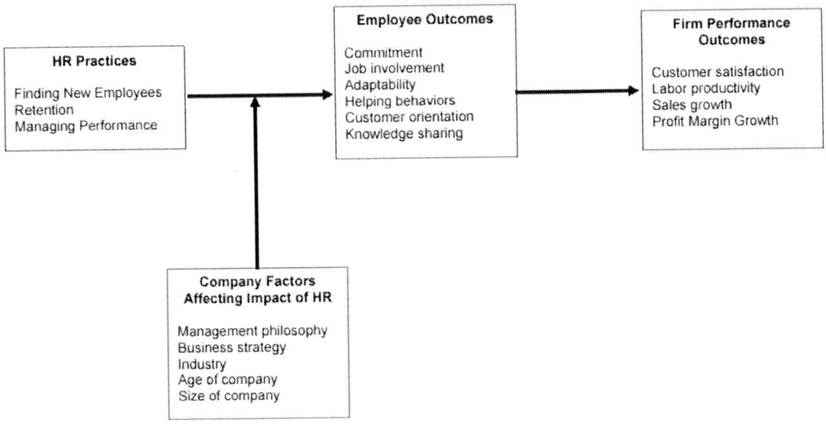

Figure 1: Model of HR and Performance In Small Companies

SECTION V: SUMMARY OF KEY FINDINGS

- Most of the contacts did not feel comfortable talking about HR practices, as they were not sure what if any HR practices their company used. Our research team found that most of the companies did use HR practices, but the HR practice label was not how they would describe the practices that they had in place. We found that the contacts were more comfortable when we described these practices as how they managed their people.
- We found evidence for only three basic models/philosophies regarding how small companies manage their employees: Autocracy; High-Commitment; Professional.

- There appear to be three recurring dimensions along which small businesses think about organizing and managing employees: (1) finding new employees, (2) retention, and (3) managing employee performance.
- The data from the interviews suggested that managers and owners of small companies are aware of and can identify the employee outcomes that affect the ability of their company to compete and succeed in their marketplace.
- Participants suggested that they attempt to use management practices to shape and affect these employee outcomes.
- 90% of the interview participants noted that they wish they better understood how to affect these employee outcomes.
- The interviews support the notion that the extent to which the company has done a good job of choosing the employee management practices that are appropriate for their company (based on management philosophy, business strategy and conditions, size of the company, etc.) should positively affect employee outcomes. In turn, these employee outcomes are likely to have strong, positive effects on the performance of the company.

Summary of the Alignment of Employee Management Practices and Management Philosophy

	Management Philosophy		
Employee Management Practices	**Autocracy**	**High-Commitment**	**Professional**
Finding Employees			
Ensure Fit to Job	X		
Ensure Fit to Company		X	
Locate Exceptional Talent			X
Retention			
Fair Compensation	X		
Interesting/Rewarding Job			X
Family Community		X	
Managing Performance			
Direct Oversight	X		
Cultural and Peer Pressure		X	
Professional Standards			X
Processes/Rules/Procedures			

REFERENCES

1. Baron, J. N. & Hannan, M. T. (2002) Organizational blueprints for success in high-tech startups: Lessons from the Stanford project on emerging companies. California Management Review, 44, 8-36.
2. Baron, J. N., Hannan, M. T., & Burton, M. D. (1999). Building the iron cage: Determinants of managerial intensity in the early years of organizations. American Sociological Review, 64, 527-547.
3. Baron, J. N., Hannan, M. T., & Burton, M. D. (2001). Labor pains: Change in organizational models and employee turnover in young, high-tech firms. The American Journal of Sociology, 106(4), 960-1012.

2

CHAPTER

The Research of Design of Human Resource Recruitment System Based on the Total Relationship Flow Management Theorems

Fangling Hu

School of Management, Jinan University, Guangzhou, China

ABSTRACT

With the development of knowledge economy, organizational strategic resource is more than the physical production such as capital, and it also includes the human resources characterized by skills, knowledge and intelligence. Recruitment as the first part of introducing talents, its quality directly influences the effect of introducing talents, more related to the long-term development of the enterprise. Therefore, building perfect recruitment system is not only an important part of the enterprise to get the resource, but also the key to support enterprise strategy implementation. Based on the total relationship flow management theory, this paper put forward suggestions to build an perfect recruitment system though designing the behaviors of the recruitment system, determining the appropriate relationship flow, and paying attention to time delay and system maintenance.

Keywords: Total relationship flow management theory, System designing, Recruitment system

1. INTRODUCTION

With the increased level of awareness of the importance of the talent, some companies are fully aware of the use of the recruitment and try their best to rely on the more professional, scientific management methods to optimize the recruitment process, and to improve the recruitment effect. Managers find that optimizing the recruitment system can not only increase the efficiency, better shape corporate image and then be able to attract more talent. However, we also find it difficult to ignore the problems in many enterprises, especially small and medium enterprises that exist in recruitment. For example, many enterprises follow the principle of "the best" rather than "optimal" in the selection process, so they are blind pursuit of highly educated and elite background. Some HR departments are lack of internal communication and coordination. These problems not only lead to recruiting costs rising and dissatisfied recruitment result, but also lead to decrease in the efficiency of the entire enterprise. In view of this, establishing a perfect recruitment system is not just the HR department's priority, but also an issue that concerns the entire organization.

2. LITERATURE REVIEW

Human resources as the most important strategic resource has attract scholars and business managers' attention. Some academic point the HR recruitment emerge, but the angles of these research are not the same. By studying literature I find two types of research about recruitment: section studies and systems research. Section research focuses on how to make the selection of talent, how to test the candidates on the list and which test methods we should use. As in 1960 the book "Career Decision" which is published by the American career guidance experts Hollander (John L. Holland) put forward the personality theory proposed career match. And domestic scholars Yongjiang Han (2007) proposed to use of analytic hierarchy process (AHP) to improve recruitment decisions [1] .

In 1940s, the famous biologist V. L. Bertalanffy founded the general systems theory which aims to study the common principles and rules that the variety of different systems obey in the different subject field [2] . Over half a century, the general systems theory has been a noticeable field. Accordingly, the human resource manage- ment system becomes more and more outstanding scholars' object. Based on systems theory, The Human Resource Management Human Resource Management is defined by Wright (1991) as the input, processing and output of the system. Xiaobing Zhang (2009) summarized the definition of human resource management system on the basis of previous research. He thought human resource management system have several common ground: 1) The activities, functions and processes that organizations use to attract, develop and maintain human resource; 2) These human resource management practices have consistent or complementary; 3) Organization through the implementation of the management practices achieve organizational goals. Recruitment system is an important part of human resource management system [3] .

According to these researches, we can regard the recruitment system means as that the organization attract, identify and recruit talents through certain plans, channels and programs. However, existing studies on the recruitment system are based on case studies or experience and don't have strong theoretical support. This paper attempts to make up for the deficiencies in the existing research under the guidance of the total relationship flow management theorems.

3. THE TOTAL RELATIONSHIP FLOW MANAGEMENT THEOREMS

Professor F. Lin proposed and developed a general systems theory: The structural theory of general systems, which are faced with problems in mathematical expression develops the general systems theory into precise theoretical content [4] . This theory is thought with the height to effectively to solve practical system problem.

The total relationship management theory is put forward by Professor Lin based of the structural theory of general systems. The theorem states that the behavior of complex systems only depend on the input relationship flow and relationship flow set $Rf_{Ord}(t)$ (the total relationship flow), especially the relationship cycle in the

system [5] . These relationships include information flow, energy flow, matter flow, fund flow, personal flow, etc. Therefore, in order to better understand and control the behavior of complex systems, we should understand and control the flow of their total relationship.

3.1. Concepts and Theorem

Relationship flow $R_{ij}(t)$ involves the action factor part e(i) one (j) at the time tin the system. Part e(i) have an

effect on the part of e(j) through the effect factor which makes a certain association between part of e(i) and e(j) just as the figure 1. From the definition of the relationship flow, we can derive the following equation:

$$f\left(s_i(t),\ R_{ij}(t),\ s_j(t)\right) = 0$$

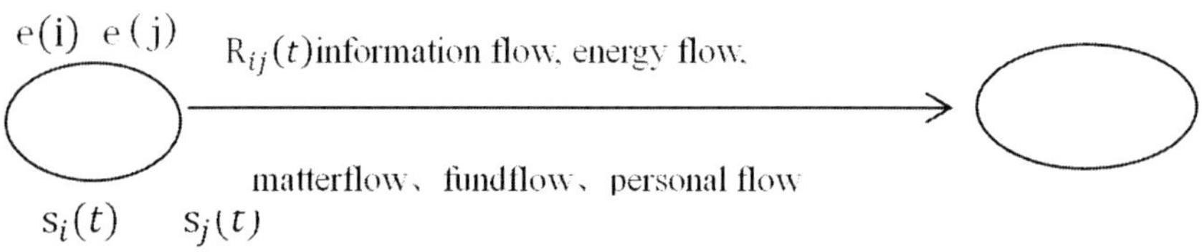

Figure 1. Relationship flow.

Theorem 1: Suppose that under the effect of the system environment, system Z(n) have m levels at the time t. Thus, the system input Rf(t), the system structure of adjacent level $R_Z(t)_C$ and $R_Z(t)_{C+1}$, C = 1, 2, ..., m – 1, and

the system behavior $H_Z(t)$ has the following relationship: $\psi\left(Rf(t),\ R_Z(t)_c,\ R_Z(t)_{c+1}\right) = 0$

Theorem 2: Suppose that under the effect of the system environment, relationship flow set $Rf_{Ord}(t)$ and the input flow's link which are at the basic level at time t can be denoted as:

$$\psi\left(Rf(t),\ Rf_{Ord}(t),\ H_{Or}(t)\right)=0$$

The Theorems 1 and 2 of the total relationship flow management theory illustrate that under the environment E(s), the organization's operating input flow Rf(t), relationship flow set $Rf_{Ord}(t)$ at the basic level and organizational behavior $H_{Or}(t)$ affect each other according to certain rules. For complex systems, its behavior only depend on the input relationship flow and relationship flow set $Rf_{Ord}(t)$. From these two theorems, we can clearly know that in a given environment the structure of the system determines the behavior of the system. And if you want to get content system behavior or function which the system designer expects, it must carefully design system's hierarchy and optimize the relationship flow.

3.2. The Total Relationship Flow Management Model

By the analysis of the above theorems, based on revealing inherent system—designing principles and logic, Professor F. Lin write the literature [6] describes how to build the total relationship flow management model, denoted as (TRFM): Firstly, define organizational behavior at time t$H_{Or}(t)$, and then determine relationship flow set $Rf_{Ord}(t)$ including the designing and implementation of relationship flow; finally delimit and find the relationship flow set Rf(t) under under the given $H_{Or}(t)$ and $Rf_{Ord}(t)$.

4. THE DESIGN OF RECRUITMENT SYSTEM

What is the relationship flow? According the total relationship flow management theory, the substance of relationship flow within the organization is cooperation and communication between the different positions. In HR recruitment system, we can understand the relationship flow as each recruitment activities' corresponding. It means that the recruitment system must be constructed to match the organization's strategic objectives in order to provide strong fresh blood for realizing organization's mission and vision. It also means the corresponding between all aspects of the recruitment process, so that the talents can match vacancies to meet human resource requirements and future needs of talent reserving. Based on the total relationship flow management model, how to build a human resource recruitment system should focus on the following aspects.

Firstly, define the expected behavior of recruitment system $H_{Or}(t)$. Recruitment starts from two basis fundamental work: human resource planning and job analysis. It is conducted by its purpose. Only to determine the number of vacancies and the quality which we need to recruit firstly will HR do better in the following process. The human resource planning is to ensure that organization gets the right people at the right time in the different positions (including personnel quality, quantity, structure and level). And job analysis refers to collect some post's comprehensive information. Job specification is the achievement of this work. Trying our best to do these two tasks is the foundation of recruitment, because they determine the expected behavior of recruitment.

Many companies employing department prefer candidates who have highly educated, elite background and famous enterprises experience to deliberately raise the threshold to beautify their image for employment sector or the company. The reason of these blindly selection is lack of job analysis and right employing concept. These conditions not only delay consequent of the recruitment and increase the turnover rate of talent, but also result in a waste of human resource. Based on the idea of the total relationship flow management theory, we must first clear expect behavior, so we should focus on human resource planning and job analysis firstly.

Secondly, determine the appropriate relationship flow set $Rf_{Ord}(t)$ and to ensure them smooth. Scientific enterprise recruitment process involves all the steps which we take in there cruitment activities. These steps are integrated with close contact. Every detail and every step is not to be ignored. If we do, the structure of the recruitment will be affected. The total relationship flow management theory point that the structure is the sum of all kinds of relations. More specifically, system structure is refers to information flow, energy flow, matter flow, fund flow, personal flow and the connection mechanism between the five flow. In the recruitment system, these flow acts as the role of the blood. Human resource planning and job analysis provide information flow and fund flow for channel selection and talent selection; channel selection provide personal flow for talent selection, etc. In order to ensure the system operate effectively, it is important to make sure that the flow is smooth and accuracy.

As shown in figure 1, the relationship flow from e(i) to e(j) can be information flow, energy flow, matter flow, fund flow, personal flow. But in fact, the information flow account for the most part of the total relationship flow in a recruitment system. However information flow in the process of access and the spread will appear some problem of information distortion and information asymmetry, for instance, the real number of absences and human resource planning statistics don't agree with each other. Thus, how to build perfect information flow is very important. But optimizing the information flow is not the whole. As is known to all, personnel flow is the information flow carrier. If only to optimize information flow and ignore the personnel flow, the system could not achieve the optimal structure. Therefore, in order to ensure information flow smooth, we still need to optimize the personnel flow configuration. In the entire recruitment process, it is not enough to rely on the power of the HR department alone. From the figure 2, we can know that there are relationships between the two adjacent level. So the participation of manager and supervisor from other department in which it has job vacancy is also necessary. The supervisor from department of job vacancies can accurately determine the specific demand for human resources and can assist HR department to do job analysis and give the appropriate comments and suggestions in the link of talent selection.

Realizing relationship flow requires a certain cost. These costs include the resources consumed, time and opportunities, capital investment, construction and deployment of hardware, personnel training, etc. For recruitment system, how to choose the way of fund flow must be considered. Today, Internet is so advanced that online recruitment by virtue of low cost, wide spread is preferred by HRs. But online recruitment is not a panacea and the recruitment of technicians and management staff is not obvious effective in this way. It shows that we must consider comprehensively.

Thirdly, pay attention to the time delay. The relationship flow $R_{ij}(t)$ from e(i) to e(j) usually requires a certain amount of time. This period of time is called delay time of $R_{ij}(t)$. Because of the existence of the delay time, the change of general relationship flow need some time. The time delay usually can have a significant impact for the organization behavior. To the recruitment system, how to control the time delay in the recruitment process is extremely important which is also a factor. When some enterprises especially large enterprises recruit managers, time interval between the adjacent two interviews is so long or the whole process lasts one month. Under this situation, many candidates can't accept such long time delay. Then they will choose to give up. So the time delay between factor in the recruitment system needs reasonable designed to make it within a certain range.

Fourthly, maintain the recruitment system. After the recruitment system according to the total relationship flow management model is designed, how do we maintain the recruitment system? We know that behavior of complex systems only depend on the input relationship flow and relationship flow set $Rf_{Ord}(t)$ (the total relationship flow), especially the relationship cycle in the system. Thus, individual behavior actually affects the total relationship flow. In order to eliminate the uncertainty and randomness of individuals and departments, rules and regulations of the recruitment system must be established.

In addition, the designed recruitment system is not constant. With the change of structural frame and organi zation or relocating, the total relationship flow in recruitment system is also to be followed by changes. At this time, we should design the relationship flow again. According to the changes of $H_{Or}(t)$, Rf(t) and $Rf_{Ord}(t)$ adjust the frame of relationship flow. Therefore, the human resources department should pay close attention to the external environment and internal organizational changes.

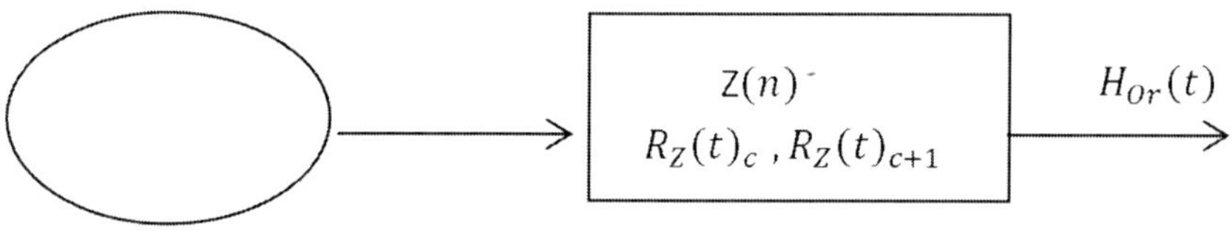

Figure 2. the association between the two adjacent level.

5. CONCLUSIONS

The recruitment system is composed of a series of workflows which interact and mutual influence with each other. Existing research about recruitment system focuses on how to combine qualitative and quantitative analysis to achieve scientific decisions. However, systems theory states that local optimum does not represent the overall optimum. Just paying attention to the selection of personnel and scientific methods rather than to internal coordinating in the human resources department, will lead the recruitment ineffective.

The total relationship flow management aims at better understanding and controlling the systems' problems. This paper under the guidance of the theory, by determining the recruitment system behavior $H_{Or}(t)$ and the appropriate relationship flow set $Rf_{Ord}(t)$, and focusing on the time delay and system maintenance gives some Fangling Hu advice on building the recruitment system, hoping to expand the existing theoretical research in the field and to provide some management implications for managers.

REFERENCES

1. Han, Y.J. (2007) Application of AHP in the Recruitment of Human Resources. Contemporary Finance.
2. Bertalanffy, L.V. (1950) An Outline of General System Theory. British Journal of Philosophy of Science, 1, 134-164.
3. Zhang, X.B. (2009) The Review and Research about Human Resource Management System and Organizational Performance. Soft Science, 3, 106-110.
4. Lin, F.Y. and Wu, J.Z. (1997) General Systems Theory and Its Application Structure. Journal of Systems Engineering, 12, 1-10.
5. Lin, F.Y. and Cheng, T.C.E. (2007) The Structural Theory of General Systems Applied in Management: The Total Relationship Flow Management Theorems. The International Journal of General Systems, 36, 673-681.
6. Lin, F.Y., Cheng, T.C.E., Cheng, H., Liang, X.H. and Zhao, J.N. (2013) Developing an Organization Design Framework Based on the Total Relationship Flow Management Theorems. IEEE Transactions on Systems, Man, and Cybernetics: Systems, 43, 1-11.

3

CHAPTER

An Assessment of the Training and Developmental Needs of Employees in Nigerian Local Government

Osabiya Babatunde Joseph

School of Management Sciences (SMS) National Open University of Nigeria Victoria- Island, Lagos, Nigeria

ABSTRACT

The importance of training and development is more obvious given the growing complexity of the work environment, the rapid change in organizations and advancement in technology, among other things. The ultimate aim of any training program is to add value and once a training program cannot add value, it should be reworked or altogether cancelled. Without training, it will be very difficult to acquire skills and without skills organizations will not achieve its objectives through people.

Keywords: Understanding training and development; Types of training and development; Relevance of training and reasons why training fail

INTRODUCTION

Training can be argued by all and sundry as an act of equipping human beings with the adequate and necessary knowledge or understanding to enable him/her perform in line with the required standards and expectations to meet up with the objectivity of his manager or organization as a whole [1]. Thus, every organization should involve in training for its employees to enable them perform their job efficiently and effectively for increased productivity.

Staff or employee occupies an indispensable position in any establishment, be it industry, commercial or educational institution. This means that without employees, organization cannot function effectively. In essence, human effort is greatly desirable and crucial in achieving the goals and objectives of the organization. Effective management is used to mean the training of personnel to improve their application of knowledge, skill, behavior or problem solving techniques which they acquire through previous education training and development experience. Training and development is a function and responsibility of the organization concerned [2]. This activity aimed at bettering the performance of individual and group settings.

Training new employees sets the tone for the employee's impression of an organization's culture. So in a sense it's a microcosm of the organization itself. Training new employee represents a golden opportunity to get things off to a good start. It sets momentum for the newly employed. This momentum can be positive for a good experience; however, an unpleasant experience can create negative momentum. This is why an outstanding training experience for newly employed and already employed is vital for both the staff and the organization. A personnel management theorist Ubeku A [3] state that "money spent on training and development of staff is money well invested. Staff, who has not received adequate training before being assigned responsibility, lacks necessary confidence with which to carry-out the job". In as much as people are regarded as a set of the major resources of work performance to a manager, therefore the successful performance of the job depends on the training given to them. To be able to get the best from workers or staff, constant and continuous training exercise should be introduced to them. Training of employee is not for potential reflection of the staff only but for the organization which includes local government council's image as well. If an employee is not given the opportunity of in-service training to better his/her educational position and develop him/her, the tendency to lack the know-how or confidence of assuming higher responsibility abounds.

Training of old and new employee are of paramount importance to boost their morals for better performance of their duty, enhancing improved productivity in realization of the management objectives. Adebayo A [4] emphasized this point, thus:

"The fact which is obvious for anyone is that the Chief Executive be he functioning as permanent Secretary, General Manager, Executive Secretary to body of organization cannot by himself alone accomplish the requirements of his office without the efficient support and assist on of other functionaries lower the ladder"

A proportionate period of the first one-month of a new employee in the organization or local government council should be used for induction purposes. This is a form of training because during the period, the employee acquits his or herself with the local government area or organizational structure and setup in form of socialization.

The overall emphasis of this research work is to implore the local government council bosses or authorities/heads of various departments to encourage employees by giving them adequate training facilities at intervals as an incentive and most recognized motivator [5]. The need for human resources training and development cannot be overemphasized, because it is an investment in human ability that leads to human capability. It should therefore occupy a unique space in the undertaking of the local government council as an indispensible part of the local government council authorities' function. Training is relevant to administration, as it is essential to overall employees. In totality, every category of staff in the Local Government Council deserves to be trained and should be desirous of being trained for his/her personal improvement and local government area achievement for desired objectives. The most conspicuous and effective lubricant to employee's efficient and productive performance of his/her job is training.

There is need for employees training and development in any organization including Local Government Councils to ensure better performance [6]. The importance and significance of training and development to organizational development has no doubt been recognized in some Local Government Council or in the Nigerian Public Services. Some of the problems of Local Government Councils include the following;

a) Non-Adherence to the recommendation of the 1988 and 1998 Civil Service Reform:

b) Local government councils of the federation had failed to adhere to the civil service recommendation which stipulates that ten percent (10%) of the total annual personnel emolument be set aside for staff training and development. The federal government and state government have equally failed in this regard in the implementation of this reform (absence of systematic training).

c) Poor awareness and exposure of Local Government Council Authorities to relevance of training and development of employee: This is a major problem, being the pilot of all affairs and owing to the fact that 80% of the workforce of the local government council is junior staff (level 1-6) and as such the council authority considers it irrelevant to spend money on training lower cadre employees.

d) Poor funding and embezzlement: this is reflected in the difference between budgetary provisions and actual funds released for various years both at federal, state and local government levels

e) High cost of training has been occasioned by lack of transparency and honest: The cost of bribes is often built into the training costs when signing contracts with training consultants and this may affect quality of training.

f) Poor utilization of trained employees: Many employees sent for training is not allowed to utilize their skills and knowledge because of bureaucratic rigidity and unwillingness to change [7].

g) Lack of proper consideration for training needs: Many times, employees are sent for training without proper consideration for the relevance to present job or future posting

h) Employees misconception on Training and development: Some employees considers training as unnecessary and waste of time, resources and energy as they believe experience is a better teacher than any training programme or exercise. Curricula and methods remain insufficiently attuned to job content due to several factors such as funding, size of the trainees etc

i) Lack of incentives for trained personnel: Being that lower cadre employees (level 1-6) constitute 80% of the workforce of the local government council, some employee sees training and development as stressful and unnecessary while some concedes that even if they undergo the training, the local government council authority may not consider them for proper placement which commensurate with their newly acquired skill or certificate.

j) The use of quack consultants by local government council authority has grossly affected the quality of training: In many instances, the council authority prefers to contract training programs to political or party associates, loyalists or family affiliates rather than competent and experienced specialist in the consulting firms.

k) Inadequate Training Facilities: Modern facilities to train and enhance development are not available neither assessed even when it is scarcely available.

LITERATURE REVIEW

Training or employee training also known as job training, occupational training or vocational instruction for employed persons by some personnel management theorist or scholars can be traced(back) to during and after World war II, when in-service training by employers became a common practice. The rapid change-over in industry from peace to war led to training schemes for semi-skilled workers, for workers transferred to new jobs, and for women newly brought into industry. Therefore, the rapid contemporary advance of technological change made training a necessity in almost all works of life. At the operating level in industry and public utilities, new techniques, new methods, new tools, new synthetic, new sources of power, and increased uses of automation have brought extensive changes in the past decades and the rate of change tends to increase as time goes on. Comparable changes are taking place in the office with extended use of computers and data processor, which provide for the storing and recall of information. All of these brought a new approach to training. Great emphasis is now placed on a good start through initial job training, supplemented by orientation sessions or by attractively produced printed materials describing the nature and objectives of the employment.

Traditionally, training and development dates back to the time of our fore fathers, who taught their children through verbal means and demonstrations (hand-work) on how to do things. An example of such verbal and demonstrative means of training used by our ancestral fathers includes occupation like blacksmithing, hunting, farming; wrestling etc and the ones who mastered these skills have always come out successfully. Therefore, the process of transferring knowledge through verbal and demonstrative means is realized today by scholars as training and development.

Virtually, all modern organization place emphasis on skilled manpower for attainment of their organizational goals and aspirations. Thus, for any organization aspiring to meet the objectives for which it is established, there must be deliberate policy to train and develop its employees.

Recruitment of qualified personnel is not synonymous with training. Every employee in any organization needs some sort of orientation and continuous development. The need for this retraining is to enable the employee meet the challenging modern industrial complexities and take on higher responsibilities and attainment of selffulfillment.

The new Civil Service Reform of 1998 clearly emphasizes the importance of training and development. The reform stressed that opportunity should be given to employees to make a career in whatever discipline they can. The reforms also emphasize that training is a right of all civil servants if they must grow.

Employees are motivated through training, which ultimately determine their utilization, productivity, commitment and growth. Many employees have been frustrated because their needs for training were not identified and provided for as an indispensible function of management.

In this regard, several authors have postulated series of works on the phenomenon of training and development

Robbins S.P [8] "training is concerned with the present development, and the future organization which cannot afford to stand still. They must be ready for change, and so must the people who comprise them".

Based on the foregoing, training and development have been directed to individuals holding managerial positions in recent years. But today, establishments, departments have now seen the need to make all caliber of employees ranging from unskilled, semi-skilled and the skilled or professionals benefit from the training programmes of such establishment as proficiency at all level of an organization goes a long way to increasing the total output of such organization.

According to Ubeku AK [3] "Training schemes for all categories of employees are vital in any organization that wants to stay in a competitive world. Machinery is becoming more and more complex and even where automation takes over; different types of skills are required. Therefore, there must be constant training and retraining of employees. With regard to managers, there are not enough managerial skills at the moment and most organizations are engaged in management training within Nigeria and abroad." Bearing in mind the complexity, and the high rate of technological and philosophical world we now live in, the need for training and development therefore becomes greatly pertinent. The days when jobs were learnt with little or no regard to technological changes are gone.

The management of employees these days' calls for higher degree of training and development of the mentality of the one charged with the administration of staff. Hence, in the local government, there are various department charged with different responsibilities. Training and development in this regard, helps in modifying the behavior of the trainee or trained officer in order to afford him the opportunity to function properly in that position.

Appleby R.C [9] "training is required to make persons behave differently or more efficiently". There is no over-stressing the fact that the skill of persons that have undergone training for specific period must improve since the objective of training and development is to enhance and increase the level of performance of the individual.

According to Jucious "training is the process of acquiring specific skills to perform a job better". It helps people to become qualified and proficient in doing some jobs.

Usually an organization facilitates the employees learning through training so that their modified behavior contributes to the attainment of the organization's goal and objectives.

Van Dersal defined training "as the process of teaching, informing, or educating people so that they may become as well as qualified as possible to do their job, (2) they become qualified to perform in positions of greater difficulty and responsibility".

Arnoff [10] observes that training and development foster the initiative and creativity of employees and help to prevent manpower obsolescence, which may be due to age, attitude or inability of a person to adapt him or herself to technological changes

Obisi [11] "training is a process through which the skills, talent and knowledge of an employee is enhanced and increased". He argues that training should take place only when the need and objective for such training have been identified

Scott, Clothier and Spriegal agree that training is the cornerstone of sound management, for it make the employees more effective and productive. They argued that training is actively and intimately connected with all the personnel and managerial activities. It would be difficult for a new employee to grow on the job and become a manager without adequate training and development.

Craig [12] in his work on training has this to say "the place of training and learning is the sky-rocketing development of knowledge and civilization has become dramatically evident".

However, with the advent of industrial revolution in the 18th century, the history of training and development that accompanied the industrial era, then fell on the increase. For organization to keep on the pace of effective and efficient management, training of personnel becomes pertinent.

In this regard, Knootz and Donnel [13] postulated that: "The lessons learned from these experiences were so valuable that managers possessed special knowledge and skills which could be explained took firm hold." With the acquiring of adequate knowledge and skills, the technicalities accompanying management in an organization become simple and well administered to ensure rapid productivity. Without training and development of personnel to meet with the increase in technology, management today would have been a difficult and complex subject to approach.

Training and development therefore becomes a process whereby planning has to be applied to make training and development manifest its true goals and objectives, by carefully, analyzing the present and critically looking into the future jobs in order that training becomes effective.

Knootz and Donnel [13] in their book say: "A good training programme is not static; it considers the training needs of managers in the present job and the next job. It also takes into accounts broad enterprise needs and plan in the distant future". The main objective is to improve current performance and provide a suitably trained staff to meet present and future needs.

Training includes seminars and workshops as well as short courses in higher institutions of learning. "Training is the systematic development of knowledge, skill and pattern required by an individual in order to perform a given task". "Training is process of learning a sequence of programme behavior". "Training is concerned with job performance and the application of knowledge and skill to present job".

In his realization of the significance of training of the public servants, Udoji [14] recommended that: "it should be a usual practice in all ministries to arrange training programme for their personnel of all grades as a way of improving efficiency and quality of the service."

Ubeku [15] speaks of training, thus: "Money spent on the training and development of employees is money well invested. Employees who have not received adequate training before being assigned with responsibilities lack the necessary confidence with which to carryout jobs. Because he believes he can do it, his enthusiasm on the job increases. It is a person in that position who can think and originate ideas as to how be the best to carry out the task of the job. People who are not trained tend to stick to what they were taught the first time then they took over the job. They are frightened of doing the job in different way, because something might go wrong and that risk they cannot take".

Garavan et al. postulated that: "Training and development encompasses three main activities: training, education and development;

Training - this is both focused upon, and evaluated against, the job that an individual currently holds,

Education - this activity focuses upon the jobs that an individual may potentially hold in the future, and is evaluated against those jobs.

Development - this activity focuses upon the activities that the organization employing the individual, or that the individual is part of, may partake in the future, and is almost impossible to evaluate".

Conroy [16] defined manpower development "as a purposive effort intended to strengthen the library's capability to fulfill its mission effectively and efficiently by encouraging and providing for the growth of its own human resources". He desired manpower development as a factor that improves the competence of personnel through opportunities for learning on the job. This implies that manpower development can be achieved through training and education of staff.

Biscoe [17] sees staff development as a two way responsibility within the organization and individual. Sodipo [18] investigated the effect of manpower development on productivity with the aim of determining the different factors that play important roles in any organizational setup for effective utilization of manpower resources available to it, its main focus is on different factors that play important role in organizational to ensure effective information management

McNamara [19] views training as involving an expert working with learners to transfer to them certain areas of knowledge or skills to improve in their current jobs. However, manpower development is not a responsibility of just an individual; rather it is a combination of different factors.

Understanding Training and Development

According to Obisi [20] the concepts of training and development are used interchangeably. However, it can be differentiated from the other. Training is for specific job purpose while development goes beyond, specifies development cover not only those which bring about growth of personality.

Steinmetz and Lawrence notes that training is a short term process, utilizing a systematic and organized procedures by which nonmanagerial personnel learn technical knowledge and skill for definite purpose. Development on the other is long term educational process utilizing procedure by which managerial personnel learn conceptual and theoretical knowledge for general purposes.

Campbell [21] says that training refers only to instruction in technical and mechanical operations while development refers to philosophical and theoretical educational concept. Training is designed for non-managers while development involves managerial personnel. Training courses are typically designed for short term stated purpose, such as the operation of some piece(s) of machinery while development involves a broader education for long-term purpose. Training is for short term while development is for long-term. Training is for specific job related purposes while development is general purpose.

Types of Training and Development

There are two (2) major types of training, On-the-job training and Off-the-job training as identified by Alo, O. (1999); On-the-job training is normally handled by colleagues, supervisors, managers, mentors to help employee adjust to their work and equip them with appropriate job related skills [22].

Armstrong [23] argues that On-the-job training may consist of teaching or coaching by more experienced people or trainers at the desk or at the bench. It may consist of individual or group assignment and projects and the use of team leaders and managers. Armstrong furthered that on-the-job training is the only way to develop and practice the specific managerial, team leading, technical, selling, manual and administrative skills needed by the organization and its has the advantaged of actuality and immediacy as the individual works, learns and develops expertise at the same time

Disadvantages of On-the-job training according to Armstrong [23]; are that the effectiveness of the learning is strongly influenced by the quality of the guidance and coaching provided on the job. Many managers and team leaders are unskilled at training and undisciplined to carry it out or to encourage it. Furthermore, relying on fellow employees in "sit by me" training has obvious disadvantages as instruction may be inadequate and the training may perpetuate bad habits. Again, the learner may be distracted by the same environment and find it difficult to acquire basic skills quickly.

According to Ejiogu [24] Off-the-job training would include vestibule training, role playing, case study, discussion and simulation. Armstrong [23] listed group exercises, team building, distance learning, outdoor and workshops as part of Off-the-job training.

He further explains that Off-the-job training may be provided by members of training department, external education and training establishments or training providers- training consultants or guest speakers. He encourages line managers to be closely involved to bring reality into the classroom, to case the transfer of learning, and to make sure that those involved in Off-the-job training are carefully selected, briefed and monitored so as to ensure that they make the right contribution

Objectives of Training and Development

Some of the main objectives of training and developing employees include:

a. To povide the knowledge and appreciation of techniques necessary to enable employee function in their jobs

b. To broaden the employee's horizon of the society in which he or she finds or lives and develops his or herself as a confident person.

c. To prepare suitable employee for more educated study leading to highly skilled work.

d. To afford the employees the opportunity of changing their schedules of duties and be able to perform equally well on them.

e. Training Benefits

When advance training was introduced some employees consider it punishment and stressful in meeting and learning something new but nowadays, employees consider training as an opportunity and as a highly regarded organizational benefit [25-29]. Employees appreciate training opportunities for many reasons including:

- They can learn something that will make their job easier or more enjoyable.
- It increases their 'stock value' within the organization. They become more desired
- It could lead to promotion, pay-rise or a new title.
- They can include it in their resume someday in the future.
- They feel needed and appreciable, relevant to the organization, because their employer is willing to invest time and money into their learning experience.
- It gives them the chance to do something different other than their daily job.
- They can be around other employees or peers and build camaraderie (familiarity and sociability).
- Therefore, it can benefit the employee in number of positive ways. Providing opportunities can also benefit the employer or organization in a number ways which includes:
- Their employees become more efficient at performing their jobs.
- It builds organization morale.
- It increases loyalty and reduces turn-over of highly regarded employees.
- It projects the organization as a preferred workplace to external or aspiring candidates.
- It enhances or stimulates employee creativity.
- It keeps the training department fresh and invigorated.

Relevance of Training and Reasons Why Training Fail

Relevance of training is a very important issue that the organization should look critically at, if they really want to improve the effectiveness of their employees [30-33]. Any training program that is not relevant should not be undertaken. Training should be designed to solve problems and to fill gaps in employee performance. Training should make things happen and bring about needed changes that would enhance organization's effectiveness. It is not proper for an organization to embark on any training program which is not relevant to it and its people [34].

Armstrong [23] agrees that for training program to be relevant, it must satisfy identified and appropriate needs.

According to Kenney and Reid planned training is the deliberate intervention aimed at receiving the learning necessary for improved job performance. Planned training according to Kenney and Reid consists of the following steps:

- Identify and define training needs
- Define the learning required in terms of what skills and knowledge have to be learnt and what attitudes need to be changed
- Define the objectives of the training
- Plan training programs to meet the needs and objectives by using right combination for training techniques and locations.
- Decide who provides the training
- Evaluate training.
- Amend and extend training as necessary.

Organization training practices can fail for many reasons. Burak, Elmar and Smith, Robert [35] give the following reasons:

- The benefits of training are not clear to employees.
- The organization hardly rewards supervisors for carrying out effective training
- The organization rarely plans and budgets systematically for training.

- Training external to the employing unit sometimes teaches techniques on method contrary to practice of the participants scheduling
- Trainers provide limited counseling and consulting services to the rest of the organization.

METHODOLOGY

The researcher used secondary data and its information was gathered from various textbooks, journals, periodicals, newspapers and magazines

CONCLUSION

Since the success of any organization depends on the available quality of human resources at its disposal, then training of employees in an organization should be a compulsory programme irrespective of their previous education or technical qualifications before their assumption of duty. "No one is a perfect fit at the time of living". Therefore training programme must be given utmost priority by every employee.

In further recognition of proper efficiency of employee job performance, up-to-date training must be given to employees. Training should be taken as a continuous process. It is therefore necessary to update the skill of manpower from time to time. Systematic, well organized and implemented training programme will afford the organization increase in productivity, heightened morale, reduce redundancy and help employees to stay longer in the organization for the realization of its objectives

RECOMMENDATIONS

The benefits accruing from employees training and development cannot be overemphasized.

Outputs and results of this study have necessitated the researcher to recommend the following for efficient management in the Local Government Council or other organizations.

1. Training programmes should be provided to cover all categories of staff that have requisite academic and professional qualification required for their proposed training.
2. On-the-job manpower development programs like in-house training, seminars, conferences, short course, workshops etc should be arranged for those employees who could not be sent on Off-the-job training or those with deficiencies.
3. The newly employed who benefited from manpower training should be promoted as soon as possible so as to give them the opportunity of assuming the level of responsibility that is commensurate with their newly acquired qualification.
4. Certain percentage of local government council subvention or allocation should be set aside for training programmes.
5. The training programme policy of the Council could be improved, more fund should be made available to enable the employees on training paid their entitlements adequately with the view to giving them the required support for the training.
6. For convenient management of manpower and organization, training program should be placed on priority list of the Local Government Council's budgets
7. The Local Government Council Authorities should recognize and appreciate outstanding employee and reward him or her hard-work accordingly.
8. The Local Government Council Authorities should encourage delegation of duties from time to time to ensure regular onthe-training.
9. Local Government Council Authorities has failed in the past in adhering to the Civil service reforms and the Federal and state government should ensure strict compliance to the reforms which encourages manpower training and development.

REFERENCES

1. Adamolekun L (1983) Public Administration: Nigeria and Comparative Perspective. Longmans, London.
2. Cole G (1982) Management Theory and Practice. 2nd Edition, D.P. Publications Ltd.
3. Ubeku A K (1975) Personnel Management in Nigeria. Ethiope Publishing Corporation, Benin City.
4. Adebayo A (1981) Principles and Practice of Public Administration in Nigeria. John Willey and Sons Ltd.
5. Craig R (1976) Training and Development Handbook. McGraw-Hill Publishing Company Ltd.
6. Fajana S (1997) Human Resources Management.Labofin and Company, Lagos.
7. Appleby R (1969) Modern Business Administration. Pitman Books Ltd, London.
8. Robbins S (1978) Personnel: The management of Human Resources. New Jersey: Prentice-Hall Inc.
9. Appleby R (1969) Modern Business Administration. Pitman Books Ltd.Scott, London
10. Arnoff J (1971) Achievement Motivations Training and Executive Advancement. Journal of Applied Science 7: 12-24.
11. Obisi C (2001) Employee Development, Issues and Dimension. Unical Journal of Public Administration1: 15-36.
12. Craig RL (1976) Training and Development Handbook. McGraw-Hill Publishing Company Ltd.
13. Knootz H, Donnel CO (1978) Essentials of Management. McGraw-Hill Book Company.
14. Udoji J (1975)The Implications of the Public Service Review Commission's Report for Management Education and Training". A Quarterly Journal of Administration 10: 5-11.
15. Ubeku A (1978) Personnel Management in Nigeria. Second edition, Ethiope Publishing Corporation, Benin.

16. Conroy B (2001) Library Staff Development and Continuing Education: Principles and Practice. Harper and Row,New York.

17. Biscoe M (2002) Human Resource Development and Utilization. Spectrum Books, Ibadan.

18. Sodipo A (2005) Manpower Development and its Effect on Productivity. McGraw Hill, Auckland.

19. Mcnamara C (1999) Employee Training and Development: Typical Reasons and Benefits.

20. Obisi C (1996) Personnel Management. Freeman Publications, Ibadan.

21. Campbell J (1971) Personnel Training and Development: Annual Review of Psychology.

22. Federal Republic of Nigeria (1976) Guidelines for Local Government Reforms.Government Printer, Kaduna.

23. Armstrong M (1995) A Handbook on Personnel Management Practices. Kogan Page Ltd, London.

24. Ejiogu A (2000) Human Resource Management towards Greater Productivity. Generation Press Ltd, Lagos.

25. Green H (1975) Adminstrative Training: Some Implication of Udoji Commission Report. Quarterly Journal of Administration10: 55-68.

26. Alo O (1999) Human Resource Management in Nigeria. Business Science Books, Lagos.

27. Koontz H, O'Donnel C, Weihrich H (1980) Management. McGraw Hill Publishing Company, Japan.

28. Atiomo A (2000) Human Resource Management. Malthouse Management Science Book, Lagos.

29. Obisi C (2001) Employee Development, Issues and Dimension. Unical Journal of Public Administration for September 1: 32-41.

30. Beach D (1980) Personnel Management of People at Work. Macmillan Publishing Company.

31. Robbins S (1978) Personnel: The management of Human Resources. Prentice-Hall Inc, New Jersey.

32. Clothier, Spriegel (1977) Personnel Management: Principles, Practices and Point of View. Tata McGraw-Hill Publishing Company Ltd. New Delhi.

33. The Presidency (1995) Revised Guidelines for Training in the Federal Civil Service.The Presidency, Lagos.

34. Cumminng C (1968) The Theory and Practice of Personnel management. Heineman, London.

35. Burak Elmar, Smith R (1977) Personnel Management: A Human Resouce System Approach. West Publishing Company, New York.

4

CHAPTER

Autoethnography as a Legitimate Approach to HRD Research: A Methodological Conversation at 30,000 Feet

Robin S. Grenier[1]

[1]University of Connecticut, Storrs, USA

ABSTRACT

I believe the field of human resource development (HRD) is missing out on the opportunity to expand our methodological approaches and ignoring the calls from others to be rebellious and look beyond our standard operating procedures. The purpose of this article is to provide an evocative "conversation" on autoethnography and to explain how HRD researchers might conduct and represent autoethnographic work. Autoethnographic methods are highly suited to the task of exploring organizational and everyday work phenomenon that can lead to the development of new theories of HRD. Through talking about the challenges associated with using an autoethnographic approach and how HRD scholars might assess such reflexive ethnography, I hope to encourage the use of rich, but neglected sources of less traditional approaches to qualitative inquiry.

Keywords qualitative research, research methodologies, ethnography

Although my roots are in adult learning and education, I have found myself drawn to the work of human resource development (HRD) scholars as they seek to better the lives of individuals through work and professional development. Since taking my first academic appointment more than 9 years ago, I have been exposed to some interesting, ground-breaking, and thought-provoking HRD research, but I have also seen the perpetuation of ingrained ways of thinking about research, methodological practice, and theory building. Moreover, I struggle to challenge many of my colleagues' thinking around what methodologies are considered rigorous or appropriate for organizational contexts.

I have a friend and colleague who I have known for more than 5 years. Valerie is a professor who writes and teaches within the field of HRD, leadership, and management. Over the years she and I have consumed a lot of coffee while debating research approaches, methodologies, and what constitutes "real research" (her words not mine). Recently she and I shared a 3-hr flight that allowed me to broach a methodological subject that sends shivers up the spines of traditional, post/positivist scholars such as her—autoethnography. I wanted to get her take on autoethnography and its application to HRD research and theory development.

In this article, I use creative nonfiction (Vickers, 2010) to provide a review of autoethnography through the application of evocative "conversation." Such an approach has previously been used as a way to cultivate an open space for narration, exploration, and growth (A. Bochner & Ellis, 2006), as well as a "way to generate social and personal knowledge" (Frentz & Hocker, 2010, p. 621). In this case, the conversation is a means to explaining how HRD researchers might conduct and represent autoethnographic work. What follows is our conversation as Valerie sought to better understand what she called "a scary idea."

. . . Flight attendants, prepare for takeoff.

Me:

I get it. Autoethnography can sound scary, especially since traditional quantitative methods are still the norm for empirical studies in HRD. I know for example, that nearly sixty percent of all the manuscript types accepted by *Human Resource Development Quarterly* (HRDQ) in 2013 were quantitative, compared to just over 12 percent of qualitative manuscripts. And despite guidance from HRD scholars like Tonette Rocco (2010) who's written pieces like

"Criteria for Evaluating Qualitative Studies" in *Human Resource Development International* (HRDI), and the creation of an AHRD qualitative inquiry SIG, HRD scholars still do not utilize the diverse collection of qualitative research methodologies at their disposal. I want to find ways to challenge my colleagues to extend our current thinking about the use of narrative and ethnographic research—and specifically autoethnography.

Valerie:

Ok, I guess it makes sense that a new idea like autoethnography should be introduced to HRD researchers.

Me:

It might be a new idea for HRD, but really autoethnography is far from new. Back in 1947, Ralph Turner presented a study based on his own military experiences in World War II. In 1959/1960, others like Donald Roy and Fred Davis explored their own work—Roy (1959/1960) as a factory worker and Davis (1959) as a cab driver. So some form of reflexive ethnography has been around for quite a while, although Hayano originated the term autoethnography in 1979.

Valerie:

But hold on. Before you said ethnography. Now you're saying autoethnography. I think you need to back up.

Me:

Fair enough, especially when you consider that despite what I see as natural links between HRD objectives and the application of ethnography, there is still a lack of understanding by scholars about how to appropriately apply ethnographic methods in the field. Ethnography is the study of social interactions, behaviors, and perceptions that occur within groups, teams, organizations, and communities. It requires the researcher to draw primarily from first-hand observations made over an extended period of time in a culture.

Valerie:

Oh, ok, I remember ethnography from my methods course, and I have read some, like Sally S. Sambrook's (2001) ethnographic case study of the British National Health System.

Me:

Yes, Sally has focused a lot methodologically on ethnography—a real standout in HRD contexts. As she could probably tell you, the benefit of ethnographies such as hers are in providing rich insights into the human, social, and cultural aspects of organizations. Now, there are three primary forms of ethnography: reflexive, holistic, and critical. The one important for understanding where autoethnography fits in is the reflexive form. In 2002, Foley noted that reflexive ethnography has no absolute distinctions between what is truth and what is fiction.

Valerie:

(with a smile and a gesture to the flight attendant) Wait a minute. I think I might need a drink for this.

Me:

In 2008, Davies talked in her book about this form of ethnography—taking into account the researcher's self as it interacts with the object of study.

Valerie:

So it's not objective?

Me:

Correct. Like all qualitative studies, the researcher is present and fully acknowledges her[1] subjectivities. Ruth Behar, in her 1996 book, called the approach vulnerable and back in 1988 Van Maanen described reflexive ethnography as confessional, and of course Ellis in 2004 called it autoethnographic. It means that the author has to gaze back on himself. Marcus (1994) outlined reflexivity as involving self-critique, as well as positionality and the understanding that representation is shaped by what he called "politics of location" (p. 571).

. . . Ladies and gentlemen, the Captain has turned off the Fasten Seat Belt sign, and you may now move around the cabin. However we always recommend to keep your seat belt fastened while you're seated.

Valerie:

It seems a bit airy-fairy, but I can't go anywhere, so I'm listening. What else should I know about reflexive ethnography?

Me:

Well, Ellis, who I will probably mention a lot, writes extensively about the methodology. She said in the 2000 *Handbook of Qualitative Research* with Bochner, and again in the 2008 *Handbook Of Constructionist Research* as a second author with Ellington, that reflexive ethnography is significant because it embraces new forms of authorship and attempts to destabilize the restrictive social scientific writing conventions (Ellington & Ellis, 2008).

Valerie:

So then you think that reflexive methods like autoethnography have the potential to broaden HRD research and its publications?

Me:

When I look at the work in our field, I would say yes. I think we have limited ourselves in terms of methodology in HRD scholarship. Autoethnography is just one means to addressing our narrow approach to research and theory building.

Valerie:

And how do you define autoethnography?

Me:

There are a number of definitions, but I think that Carolyn Ellis' (2004) is a good one. She describes autoethnography as "research, writing, story, and method that connect the autobiographical and personal to the cultural, social, and political" (p. xix). But it is of course more nuanced. See, according to Ellis and Bochner (2000), autoethnography writing and research presents several layers of consciousness. Rambo, in 2005, said that by layering accounts you could increase evocativeness and the aesthetic quality of the text. This allows the author to incorporate multiple voices like theory, subjective experience, and even fantasy.

Valerie:

So I am trying to imagine when autoethnography would be appropriate in HRD.

Me:

First, I think autoethnography has the ability to connect the seemingly common and everyday experiences of the author to broader political, social, and organizational implications and it can also expose and highlight the tacit knowledge and memory not easily accessed through traditional methodologies. It is in some ways the highest form of an emic, or insider's viewpoint.

Valerie:

That means that it is considered a reflexive form of ethnography, right? Because the researcher's interaction with the phenomenon is considered?

Me:

You're catching on. Babcock, in 1980, said that in autoethnography the researcher turns the study back upon herself in order to describe and systematically analyze one's personal experience in order to understand the cultural experience. Take for example, "Going Global: Professional Mobility and Concerns for LGBT Workers". It's an autoethnography that includes the authors' (Gedro, Mizzi, Rocco, & van Loo, 2013) experiences "as sexual minorities relocating for professional reasons" (p. 282) and how those experiences are shaped by legal, social, and cultural effects. It is a study that provides unique insights into psychological and physiological responses and has implications for HRD, as well as furthering theory development including Fontaine's (1996) emerging model of skills for success abroad.

Valerie:

So that's where the -auto, -graphy, and -ethno come together.

Me:

Exactly. And the result is what Reed-Danahay (1997) described in his book as highly personalized based on the researcher's experiences and understanding of a particular culture. Remember I mentioned that qualitative researchers embrace their subjectivities? Well, in 2008, Holt noted that autoethnographers in particular challenge the dominant views about silent authorship by capitalizing on their subjectivities. In this way these researchers are confronting common scholarly discourses that Ellis and Bochner (2000) said often "privilege arguments, theories, abstractions and jargon over feelings, stories, concrete events, and accessible prose" (p. 746).

Valerie:

What you're saying is that you want to evangelize autoethnography because it can provide a unique voice that is missing from HRD scholarship?

Me:

Yes, and in particular, with regard to theory, I think it can be used to confirm or explore (Guest, MacQueen, & Namey, 2012) both emerging and established theories. For example, A. S. Sambrook, Jones, and Doloriert (2014) explore the application of autoethnography in furthering our understanding of personal engagement at work, and in particular its use in exploring Kahn's (1992) conceptual framework of personal engagement. But, I must admit that I want to encourage all sorts of rigorous qualitative research. I think it is important to see the value in not just autoethnography, but how constructivist epistemologies can contribute to HRD theory and practice. Today in HRD scholarship, besides the overwhelming amount of quantitative studies, there is a smaller body of qualitative inquiry. Most common are studies that focus on understanding such things as a phenomenon, process, or people's perspectives. These are what Sharan Merriam (2014) calls basic interpretive. A few have used phenomenology, but when I looked recently, HRDQ hadn't published one since 2013, although HRDI published a phenomenological study at the start of 2015 by Belle, Burley, and Long called "Where Do I Belong: High-Intensity Teleworkers' Experience of Organizational Belonging." There are also a number of qualitative case studies, like Rod Githens' 2012 study of lesbian, gay, bisexual, transgender, and queer (LGBTQ) employees creating formal and informal groups in workplaces to provide social support and foster organizational change. His study used narrative descriptions and historical research methods.

Valerie:

And what about ethnography?

Me:

HRD scholars have applied ethnography. The chapter by Beattie (2002) in *Understanding Human Resource Development: A Research-Based Approach* is worth reading. Besides that, there are a number of very good applications of ethnography in HRD including the one I mentioned from S. Sambrook (2001) and others (see Howell, Carter, & Schied, 2002; Lawless, Sambrook, & Stewart, 2012).

Valerie:

But how is autoethnography different from ethnography or the other methodologies you just mentioned?

Me:

Well, all qualitative approaches are initiated by a purpose of seeking deep understanding of a phenomenon usually in a natural setting. By using interviews, observations, artifacts, or a combination of the three, a researcher is likely to answer a question such as, how do older, professional men cope with the life transition of involuntary job loss? Or, what influences learners' perceptions, interpretations, and application of feedback during formal workplace training? These are qualitative in that they employ a constructivist ontology, but I would say autoethnography is farther along the qualitative continuum in that it has a strong foundation in a critical paradigm. My autoethnographic work is predicated on the research being, what Adams and Holman Jones in 2008 called a political, socially just, and socially conscious act that values the researcher as full participant, which takes it beyond traditional ethnography. An example is the autoethnography by Jamie Callahan in 2009. She explored the role of training practices at the United States Air Force Academy in perpetuating power and control issues and she did this by examining her own experiences as a cadet in the hegemonic masculine culture of the Academy. She did not simply share her story, she used public documents along with her own personal experiences to critically examine eating disorders and sexual harassment at the Academy and raise questions confronting socially constructed gender roles in the military. It is an excellent example of the socially conscious dimensions I described.

Valerie:

I will have to read that one.

Me:

I should also tell you that Jamie (Callahan, 2010) had to defend her epistemological choices against a positivist's commentary (Rosenstein, 2010) to her autoethnography. In her defense, Jamie was clear when she wrote,

It is now common for scholars to argue that the only relevant data are those based in the personal experience of the researcher—such as autoethnographic research, which served as an informing foundation for my approach to the exploration of the manuscript topic. (Callahan, 2010, p. 1188)

Valerie:

I see and can appreciate what sounds like a critical paradigm, but the scholar part of my brain still has trouble though, especially if you want to publish an autoethnography in a journal or as a dissertation. I still don't have a clue how the autoethnographic process works. Is it like writing an autobiography?

Me:

I get that question a lot from students in my qualitative classes. Autoethnography is an unconventional methodology largely because authors attempt to shake up science and art. With that said, Ellis, Adams, and Bochner (2010) are clear that the work should be rigorous, theoretically grounded, and analytical while at the same time not avoiding what is emotional and therapeutic or personal. Also, it is more about who reads the work, how the reader is affected by the phenomenon and research, and how it stimulates or furthers conversations. Much like more general ethnography, Chang (2008) describes autoethnography as depending largely on participant observation, wherein the researcher is engaged in a social or cultural group or the lives of participants while observing behavior. In 2010, Ellis and her co-authors also stressed that autoethnographers use methodological tools and existing scholarship to analyze the experience as a whole, while at the same time using personal experience to illustrate facets of his own existence in order to make characteristics of the culture familiar for insiders and outsiders. This requires the researcher to purposefully reflect on, record, and observe her own behaviors, while actively engaged in the research setting during participant observation. Chang (2008) talks about the process involving interactive introspection and introspective self-observation.

Valerie:

Say that again?

Me:

Interactive introspection calls for collaboratively interviewing others in order to relive and describe previous experiences, and introspective self-observation is useful for surfacing tacit knowledge and mental models that may be taken for granted and shed light on one's engrained or elusive experiences—like your emotions, motivations, or actions. The beauty for Ellis and her colleagues (2010), and me, is that this reflective process can reveal my actions that might otherwise be concealed and allow me to weigh those experiences against existing research, theory, and relevant cultural artifacts.

Valerie:

How do you keep track of this data—both the "real" stuff and your own thoughts?

Me:

(smiling) The use of field texts, a term from Clandinin and Connelly (2000) is the most basic form and these "help fill in the richness, nuance, and complexity of the landscape, returning the reflecting researcher to a richer, more complex, and puzzling landscape than memory alone is likely to construct" (p. 83). The autoethnographer's field texts allow for the collecting and organizing of data to manage the variety of data sources that the study is likely to draw from. You read my 2008 article with Morag Burke right? She and I worked together and used a lot of different techniques like a diary of daily life, sketches, lists of facts, people, places, and events, correspondence, photographs, and artifacts. More recently there is an emergence of digital data sources that can supplement traditional texts such as blogs, video footage or diaries, webpages, and music. I used some of those in the autoethnography I wrote about my experiences as a sojourner in Iceland (Grenier, under review).

Valerie:

Oh yeah. I read those. But wait, how can the one with Morag be an autoethnography if you and she wrote the paper together?

Me:

We struggled with that question too. We collected data separately and analyzed our own data before coming together, so it certainly felt like it was autoethnographic, but it was not "auto." We settled on calling it co-constructed ethnography (Grenier & Burke, 2008), and I later learned that others have done similar work. As a matter of fact, I saw a poster presentation at UFHRD in Scotland (Ekeh, Leitch, & Iyer, 2014) that used a similar technique, but they called it an auto-ethnographic bricolage. But hold on, I don't want to get ahead of myself.

Valerie:

Ok, just promise to come back to the co-constructed thing.

Me:

I will, but first let's talk writing and representation, which is just as important as the data collection. In order for an autoethnographer to represent his research in a way that is both personal and culturally meaningful to an audience beyond the immediate scholarly community, Richardson and St. Pierre (2005) said it is important to engage in creative analytic practices that incorporate evocative or aesthetic styles of writing. Remember what Ellis and her co-authors (2010) said; this is central to autoethnography since the researcher is attempting to communicate more than that found in traditional genres.

Valerie:

So are there rules or standards like in traditional scholarly writing? You know—intro, problem, research questions, lit, methods, et cetera?

Me:

Well, autoethnographies, like other qualitative research, are written in first person, but beyond that there are seemingly no rules. Of course there are approaches that are preferred by scholars, and Ellis et al. (2010) do a good job explaining these. First, there's dialogue as a genre. It uses narrative written as an interview, dialogue, or conversation between two or more people. Ellis wrote one in 1999 using a conversation format between herself and a graduate student. As a matter of fact I was thinking of using something like that for the *Human Resource Development Review* (HRDR) article. Next, there is co-generative or co-created narratives that stray from the single author tradition of autoethnography to incorporate the writing from two or more authors to present a transformative experience into a share text.

Valerie:

Like the one you did with Morag about being pregnant in graduate school!

Me:

Exactly. Besides those two techniques, there is a layered account that uses an authorial voice splicing together ethnographic and autoethnographic content, self-reflective voice, and researcher arguments. David Boje and Jo Tyler wrote one in 2009 on workaholism that ties these components together in a really meaningful way. Or autoethnographers might use self-contained, evocative vignettes based in epiphanies that vividly portray the richness of an event that might otherwise be abstract, like Erika Vasconcelos' (2011) look at her teacher-student self. A final likely approach to writing autoethnography is the application of extreme cases—you should read Johanna Uotinen's (2011) paper in *Qualitative Health Research* about his experiences as a patient in an intensive care unit (ICU). He uses narratives founded in unexpected or surprising experiences to present the contradictions, paradoxes, and irregularities in the phenomenon.

Valerie:

So then there are five forms.

Me:

Those are the most common, but as Boyle and Parry (2007) point out, there are ever expanding writing approaches including personal essays, poetry, short stories, journals, stream of consciousness, detailed unstructured interview narratives, visual presentations, and fragmented writing forms like polyvocal texts. Journals like *Cultural Studies ⇔ Critical Methodologies*, the *Journal of Ethnographic and Qualitative Research*, and *Qualitative Research* are good starting points for all sorts of autoethnographic writing. Regardless of the finished structure, the key is to avoid the prescription of standard writing conventions and structures that inhibit the emancipation of the researcher's voice.

Valerie:

So autoethnography needs to be out there? And all about the researcher.

Me:

(with a chuckle) Many would say yes, but I think that is way too narrow of an interpretation. As an aside, it would be wrong of me not to mention the analytic ethnographic paradigm. It is a term Leon Anderson presented in 2006 in the *Journal of Contemporary Ethnography* to counter evocative ethnography. Actually, you might like this. Evocative autoethnography, what you would call more "out there," intentionally separates itself to "fracture the boundaries that normally separate social science from literature . . . the narrative text refuses to abstract and explain" (Ellis & Bochner, 2000, p. 377). In contrast, analytic autoethnography has a more, what I think to be, post-positivist element. Like evocative autoethnography, it situates the writer as both subject and object of the text, but it refuses to use the self as the only locus of information and calls for more critical analysis.

Valerie:

So less self-absorbed?

Me:

I guess some would say that, but that's only a piece of it. Anderson (2006) said, "The definitive feature of analytic autoethnography is this value-added quality of not only truthfully rendering the social world under investigation but also transcending that world through broader generalization" (p. 388). Just keep in mind that in some approaches the ethnographic process has more value and in others it might be the cultural interpretation, analysis, or representation of self.

Valerie:

I see, but I think I'll check out the analytic autoethnography some time—it might ease me into more evocative approaches. But I want to go back a minute to the writing techniques. What does it look like on paper?

Me:

Oh, ok. O'Riordan wrote a conference paper in 2014 that included a review of autoethnographies and he outlined the most likely techniques in writing. He found extensive use of figurative language like similes and metaphor to illustrate unfamiliar concepts, but of course that's common in many qualitative approaches. There was the author's use of foreshadowing, tense shifting, and single or multiple plot lines to create interest. There was even the use of an additional narrator other than the author or the addition of different formatting and stylistic applications like using varied fonts, indentations, or icons and symbols in order to clarify the purpose of each textual element.

Valerie:

That might be tough for someone like me who is used to reading and writing in one form, or for journal reviewers, but it sounds interesting and must make it more accessible for non-academics.

Me:

I think so. I know that once students in my qualitative methods course get use to the idea, they love those novel approaches to representing research. And when I talk to other qual researchers they often recount getting more feedback on their autoethnographies as opposed to their more traditional research.

Valerie:

Wow, someone reads the papers that doesn't have to? And likes it? That's enough to sell me—a little. I say a little, because I still tend to be a traditionalist, and I know many of my colleagues in the School of Business would have a fit. How do you address issues of things like generalizability, or validity and reliability?

Me:

I get your point. Take for example a doctoral student who wants to write an autoethnography, there are some things you can expect from the work as you start to review it. First off, it should be rich and thick.

Valerie:

(with a smirk) Like barbeque sauce?

Me:

Sort of! If you think of it in terms of the work being rich and thick so it sticks with you so to speak, and makes you want more. It should also go beyond just writing about the self and instead be critical about the experience using what Ellis in 2007 describes as "a back-and-forth movement between experiencing and examining a vulnerable self and observing and revealing the broader context of that experience" (p. 14). An autoethnography should also have, according to Richardson (2000), aesthetic merit, impact on the reader, and make a substantive contribution. One other thing—I think it is important to also expect a high level of integrity and ethical practice. In 2006, Megford proposed that the crucial ethical standard against which any autoethnography should be evaluated is what he called an ethic of accountability. The researcher should write her truth as if all the people involved in those events were reading.

Ladies and gentlemen, the Captain has turned on the fasten seat belt sign. We are now crossing a zone of turbulence. Please return your seats and keep your seat belts fastened. Thank you.

Valerie:

And what about validity, reliability, and generalizability? How do those fit into qualitative methods like autoethnography?

Me:

Be assured, despite what you might have heard, qualitative researchers hold narrative *truth* in high regard. A. P. Bochner (1994) emphasizes that methodologists recognize the significance of that truth as it relates to how the writing is understood, used, and the reactions it provokes, but as qualitative researchers will attest, there are multiple truths that can change over time or even with how those truths are represented in writing (Ellis et al., 2010). Therefore, when you ask about reliability, validity, and generalizability it can get a little tricky—especially since these are positivist terms designed to address quantitative research. So instead let's use Guba and Lincoln's (1981) terms of dependability, credibility, and transferability. First off, is the work honest and transparent? At the heart of it is, are the researcher's motives and intentions sincere and Guba and Lincoln would ask to what extent is the work auditable? In other words, can the reader evaluate the depth of the researcher's immersion in the experience and if data, and what is presented, is sufficient for exploration (Atkinson & Hammersley, 1994)?

Valerie:

That's where the barbeque sauce comes in! With rich description a reader can judge for himself if the research is dependable.

Me:

You got it! We're also talking about confidence in the *truth* of the findings, or more likely in the case of autoethnographies, does the reader find value in the work? Despite the limits of one researcher's unique experience, the reader is able to see the applicability of the findings in other contexts—including her own. It should also help readers communicate with others different from themselves or provide ways to improve lives. Ellis and her co-authors (2010) call this seeking verisimilitude. The researcher's work is believable and lifelike, and there is a sense that what has been represented is truthful. Does it have a naturalistic generalization (Stake & Trumbull, 1982)—bring "felt" news from one world (the researcher's) to another (the reader's) and give opportunities for vicarious experiences?

Valerie:

This approach seems to put a lot on the reader.

Me:

Qualitative inquiry as a whole does. There is a trust with the readers that in the end they are the ones who will decide the value, use, and meaning of the researcher's work—but shouldn't that be the case for all research?

Valerie:

(just smiles and takes a drink)

Me:

And let me be clear, I know that autoethnography isn't perfect or right for everybody. It is not easy to put yourself out there and be exposed. There are both personal and professional risks in doing so and some like Lee (1995) have called it the most dangerous form of research.

Valerie:

But who knows, emerging scholars might be more open to an autoethnographic approach since they are accustomed to creating and presenting themselves and their experiences through social media like Instagram, Twitter, and YouTube. All right, I might not be running out the door to start my first autoethnography, but I do have a better idea of what it is and how it fits into the larger area of qualitative research, but I am still curious what that would look like in HRD.

Me:

First off, Reed-Danahay back in 2001 suggests that a new wave of ethnographic writing might come from careers including mentorship, issues around work-life balance, and education and employment issues, as well as professional success and failure. I think autoethnography is well suited to the work of HRD scholars and scholar practitioners, and is useful in the exploration of professional experiences and one's place in organizational structures and communities. Some would agree. Doloriert and Sambrook in 2012 wrote an excellent overview of organizational autoethnography in the *Journal of Organizational Ethnography* and in that article they advocate for the application of autoethnography in order, "to open up the discursive space for exploring the culture of self, work and relationships" (p. 89) within higher-ed organizations. And Karra and Phillips (2008), researching in international management, maintain that a growing portion of work in their field is taking on the characteristics of autoethnography with researchers collecting data locally, or when they return home, and then publishing the results internationally.

Valerie:

You know, I can see the appeal. A researcher could write about a previous experience or challenge he faced during a consulting job. Or maybe a scholar-practitioner might use autoethnography to capture her role in a change process or new initiative. I could even write one on introducing a course on reflexive ethnography to the business school—if I found the courage (smiling).

Me:

Ha! I knew I could drag you to the dark side. Now you're getting it. A second implication is related to what Richardson wrote in 1994 as key to why HRD scholars should care about narrative methods in general and autoethnography in particular. He said, "by writing in different ways, we discover new aspects of our topic and our relationship to it" (p. 516). Although HRDR on occasion includes interesting and novel methodological approaches like Glibkowski, McGinnis, Gillespie, and Schommers' (2014) introduction of narratology, I don't often see those methods applied in empirical studies or theory building. I look at our journals and I see much of the same thing; the writing and methodology lacks the rebelling ideas Greg Wang talked about in his 2011 editorial in HRDQ.

Valerie:

Wasn't Wang's editorial a response to Gary McLean's editorial the previous year?

Me:

Yes. Gary gets at this idea of experimenting and exposing ourselves to novel and innovative research. He said, we as a field "need to find ways to encourage thinking that is outside the box. It might not be continuous with existing theoretical frameworks, and that may help us to think in new ways to keep HRD dynamic, growing, and barrier busting" (p. 320).

Valerie:

I agree about the methods I see in HRD journals. Maybe we're guilty of playing it safe by going for what will be easy and acceptable for review and not pushing the field forward. Jamie Callahan addresses something similar in her 2012 editorial in HRDR. She was talking about organizational spaces, but the sentiment fits. She doesn't "want the field to be satisfied with what we think we 'know' is HRD" (p. 136).

Me:

And I don't want the field to be satisfied with what we think we know about methodological approaches to studying HRD. I know there will be those who might not think autoethnography is rigorous, or worse, like Sparkes in 2002 who called autoethnographers self-absorbed narcissists. I am just optimistic that my peers, both from quantitative and qualitative camps, will read an article using autoethnography regardless of their reliance on powerful academic conventions (Wall, 2006) in order to, in some small way, "change the culture that is keeping us from breakthrough impact on our field's research and practice" (McLean, 2010, p. 318).

Valerie:

Do you see any other implications for the use of autoethnography in HRD research?

Me:

Since autoethnography focuses on exploring the self in relation to other and the space created between the two, I see HRD as ideal for autoethnographic study because in many ways knowledge, identity, and organizational culture are inherent in the field. Autoethnography often places emphasis on a transformative or emancipatory process for the individual. Given the large number of scholar-practitioners in the field, the transformative value of autoethnography can create opportunities for in-depth analysis of the complex lived experiences of these researchers as they explore their emergent identities in relation to others and the organizations in which they operate. Those who are immersed in understanding organizational processes and individual development, and more importantly are responsible for the direction of each, benefit from locating themselves within the study of HRD in order to build a foundation for transformative and emancipatory learning.

Valerie:

Seems to me that autoethnography would allow HRD scholars and practitioners the chance to effectively acknowledge the pragmatic demands of their work and scholarship, to take stock of their experiences, and express how those shape both practice and research.

Me:

I also think that autoethnography is an excellent fit for HRD scholars because they are so passionate and invested in their work. Ellis (1991) once asked, "Who would make a better subject than a researcher consumed by wanting to figure it all out?" (p. 30). I tend to agree. Because of the researcher's use of self, many methodologists argue that autoethnography is more authentic than traditional methodologies. Autoethnographies, like ones that can be produced by those in HRD, "are likely to present fuller pictures [thick description], ones in which the meanings of events and relationships are more likely to be told than inferred" (Laslett, 1999, p. 391). This is particularly important if we are seeking ways to represent the depth of research that is often missing in more traditional, quantitative studies of organizations and employees.

Valerie:

OK, so I can see the appeal, but I am not sure why you want to write a manuscript for HRDR.

Me:

In some ways I was inspired by Turnbull's 2002 HRDR article. She warned against "deep entrenchment in a single paradigm [that] can limit the possibilities of building new and exciting theory" (p. 113). She called for, "a liberal and pragmatic approach to HRD theory building, which, although still retaining academic rigor, celebrates difference and allows learning from more than one paradigm" (p. 113).

Valerie:

That's a good point. I remember reading an article by Alvesson and Skoldberg (2000) and in it they suggested that good qualitative theory building should be interpretively rich. This seems to align with your contention that autoethnography could aid in theory building, because it avoids definitive statements about how things are and instead emphasizes the need to examine things in a particular way in order to allow for new understandings to emerge. They said that for this to occur, both imagination and creativity are required to allow the possibilities that arise from ambiguous empirical material to emerge. At the time I rejected this idea out of hand, admittedly because I didn't fully understand what that might look like.

Me:

It is not always easy to make the connections about methodological choices to theory building. I like to remind my students that generally, quantitative studies are for hypothesis testing, while qualitative studies, like autoethnographies, are excellent approaches for hypothesis generating—which is an essential step to theory building. Plus, as Pedro Bendassolli (2013) points out, qualitative research can provide a way to refine existing theories, as well as develop new inductive theories and present counterfactual inferences. And one more thing; I was recently reminded of Rich Torraco's (2004) call for "publishing peer-reviewed accounts of the researcher's experiences in developing a theory" since this "would offer insights into the process of how the researcher developed a theory" (p. 181). It is another way that autoethnography can contribute to the theory building in HRD by being a critical means for exploring the theory development process used by scholars.

Valerie:

OK, so autoethnography seems a lot less scary now. I understand where it comes from and I get how it's conducted. I also see why you would want to share it in a journal article. It certainly has implications for those conducting research and developing theory in the field of HRD. To be honest, I think I, like so many of my colleagues, are not necessarily opposed to innovative methodologies, on the contrary, I think it is more likely what Hatcher and Guerdat described in their 2008 editorial in HRDQ, "The reason innovative methods are not used is probably more about expertise than reluctance to send the results of innovative research to an HRD research journal" (p. 2).

Me:

I think you're right. And I remember that editorial. Their push for innovation seven years ago bears repeating, "If we are going to lead the field through research, then we need significant breakthroughs that take us to the next version, generation, or level of understanding" (Hatcher & Guerdat, 2008, p. 1). We need to take off our blinders and become accepting of and encourage new and different research. Scholars and scholar-practitioners will then be agreeable to new research that includes supporting the use of innovative or uncommon research methods and motivated to send their innovative research to HRD journals rather than to hybridized journals that have become the catch-all for what doesn't fit a field's dominant paradigm.

> *. . . *Ding* Ladies and gentlemen, as we start our approach, please make sure your seat backs and tray tables are in their full upright position. Make sure your seat belt is securely fastened and all carry-on luggage is stowed underneath the seat in front of you or in the overhead bins. Thank you.*

Declaration of Conflicting Interests The author declared no potential conflicts of interest with respect to the research, authorship, and/or publication of this article.

Funding The author received no financial support for the research, authorship, and/or publication of this article.

NOTES

1. To maintain the conversational style, I have intentionally chosen to alternate the use of gendered pronouns throughout the paper.

REFERENCES

1. Adams T. E., Holman Jones S. (2008). Autoethnography is queer. In Denzin N., Lincoln Y., Smith L. T. (Eds.), Handbook of critical and indigenous methodologies (pp. 373-390). Thousand Oaks, CA: Sage.
2. Alvesson M., Skoldberg K. (2000). Reflexive methodology. London, England: Sage.
3. Anderson L. (2006). Analytic autoethnography. Journal of Contemporary Ethnography, 35, 373-395.
4. Atkinson P., Hammersley M. (1994). Ethnography and participant observation. In Denzin N., Lincoln Y. (Eds.),

Handbook of qualitative research (pp. 248-261). Thousand Oaks, CA: Sage.

5. Babcock B. A. (1980). Reflexivity: Definitions and discriminations. Semiotica, 30(1-2), 1-14.

6. Beattie R. (2002). Going native: Ethnographic research in HRD. In Stewart J. J., Watson S. (Eds.), Understanding HRD: A research based approach (pp. 315-338). London, England: Routledge.

7. Behar R. (1996). The vulnerable observer: Anthropology that breaks your heart. Boston, MA: Beacon.

8. Belle S. M., Burley D. L., Long S. D. (2015). Where do I belong? High-intensity teleworkers' experience of organizational belonging. Human Resource Development International, 18, 76-96.

9. Bendassolli P. F. (2013, January). Theory building in qualitative research: Reconsidering the problem of induction. Forum Qualitative Sozialforschung/Forum: Qualitative Social Research, 14(1). Retrieved from http://www.qualitativeresearch.net /index.php/fqs/article/view/1851/3497

10. Bochner A., Ellis C. (2006). Communication as autoethnography. In Shepherd G. J., John J.St., Striphas T. (Eds.), Communication as . . . Perspectives on theory (pp. 110-122). Thousand Oaks, CA: Sage.

11. Bochner A. P. (1994). Perspectives on inquiry II: Theories and stories. In Knapp M. L., Miller G. R. (Eds.), Handbook of interpersonal communication (pp. 21-41). Thousand Oaks, CA: Sage.

12. Boje D., Tyler J. A. (2009). Story and narrative noticing: Workaholism autoethnographies. Journal of Business Ethics, 84, 173-194.

13. Boyle M., Parry K. (2007). Telling the whole story: The case for organizational autoethnography. Culture and Organization, 13, 185-190.

14. Callahan J. L. (2009). Manifestations of power and control: Training as the catalyst for scandal at the United States Air Force Academy. Violence Against Women, 15, 1149-1168.

15. Callahan J. L. (2010). The Importance of epistemology: A response to Rosenstein's commentary. Violence Against Women, 16, 1186-1193.

16. Callahan J. L. (2012). Occupy . . . HRD? Expanding our vision of the field into nontraditional spaces. Human Resource Development Review, 11, 138-155.

17. Chang H. (2008). Autoethnography as method. Walnut Creek, CA: Left Coast Press.

18. Clandinin D. J., Connelly F. M. (2000). Narrative inquiry: Experience and story in qualitative research. San Francisco, CA: Jossey-Bass.

19. Davies C. A. (2008). Reflexive ethnography: A guide to researching selves and others. New York, NY: Routledge.

20. Davis F. (1959). The cabdriver and his fare: Facets of a fleeting relationship. American Journal of Sociology, 65, 158-165.

21. Doloriert C., Sambrook S. (2012). Organisational autoethnography. Journal of Organizational Ethnography, 1, 83-95.

22. Ekeh A., Leitch J., Iyer S. (2014, June). Cultural influences on learning technologies in the US health care industry: An auto-ethnographic bricolage from HRD practitioners. Poster presented at the University Forum for Human Resource Development, Edinburgh, Scotland.

23. Ellington L., Ellis C. (2008). Autoethnography as constructionist project. In Holstein J. A., Gubrium J. F. (Eds.), Handbook of constructionist research (pp. 445-465). New York, NY: Guilford Press.

24. Ellis C. (1991). Sociological introspection and emotional experience. Symbolic Interaction, 14, 23-50.

25. Ellis C. (1999). Heartful autoethnography. Qualitative Health Research, 9, 669-683.

26. Ellis C. (2004). The ethnographic I: A methodological novel about autoethnography. Walnut Creek, CA: Alta Mira Press.

27. Ellis C. (2007). Telling secrets, revealing lives: Relational ethics in research with intimate others. Qualitative Inquiry, 13, 3-29.

28. Ellis C., Adams T. E., Bochner A. P. (2010). Autoethnography: An overview. Forum Qualitative Sozialforschung/Forum: Qualitative Social Research, 12(1), Article 10. Retrieved from http://www.qualitative-research.net/index.php/fqs/article/view/1589/3095

29. Ellis C., Bochner A. P. (2000). Autoethnography, personal narrative, reflexivity: Researcher as subject. In Denzin N. K., Lincoln Y. S. (Eds.), Handbook of qualitative research (2nd ed., pp. 733-768). Thousand Oaks, CA: Sage.

30. Foley D. E. (2002). Critical ethnography: The reflexive turn. International Journal of Qualitative Studies in Education, 15, 469-490.

31. Fontaine G. (1996). Social support and the challenges of international assignments. In Ward C., Bhagat R. S. (Eds.), Handbook of intercultural training (pp. 264-281). Thousand Oaks, CA: Sage.

32. Frentz T. S., Hocker J. L. (2010). Layered reflections on a written story through real-time conversation. Qualitative Inquiry, 16, 621-629.

33. Gedro J., Mizzi R. C., Rocco T. S., van Loo J. (2013). Going global: Professional mobility and concerns for LGBT workers. Human Resource Development International, 16, 282-297.

34. Githens R. P. (2012). Organization change and social organizing strategies: Employee-initiated organization development. Human Resource Development Quarterly, 23, 487-518.

35. Glibkowski B. C., McGinnis L., Gillespie J., Schommer A. (2014). "How" narratology narrows the organizational theory-practice gap. Human Resource Development Review, 13, 234-262.

36. Grenier R. S. (under review). A sojourn experience in the Land of Fire and Ice: Examining cultural competence and employee well-being through an autoethnographic exploration.

37. Grenier R. S., Burke M. C. (2008). No margin for error: A study of two women balancing motherhood and Ph.D. studies. The Qualitative Report, 13(4), 581-604. Retrieved from http://www.nova.edu/ssss/QR/QR13-4/grenier.pdf

38. Guba E. G., Lincoln Y. S. (1981). Effective evaluation: Improving the usefulness of evaluation results through responsive and naturalistic approaches. San Francisco, CA: Jossey-Bass.

39. Guest G., MacQueen K. M., Namey E. E. (2012). Applied thematic analysis. New York, NY: Sage.

40. Hatcher T., Guerdat K. (2008). Where is innovation in HRD research? Human Resource Development Quarterly, 19, 1-5.

41. Hayano D. M. (1979). Auto-ethnography: Paradigms, problems, and prospects. Human Organization, 38, 113-120.

42. Holt N. L. (2008). Representation, legitimation, and autoethnography: An autoethnographic writing story. International Journal of Qualitative Methods, 2, 18-28.

43. Howell S. L., Carter V. K., Schied F. M. (2002). Gender and women's experience at work: A critical and feminist perspective on human resource development. Adult Education Quarterly, 52, 112-127.

44. Kahn W. A. (1992). To be fully there: Psychological presence at work. Human Relations, 45, 321-349.

45. Karra N., Phillips N. (2008). Researching "back home" international management research as autoethnography. Organization Research Methods, 11, 541-561.

46. Laslett B. (1999). Personal narratives as sociology. Contemporary Sociology, 28, 391-401.

47. Lawless A., Sambrook S., Stewart J. (2012). Critical human resource development: Enabling alternative subject positions within a master of arts in human resource development educational programme. Human Resource Development International, 15, 321-336.

48. Lee R. M. (1995). Dangerous fieldwork. Newbury Park, CA: Sage.

49. Marcus G. (1994). What comes (just) after "post"? The case of ethnography. In Denzin N., Lincoln Y. (Eds.), Handbook of qualitative research (pp. 563-574). Thousand Oaks, CA: Sage.

50. McLean G. N. (2010). Human resource development scholar as rebel. Human Resource Development Quarterly, 21, 317-320.

51. Megford K. (2006). Caught with a fake ID: Ethical questions about slippage in autoethnography. Qualitative Inquiry, 12, 853-864.

52. Merriam S. B. (2014). Qualitative research: A guide to design and implementation. New York, NY: John Wiley.

53. O'Riordan N. (2014, June). Autoethnography: Proposing a new method for information systems research. Paper presented at the Twenty Second European Conference on Information Systems, Tel Aviv, Israel.

54. Rambo C. (2005). Impressions of grandmother: An autoethnographic portrait. Journal of Contemporary Ethnography, 34, 560-585.

55. Reed-Danahay D. E. (1997). Auto/ethnography. New York, NY: Berg.

56. Richardson L. (1994). Writing: A method of inquiry. In Denzin N. K., Lincoln Y. S. (Eds.), Handbook of qualitative research (pp. 516-529). Thousand Oaks, CA: Sage.

57. Richardson L. (2000). Evaluating ethnography. Qualitative Inquiry, 6, 253-255.

58. Richardson L., St. Pierre E. (2005). Writing: A method of inquiry. In Denzin N., Lincoln Y. (Eds.), Handbook of qualitative research (3rd ed., pp. 959-978). Thousand Oaks, CA: Sage.

59. Rocco T. S. (2010). Criteria for evaluating qualitative studies. Human Resource Development International, 13, 375-378.

60. Rosenstein J. E. (2010). Commentary on Jamie L. Callahan's "manifestations of power and control: Training as the catalyst for scandal at the United States air force academy. Violence Against Women, 16, 1173-1185.

61. Roy D. E. (1959/1960). Banana time: Job satisfaction and informal interaction. Human Organization, 18, 158-168.

62. Sambrook A. S., Jones N., Doloriert C. (2014). Employee engagement and autoethnography: Being and studying self. Journal of Workplace Learning, 26, 172-187.

63. Sambrook S. (2001). HRD as an emergent and negotiated evolution: An ethnographic case study in the British National Health Service. Human Resource Development Quarterly, 12, 169-193.

64. Sparkes A. C. (2002). Autoethnography: Self-indulgence or something more. In Bochner A., Ellis C. (Eds.), Ethnographically speaking: Autoethnography, literature, and aesthetics (pp. 209-232). New York, NY: Alta Mira Press.

65. Stake R. E., Trumbull D. J. (1982). Naturalistic generalizations. Review Journal of Philosophy and Social Science, 7, 1-12. Retrieved from http://education.illinois.edu/circe/publications /naturalistic.pdf

66. Torraco R. J. (2004). Challenges and choices for theoretical research in human resource development. Human Resource Development Quarterly, 15, 171-188.

67. Turnbull S. (2002). Bricolage as an alternative approach to human resource development theory building. Human Resource Development Review, 1, 111-128. Abstract

68. Turner R. (1947). The navy disbursing officer as a bureaucrat. American Sociological Review, 12, 342-348.

69. Uotinen J. (2011). Senses, bodily knowledge, and autoethnography unbeknown knowledge from an ICU experience. Qualitative Health Research, 21, 1307-1315.

70. Van Maanen J. (1988). Tales of the field: On the writing of ethnography. Chicago, IL: University of Chicago Press.

71. Vasconcelos E. F. D. S. (2011). "I can see you": An autoethnography of my teacher-student self. Qualitative Report, 16, 415-440. Retrieved from http://nsuworks.nova.edu/tqr/vol16/iss2/6

72. Vickers M. H. (2010). The creation of fiction to share other truths and different viewpoints: A creative journey and an interpretive process. Qualitative Inquiry, 16, 556-565.

73. Wall S. (2006). An autoethnography on learning about autoethnography. International Journal of Qualitative Methods, 5, 146-160. Retrieved from http://ejournals.library. ualberta.ca/index.php/IJQM/article/viewArticle/4396

74. Wang G. G. (2011). The human resource development scholar as a disciplined rebel. Human Resource Development Quarterly, 22, 1-5.

5

CHAPTER

Investigating The Factors Affecting Job Satisfaction and Turnover: Case of Sultan Qaboos University

Adel Ismail Al-Alawi[1] , Amal Suliaman Al-Azri[2] and Hisham Naseem Mohammad[3]

[1] *University of Bahrain, College of Business Administration, Department of Management and Marketing, Kingdom of Bahrain*

[2] *Sultan Qaboos University, Oman*

[3] *Ministry of Education, Manama, Kingdom of Bahrain*

ABSTRACT

Job satisfaction has received wide attention as one of the core elements of an organization that is successful in achieving its purposes. This study aims to investigate the job satisfaction of Sultan Qaboos University (SQU) administrative staff by measuring the job satisfaction level of non-academic staff. The study is concerned with the problem of turnover amongst administrative employees in 2014 which was believed to be high by Majlis Al- Shura (Oman Parliament), this drove the university to create an incentive program through increasing salaries. This is a descriptive quantitative cross sectional applied research where data were collected by using a structured questionnaire consisting of 42 items covering seven domains of job satisfaction. The overall response rate (150 completed questionnaire) was 68%, 137 (47.4% males, 52.6% females) were usable. The outcome showed that administrative staffs were satisfied with their job. It also revealed that job satisfaction was affected by staff's gender, where males showed higher job satisfaction than females. It also showed that those who have shorter experience are more satisfied than those who have longer experience and those who hold lower qualifications and lower job levels have higher job satisfaction compared to those who have higher qualifications and job level.

Keywords: Factors affecting job satisfaction, Turnover, Qaboos University, Work motivation, Work quality, Workforce environment, Working conditions, Incentive programs.

INTRODUCTION

Job satisfaction has received wide attention as one of the core elements of an organization which is successful in achieving its purposes. The concept of job satisfaction was defined by some researchers such as Locke (1976, p1304) who defined it as "a pleasurable or positive emotional state resulting from the appraisal of one's job or job experiences", while Lofquist and Davis (1991, p27) defined it as "an individual's positive affective reaction of the target environment...as a result of the individual's appraisal of the extent to which his or her needs are fulfilled by the environment." It is also defined by Luthans (1994) as "an attitude developed by an individual towards the job and job conditions." Spector (1997) enhanced the definition as "an attitudinal variable that measures how a person feels about his or her job, including different facets of the job." According to these definitions, job satisfaction could be viewed as the status of how employees feel regarding their working environment.

Job satisfaction is a very important factor as it affects employees' working behavior, loyalty to the institution and their decisions about turnover (Clark 2001, Shields and Ward 2001). It also positively affects the employees' internal work motivation, work quality, performance, absenteeism and turnover (Bruce and Blackburn 1992; Fajana 2002).

Nguyen et al, (2003) found that high levels of job satisfaction cause employees to be happier with their job environment, income, communication and workload and to be willing to act positively.

Therefore, the success of an institution in achieving its aims is directly linked to the satisfaction expressed by its employees (Freeman 2005). A study by Carpitella (2003) found that job satisfaction reduces turnover by 50% from the norms, increases customers' satisfaction to an average of 95% and lowers the cost of labor by 12%. Harter et al (2002) found positive and substantive correlation between employees' level of satisfaction and the unit outcomes of productivity, profits, workplace accidents and customers' satisfaction.

To achieve the satisfaction of employees, the institution uses incentive programs to ensure the productivity, loyalty and low turnover rate of its employees (Toloposky, 2000). Alam et al,(2012, p35-36) suggested nine domains of job satisfaction which can be used to measure job satisfaction levels:"(1) Organization development; (2) Policies of compensation and benefits such as wage, salary reward and penalties; (3) Promotion and career development such as opportunity for promotion, equal opportunity, training programs; (4) Job satisfaction such as job design, responsibility, task identity, quantity of work; (5) Security which give employees assurance to keep their current job; (6) Working environment, such as feeling safe, comfortable, having a clean office, good services; (7) Relationship with supervisor; (8) Working group; (9) Leadership styles."(Küskü, 2003).

As job satisfaction has such an effect on the success of institutions, many researchers have conducted studies in different institutions; however, few of these studies have been concerned with higher education and particularly with administrative staff in universities. Küskü (2003) stressed the importance of evaluating the job satisfaction level of these employees because most research is mainly concentrated on profit-making in industrial and service organizations and there is a growing interest in investigating job satisfaction of employees in higher education to achieve quality management. He also explained that the higher education institutions have intensive labor and their budgets depend on the effectiveness of their employees.

Several studies have been conducted about the job satisfaction of academics in higher education, yet few of them have been concerned with administrative staff in universities. These studies found high levels of job satisfaction (Olorunsola2010). Others found that employees are satisfied with university arrangements such as promotion and tenure process but not satisfied with their workload and salary (Leckie and Brett 1997). Some studies showed relationships between job satisfaction and work environment, salary, and relationships with colleagues (Küskü2003). Some studies found that job satisfaction correlates strongly with promotion (Ellickson and Logsdon 2002; Peterson et al 2003).

The effects of demographic variables on job satisfaction have been examined by some researchers. The results related to gender are varied; some showed that males had higher levels of job satisfaction (McIntyre and McIntyre 2010), while others showed that females' job satisfaction was higher than that of males (Smith 2009; Tulen and Serife 2012). While a research study by Al-Alawi and Al-Alawi (2014) in Bahrain stated that "Perceived levels of stress were statistically significantly associated with gender. Staff with moderate to high perceived levels of stress was more likely to be male compared to staff with low perceived levels of stress that were more likely to be female". Other studies showed no significant differences (Brown and Sargeant 2007). Some studies examined the effect of experience and found that those who have long experience tend to be less interested in institutions' turnover due to emotional attachment, which shows affective commitment and satisfaction (Mathieu and Zajac 1990; Meyer et al 2002).

The current study is concerned with examining the job satisfaction of Sultan Qaboos University's administrative staff. The basis of this study was the problem of turnover of administrative staff in the last few years, which drove the university to create an incentive program through increasing salaries in January 2014. However, Pfeffer, and Davis-Blake (1992), Ma, Samuels, and Alexander (2003), Trevor, Reilly and Gerhar (2012), Alam, Sameena, and Puja (2012) and Al-Alawi and Al-Alawi (2014) indicated that salary is not the only factor for turnover but that there are other factors. This study tries to investigate job satisfaction from different domains of job satisfaction to come up with a clear picture about the situation regarding job satisfaction at SQU.

The selection of SQU was based on the fact that it is the only governmental university in the Sultanate of Oman and government is highly involved with this university. The budget of the university has reached 140 million Omani Riyal in the year 2014 (1.00 Omani Riyal equals 2.60 US Dollars). The university is seeking success in obtaining international accreditation, so it is highly concerned about developing all facilities, services, work quality, products quality and achieving all that is required to satisfy the requirements.

This study aims to determine the level of job satisfaction of Sultan Qaboos University administrative staff and to identify the effect of some independent variables on the level of job satisfaction of University administrative staff. The study addressed two related research questions: (1) what is the level of job satisfaction of Sultan Qaboos University administrative staff? (2) What are the affecting job satisfaction factors of Sultan Qaboos University administrative staff according to their gender, experience, qualification and job level?

Hence, there is a lack of research studies in the field of higher education administrative staff in the Arab world, however, this study attempted to measure the job satisfaction and turnover of higher education non-academic administrative staff in the Omani governmental university. Consequently, the significance of the study is to provide information about the level of job satisfaction of Sultan Qaboos University administrative staff and to provide an overview of the factors affecting the levels of job satisfaction and the possible reasons for the high turnover rate of staff.

METHODOLOGY

In this section, participants, data collection, instrument and results are presented as follows:

Participants

The questionnaire was distributed randomly to 150 responses but only 137 (47.4% males, 52.6% females) were usable and the remaining 13 questionnaires were not filled completely. Data were completed with a response rate of 68 %. These participants were selected randomly from those who agreed to participate and from those whom the researchersmet in reception and meeting areas. Convenience sampling techniques were used in this research. This method involves acquiring participants in the place of work typically wherever they are available to participate. Descriptive Data Analysis in Table-1 shows there are more female participants in the study with response rate of 52.6% and the majority of responses have bachelor's degree (50.4%). The table also illustrated that the majority (66.4%) are only staff and it also indicated that a greater portion of participants (40.9%) have 1 to 6 years of experience.

Table 1: Number &Percentage of Variables

Variables		N	%
Gender	Male	65	47.4
	Female	72	52.6
	Total	**137**	**100**
Qualification	Secondary	8	5.8
	Diploma	39	28.5
	BA	69	50.4
	MA	21	15.3
	Total	**137**	**100**
Job Level	Manager	9	6.6
	Manager's assistant	14	10.2
	Head of Department	23	16.8
	Staff	91	66.4
	Total	**137**	**100**
Experience	1 to 6 years	56	40.9
	7 to 15 years	38	27.7
	Above 15 years	43	31.4
	Total	**137**	**100**

Limited Number of Respondents

Data were collected from only 137 out of 3220 administrative staff from Sultan Qaboos University. The current study had targeted to reach 500 respondents but due to the shortage of time it only acquired 200. Though, the returned amount was 150 as some of them were eliminated because they were incomplete.

Instrument

A questionnaire was used to gather data from the administrative staff. The questionnaire was developed by the researchers and was based on the previous studies such as Küskü (2003); Marvin (2006); Rita and Irena (2012). The questionnaire consisted of 42 items divided into seven domains.

The questionnaire was validated by a group of judges from 2 human rescores managers, and 2 professors in Sultan Qaboos University and the 3 management professors from the University of Bahrain. The judges were asked to evaluate appropriateness of items to the purpose of the study, clarity items, as well as their correlation to each domain and formulation of every item. Based on the judges' comments and recommendations, the questionnaire was enhanced by modifying and rephrasing some items, and finally by adding new ones. The questionnaire reliability was obtained by piloting it to 20 staff and assessed by using Cronbach's Alpha test (.929).

RESULTS

The analyses of the following research questions are below:

- What is the level of job satisfaction of Sultan Qaboos University administrative staff?

Table 2 shows the mean and standard deviations of the job satisfaction of Sultan Qaboos University administrative staff. Mean interpretation: 1-1.49 (very unsatisfied), 1.5-2.49 (unsatisfied), 2.5-3.49 (uncertain), 3.5-4.49 (satisfied), 4.5-5 (very satisfied).

Table 2: Means and standard Deviations of Staff Job Satisfaction

Satisfaction domains	N	Mean	Std. Deviation
Job Mission and evaluation system	137	3.98	1.27
Work environment	137	3.76	0.91
Satisfaction about working at SQU	137	3.57	0.612
Salary Progression	137	3.54	0.832
Office Services	137	3.43	0.727
Administration system	137	3.37	0.898
General Services	137	3.17	0.91
Total	137	3.55	0.612

The result showed that SQU administrative staff were satisfied with their job and working at SQU. They were highly satisfied about job mission and evaluation systems, working environment and financial promotion but they were uncertain about general services and administration system.

Analyses of the questions relevant to the role of gender, experience, qualification and job are presented below:

– The effect of Gender on Job Satisfaction:

Table 3 indicates the mean and standard deviation values, independent samples and t-test analysis of variance of the responses given by the participants concerning their job satisfaction with respect to their gender.

Table 3. Means, STD and t-test for the Gender

Table 3. Means, STD and t-test for the Gender

Satisfaction domains	Gender	N	Mean	Std. Deviation	t	df	Sig. (2-tailed)
Administration system	Male	65	3.33	0.643	0.43	135	0.668
	Female	72	3.4	1.082		117.495	
Job Mission and evaluation system	Male	65	4.16	1.585	1.617	135	0.108
	Female	72	3.81	0.9		99.104	
Work environment	Male	65	3.98	0.928	2.728	135	.007 ✱
	Female	72	3.56	0.853		130.453	
Office Services	Male	65	3.57	0.66	2.293	135	.023 ✱
	Female	72	3.29	0.762		134.768	
Financial promotion	Male	65	3.63	0.793	1.216	135	0.226
	Female	72	3.46	0.863		134.953	
General Services	Male	65	3.12	0.889	0.566	135	0.573
	Female	72	3.21	0.933		134.601	
Satisfaction about working at SQU	Male	65	3.63	0.557	0.955	135	0.341
	Female	72	3.53	0.659		134.422	
Total	Male	65	3.63	0.544	1.599	135	0.112
	Female	72	3.47	0.662		133.887	

✱ **Significant Difference (α0.05).**

The results showed that there are no significant differences due to the staff gender except in working environment and office services in favor of male staff. Males showed high level of job satisfaction compared to females.

– The effect of Experience on Job Satisfaction:

Table 4 indicates the results of ANOVA test of variance of the mean given by the participants concerning their job satisfaction with respect to their experience.

Table 4: Results of ANOVA Test for the Staff experience

Domains		Sum of Squares	df	Mean Square	F	Sig.
Administration system	Between Groups	7.821	2	3.91	5.134	.007*
	Within Groups	102.067	134	0.762		
	Total	109.888	136			
Job Mission and evaluation system	Between Groups	9.06	2	4.53	2.84	0.062
	Within Groups	213.712	134	1.595		
	Total	222.771	136			
Work environment	Between Groups	1.796	2	0.898	1.085	0.341
	Within Groups	110.917	134	0.828		
	Total	112.713	136			
Office Services	Between Groups	5.827	2	2.914	5.907	.003*
	Within Groups	66.092	134	0.493		
	Total	71.92	136			
Financial promotion	Between Groups	1.787	2	0.894	1.294	0.278
	Within Groups	92.519	134	0.69		
	Total	94.306	136			
General Services	Between Groups	7.957	2	3.979	5.084	.007*
	Within Groups	104.863	134	0.783		
	Total	112.82	136			
Satisfaction about working at SQU	Between Groups	2.765	2	1.382	3.833	.024*
	Within Groups	48.329	134	0.361		
	Total	51.094	136			
Total	Between Groups	4.059	2	2.029	5.786	.004*
	Within Groups	46.998	134	0.351		
	Total	51.057	136			

*Significant Difference (α0.05).

With respect to the experience variable, statistical differences were found in staff's level of job satisfaction in most domains except in job mission and evaluation systems and financial promotion which showed no difference. It revealed that those who have less experience (1 to 6) showed higher levels of job satisfaction compared with those who have more experience.

– The effect of Qualification on the Job Satisfaction

Table 5 indicates the results of ANOVA test of variance of the mean given by the participants concerning their job satisfaction with respect to their qualifications. There is a significant relationship (p < .05) between administrative staff qualification with general services. There is also a significant relationship between admin staff qualification (p>.05) with the level of satisfaction working in the SQU. The study shows that there is no significant relationship found with other domains such as administration system, job mission and evaluation system, work environment and office services.

Table 5. Results of ANOVA Test for Staff Qualifications

Domains		Sum of Squares	df	Mean Square	F	Sig.
Administration system	Between Groups	5.628	3	1.876	2.393	0.071
	Within Groups	104.26	133	0.784		
	Total	109.888	136			
Job Mission and evaluation system	Between Groups	11.78	3	3.927	2.475	0.064
	Within Groups	210.991	133	1.586		
	Total	222.771	136			
Work environment	Between Groups	2.241	3	0.747	0.899	0.443
	Within Groups	110.472	133	0.831		
	Total	112.713	136			
Office Services	Between Groups	2.478	3	0.826	1.582	0.197
	Within Groups	69.442	133	0.522		
	Total	71.92	136			
Financial promotion	Between Groups	4.374	3	1.458	2.156	0.096
	Within Groups	89.931	133	0.676		
	Total	94.306	136			
General Services	Between Groups	7.491	3	2.497	3.153	.027*
	Within Groups	105.33	133	0.792		
	Total	112.82	136			
Satisfaction about working at SQU	Between Groups	3.931	3	1.31	3.695	.014*
	Within Groups	47.163	133	0.355		
	Total	51.094	136			
Total	Between Groups	3.711	3	1.237	3.474	.018*
	Within Groups	47.346	133	0.356		
	Total	51.057	136			

*Significant Difference (α0.05).

In respect of the qualification variable, statistical differences were found in general services, satisfaction about working at SQU. It revealed that those who have Secondary Diploma and BA were more satisfied than those who have an MA degree.

The effect of job level on Job Satisfaction

Table 6 indicates the results of ANOVA test of variance of the mean given by the participants concerning their job satisfaction with respect to their job level.

Table 6. Results of ANOVA test for Staff Job Level

Domains		Sum of Squares	df	Mean Square	F	Sig.
Administration system	Between Groups	3.347	3	1.116	1.393	0.248
	Within Groups	106.541	133	0.801		
	Total	109.888	136			
Job Mission and evaluation system	Between Groups	7.507	3	2.502	1.546	0.206
	Within Groups	215.264	133	1.619		
	Total	222.771	136			
Work environment	Between Groups	1.671	3	0.557	0.667	0.574
	Within Groups	111.042	133	0.835		
	Total	112.713	136			
Office Services	Between Groups	0.156	3	0.052	0.096	0.962
	Within Groups	71.764	133	0.54		
	Total	71.92	136			
Financial promotion	Between Groups	2.295	3	0.765	1.106	0.349
	Within Groups	92.01	133	0.692		
	Total	94.306	136			
General Services	Between Groups	16.571	3	5.524	7.633	.000 *
	Within Groups	96.249	133	0.724		
	Total	112.82	136			
Satisfaction about working at SQU	Between Groups	1.822	3	0.607	1.639	0.183
	Within Groups	49.273	133	0.37		
	Total	51.094	136			
Total	Between Groups	2.06	3	0.687	1.864	0.139
	Within Groups	48.997	133	0.368		
	Total	51.057	136			

* Significant Difference (α0.05).

In respect of the job level variable, no statistical differences were found in staff job satisfaction in most of the domains except in general services which showed a difference. It revealed that managers, manager assistants and directors were less satisfied about general services when compared with ordinary staff.

DISCUSSION

The results of the study indicated that Sultan Qaboos University administrative staffs were satisfied with their job. This result could be due to the fact that the university is extremely concerned about providing a positive working environment to make its employees happier and more productive and about reducing turnover rates. It also could be because SQU is the only governmental university and it is highly supported by the government and under the eye of the government to maintain its quality and reputation as it carries the name of His Majesty. The university buildings and facilities have their effect on the levels of job satisfaction where the design of the university was well structured to provide a suitable working environment. Moreover, Yahy (2012) stated that it also could be due to the religious and cultural aspects which encourage the staff to be more positive in their work and to cooperate with others.

The satisfaction is a result of the university policies to maintain the quality of its products and services to compete with another private university which has become recently a competitor of SQU. It also is due to accelerated development in services such as new buildings which provide more offices, introducing new services for staff, and introducing all services electronically. It also is due to the service evaluation system which allows staff to evaluate the quality of all provided services through online questionnaires every year, which has led to the development of many of these services. The satisfaction is furthermore a result from the high increase in the staff salaries which took place in January 2014 and expectation of further increases in July 2014. The university policies were effective in raising the level of job satisfaction as literature showed a relationship between job satisfaction and work environment, salary, and relationships with colleagues (Küskü, 2003), and the correlation between job satisfaction and promotion (Ellickson and Logsdon 2002, Peterson, et al., 2003).

Based on the results, SQU, according to the literature, has achieved one of the main elements of an institution's success, which is employees' satisfaction (Freeman, 2005). Such levels of satisfaction for SQU are illustrated in Table 2.According to Clark (2001); Shields and Ward (2001) positively reflected on SQU staff's working behavior, loyalty and their interest in working instead. It will also lead to strengthening the relationships between staff, increasing cooperation, motivation and work quality and their performance (Bruce and Blackburn, 1992; Fajana 2002).

The results also showed that job satisfaction was affected by gender. The finding of this study supports the results of some previous studies which showed that males had higher levels of job satisfaction than females (McIntyre and McIntyre, 2010). This difference is mainly in working environment and office services which could be due to the fact that some females share offices with male staff, which may not be comfortable for them. It could also be because females feel greater pressure in relation to work, and they were less trusted by their leaders. They were also less trusted because of the speed of providing service.

In this research, respondents with lower job experience showed higher job satisfaction levels. This result contradicts with the literature which showed that those who have more experience have higher levels of job satisfaction (Mathieu and Zajac, 1990; Meyer et al., 2002). This result could be because those who have more experience have higher ambitions for getting better services were interested in developing administration systems. A study by Gesinde and Adejumo (2012) indicated that there was significant positive relationship between age and work experience and job satisfaction. Whereas, in a contradictory study by Hong, Hamid and Salleh (2013) indicated that age factor negatively affects the employee job satisfaction. The results may benefit organizations in enhancing overall job satisfaction and in empathizing organizational issues such as high turnover (Kerber and Campbell, 1987).

The result also revealed that administrative staff job satisfaction was affected by their qualification and job level. This result could be due to the high expectations of those who hold higher degrees and higher job level compared to those who hold lower degrees and lower job level. Such results could be due to comparisons in which these employees compare the services provided with other institutions which provide better services. It also could be due to the fact that the service provided is less than their expectations according to their qualification and working position.

Study Limitations, Further research and Conclusion

Limitations

The limitations of this study were as follow:

1. The data were limited to Sultanate Oman.
2. This research is limited to only one governmental university Sultan Qaboos University
3. Limited to non-academic staff — The research was collected solely from administrative employees of Sultan Qaboos University in Oman.

Further Research

Therefore, further study, in expanding the sample size of administration staff to be greater than the number who participated in this study is crucial in order to verify the generalizability of the findings to a larger population of Sultan Qaboos University. A more balanced ratio of men to women responses in this study could possibly provide more significant results to further understand perceived job satisfaction of males and females in relation to turnover and job satisfaction. Additionally, the study should also focus on comparisons between faculty members and administrative staff to measure the job satisfaction and turnover.

CONCLUSION

The study indicated that Sultan Qaboos University administrative employees were satisfied with their job and with working in a good workplace environment, which made the staff more productive and secure, and thus reducing the turnover rate. Furthermore, SQU believes that their staff is the number one asset, with the highest degrees of competence, integrity and professionalism. Although SQU instills in its people the principles of entrepreneurship and decision-making, the university needs to stress the positive aspects of job satisfaction and sort out the negative aspects which may affect staff job satisfaction currently or in the future. Furthermore, the Omani culture and the loyalty aspect inspire the workforce to be more confident in their job environment and to collaborate. Nevertheless, the job satisfaction may also result from the enhancement of the employees' salaries during the data collection time of this study.

ACKNOWLEDGEMENTS

The researchers thank all the staff who responded to their study's questionnaire and all the staff who helped them to distribute and gather questionnaires from different departments. They also appreciate the comments provided by Dr Nehal Elnaggar from Royal University for Woman in Bahrain and Dr Ebtisam Al-Alawi from Brunel University in the UK and Ms Sara Al-Bassam from Arabian Gulf University in Bahrain.

REFERENCES

1. Al-Alawi, A. I. and Al-Alawi, E. I. (2014). "Measuring Occupational Stress among Management Information Systems Workers and Users in the Financial Services Sector: The Case of Bahraini Bankers", International Journal of Scientific and Research Publications, 4(8) ISSN 2250-3153.
2. Alam, S., Sameena, R. and Puja, A. (2012). "Identification of Variables Affecting Employee Satisfaction and Their Impact on the Organization", IOSR Journal of Business and Management. 5(1) 32-39.
3. Brown, D. and Sargeant, M. (2007). "Job satisfaction, organizational commitment, and religious commitment of full time university employees",Journal of Research on Christian Education, 16, 211-241.
4. Bruce, W. M., and Blackburn, J. W. (1992) . Balancing job satisfaction and performance. Westport, CT: Quorum Books.
5. Carpitella, Bill. (2003). Make residential construction the industry of choice. Professional Builder, Oct 2003.
6. Clark, A.E. (2001). "What Really Matters in a Job? Hedonic Measurement Using Quit Data",Labour Economics, 8, 223-242.
7. Ellickson, M. and logsdon , K. (2002). "Determinants of Job satisfaction of municipal government employees", Public personnel management, 31(3), 343 — 358.

8. Fajana, S. (2002). Human Resource Management: An Introduction. Lagos: Labofin and Company.

9. Kusku, F. (2003). "Employee satisfaction in higher education: the case of academic and administrative staff in turkey", Career Development International, 8 (7), 347-356.

10. Freeman, S. (2005), "Employee satisfaction: The key to a successful company", [online], [Retrieved on March 15, 2016], http://library.lp.findlaw.com/articles/file/00301/008927/title /Subject/topic/Employment.

11. Gesinde, A. M., and Adejumo, G. O. (2012). "Effects of Age and Work Experience on Job Satisfaction of Primary School Teachers: Implications for Career Counseling". International Journal of Asian Social Science, 2(3), 302-309

12. Harter, J., Schmidt, F. L., and Hayes, T. (2002). "Business-unit level relationship between employee satisfaction, employee engagement, and business outcomes: A meta-analysis", Journal of Applied Psychology, 87, 268-279.

13. Hong, L. C., Hamid, N. I. N. A., and Salleh, N. M. (2013). "A study on the factors affecting job satisfaction amongst employees of a factory in Seremban, Malaysia". Business Management Dynamics, 3(1), 26-40.

14. Kerber, K. W., and Campbell, J. P. (1987). Job satisfaction: Identifying the important parts among computer sales and service personnel. Journal of Business and Psychology, 1(4), 337-352.

15. Leckie Gloria J. and Brett, Jim. (1997). Job satisfaction of Canadian University Librarians: A national survey.College and Research Libraries 58, January, 31-47.

16. Locke, E. A. (1976). The nature and causes of job satisfaction. In M. D. Dunnette (Ed.), Handbook of industrial and organizational psychology (pp. 1297—1349). Chicago: Rand McNally.

17. Lofquist, L. and Dawis, R. (1991). Essentials of person environment correspondence counselling, University of Minnesota Press. Minneapolis.

18. Lu, H., While, A. E., and Barriball, K. L. (2005). "Job satisfaction among nurses: A literature review", International Journal of Nursing Studies, 42, 211—227.

19. Luthans, F. (1994). Organizational Behavior. New York: McGraw-Hill.

20. Ma, C. C., Samuels, M. E., and Alexander, J. W. (2003). "Factors that influence nurses' job satisfaction". Journal of nursing Administration, 33(5), 293-299

21. Mathieu, J. E. and Zajac, D. M. (1990), "A review and meta-analysis of the antecedents, correlates, and consequences of organizational commitment", Psychological Bulletin, 108, 171-194.

22. Mclntyre, T. M., and Mclntyre, S. E. (2010). "Measuring job satisfaction in Portuguese health professionals: Correlates and validation of the job descriptive index and the job in general scale", International Journal of Selection and Assessment, 18, 425-431.

23. Meyer, J. P., Stanley, D. J., Herscovitch, L. and Topolnytsky, L. (2002)."Affective, continuance, and normative commitment to the organization: A meta-analysis of antecedents, correlates, and consequences", Journal of Vocational Behaviour, 61, 20-52.

24. Nguyen, N., Taylor, J. and Bradley, S. (2003)."Relative pay and job satisfaction: some new evidence",Working paper 045, Department of Economics, Lancaster University Management School.

25. Olorunsola, E. (2010). "Job Satisfaction and gender factor of administrative staff in South West Niggria University",Contemporary Issue In Education Research, 3(10) 51 — 56.

26. Peterson, D. K., Puia, G. M and Sues, F. R. (2003). "YoTengo La Cainisela (I Have the Shint On)", "An Exploration of Job satisfaction and Commitment among Workers in mexico",Journal of Leadership and Organizational studies, 10(2), 73 — 88.

27. Rita, B and Irena, B. (2012). "Determinations of different group employees' job satisfaction: Litunia's University case", Human Resources Management and Ergonomics, I, 6 — 17.

28. Ryan, E. and Marvin, P. (2006). "Examining Herzberg's theory: improving job satisfaction among non-academic employees at a university", Research in Higher Education, 48 (2), 229 — 250.

29. Smith, P. C. and Stanton, J. M. (1999). "Perspectives of the measurement of job attitudes: The Longview", Human Resource Management Review, 8(4), 367-386.

30. Shields, M. A. and Ward, M. (2001). "Improving nurse retention in the National Health Service in England: The impact of job satisfaction on intention to quit", Journal of Health Economics, 20, 677-701.

31. Spector, P.E. (1997). Job Satisfaction: Application, Assessment, Causes and Consequences. Thousand Oaks, CA Sage.

32. Toloposky, A. (2000). What every supervisor should know. New York: McGraw-Hill.

33. Tulen, S. and Serife, Z. (2012). "Have gender differences in job satisfaction disappeared? A study of Turkish universities in North Cyprus, African", Journal of Business Management 6(1), 250-257.

34. Yahy, M. (2012). "Value of work in Islam and its contribution in sustainable development", International Symposium about sustainable development facilities in Islamic Economic, 3-4 December 2012 [online], [Retrieved June 12, 2014]. http://iefpedia.com/arab/wp-content/uploads

35. Trevor, C. O., Reilly, G., and Gerhart, B. (2012). "Reconsidering pay dispersion's effect on the performance of interdependent work: Reconciling sorting and pay inequality". Academy of Management Journal, 55(3), 585-610.

36. Pfeffer, J., and Davis-Blake, A. (1992). "Salary dispersion, location in the salary distribution, and turnover among college administrators". Industrial and labor relations review, 45(4), 753-763.

6

CHAPTER

Perceptions of Key Success Factors for Managers in France

Semra Karakas

Université Paris Panthéon Sorbonne, Prism-Sorbone, Paris, France

ABSTRACT

In France, graduates of business or engineering schools and university graduates represent a population of managers with potential or with high potential. That is why the study of this population is an important issue for companies. First of all, we need to recall the situation of higher education in France which is divided between the "grandes écoles" and public universities. The "grandes écoles" represent elite higher education establishments because they are very selective in their admission of students. These schools include business schools (for example HEC, ENS, etc.) and engineering schools (for example *Polytechnique, les Mines, Arts et métiers,* etc.). The objective of this paper is to study the effect of degree (a"grandes écoles" degree vs a university degree), gender and age on the perceptions of key success factors for promotion. We have also drawn a comparison between managers according to different criteria (sex, degree, etc). Our results have shown that in general, the managerial characteristics are perceived as crucial for promotions. However, women and university graduates attach more importance to technical competencies than men and "grandes écoles" graduates. Whereas older managers are more inclined to geographical mobility and risk taking and would attach less importance to support needs.

Keywords: Executive management, perceptions of promotions keys success, degree, sex, age

INTRODUCTION

The study of managers aroused and still arouses the interest of researchers and organizations. In management, career is particularly widely discussed through the analysis of the manager's population. Indeed, companies are concerned about manager career progress to attract, motivate and retain a quality workforce (Sturge et al., 2002). With the evolution of economic and organizational contexts, the concept of career has evolved. Paradigms have emerged and highlighted the changing behavior, attitudes and strategies of individuals to their careers. Managers have a greater role in managing their careers and the protean career highlights the proactive aspect of individuals in their careers. Also, it is interesting to analyze their perception on factors that could influence their career advancement or promotion because this will allow better understanding and management of this qualified personnel. Studies on promotions or hierarchical advancement have attracted a significant number of works in the management literature, and with the democratization of education and the massive entry of women in the labor market, there have been many studies on women's careers.

Furthermore, the socialization in different environments (school, family, etc.) can notably influence the beliefs, values, personality traits, behaviors and trajectories of individuals. Thus, socialization can be characterized as "*the process by which individuals acquire some of the values, attitudes, interests, skills and beliefs of the groups to which they belong to*" (Safavian-Martinon, 1998, p.124). The education system would therefore provide skills and would also contribute to the construction of the professional identities of individuals.

In France, the "grandes écoles" graduates and the university graduates represent a population of managers with potential or with high potential. The objective of this work is to study the effect of the degree ("grandes écoles" degree and university degree), gender and age on the perceptions of individuals on work behaviors and characteristics that would influence the progress of career through comparisons of certain framework categories (man, woman, "grandes écoles" graduates, etc.). For example, Heisler and Gemmill (1978) identified the perceptions of students and managers on behavior allowing career advancements. In our research, particularly, we have shown that managerial characteristics are perceived generally as determining for the promotions. But women and university graduates attach more importance to technical skills than men and "grandes écoles" graduates. Whereas with age, individuals are more inclined to geographical mobility and risk taking and would give less importance to support needs in more advanced positions.

Theoretical framework

The perception of promotion procedures can have effects on attitudes, motivations and behaviors of individuals at work (Beehr and Taber, 1993). The expectancy theory or VIE model (valence, instrumentality, expectancy) developed by Vroom (1964) is one of the best known theories of behavioral research. Vroom (1964) was one of the first theorists to adopt a perception of motivation as an active process; its approach corresponds to a process theory (Plane, 2012). The VIE model allows highlighting the "behavioral strategy" of individuals who act to get a reward trough a rational choice (Safavian-Martinon, 1998), so it "*aims to explain the choice of the individual at work according to their perceptions and efforts to contribute to the achievement of a task* "(Plane, 2012, p.91). Promotion or career advancement is both a system of reward and a system of employee motivation. That's why it is important to study what individuals perceive as important factors for promotion to better understand their choices and eventually to highlight the differences between the perception of employees and the organizational promotion system.

Therefore, several authors have studied the various factors and characteristics that can facilitate or, on the contrary, hinder career advancement. Thus, women and ethnic minority groups seem to face barriers in their ascent to higher positions (Daley, 1996). Some behaviors may also influence promotions. And the career advancement (or promotion) can be defined as a set of promotions and evolutions in the direction of the top of the hierarchy (Hall, 1976). For example, Heisler and Gemmill (1978) have identified the perceptions of students and managers on behavior allowing career advancements or hierarchical advances.

For students, the 3 most important factors are the task/communication effectiveness, managerial proficiency and organizational demeanor. For managers, the 3 most important factors are the managerial competences, organizational demeanor and superficial presentability. Thus, according to Heisler's and Gemmill's (1978) study, both groups would give more importance to factors linked to skills. Blevins et al. (1989) have also focused on the perceptions of promoting factors by comparing students in management and managers. Furthermore, Beehr and Taber (1993) worked on the perception of intra-organizational mobility and their model have demonstrated two channels:

- Performance-based channels : Performance-based channels include "exceptional performance" (such as having good ideas and initiative, coming up with lots of ideas, leadership ability, working long hours, etc.) and "reliable performance" (such as doing a good job, good attendance, experience and ability, etc.)
- Role-irrelevant channels : Role-irrelevant channels include "personal characteristics" (race, sex, educational level, personality and appearance) and "luck and favoritism" (such as getting the right breaks, having friends or relatives higher up, etc.)

Objective and Methodology

The objective of this work is to study the perceptions of managers on factors affecting promotions and to compare individuals according to the type of degree (a "grandes écoles" degree vs a university degree), age (three age groups: less than 35 years, 35-50 years, and over 50 years) and sex possibly to highlight differences. Our hypotheses are therefore as follows:

- The perception of the factors influencing promotions differs by degree of individuals
- The perception of the factors influencing promotions differs by age individuals
- The perception of the factors influencing promotions differs by gender

Using the factors of Beehr and Taber (1993) and Heisler and Gemmill (1978), which are questionnaires found in the literature, Savafian-Martinon (1998) conducted a selection of items that seemed most relevant to its population of “grandes écoles” graduates and university graduates and she completed the series with her qualitative study.

Our sample is similar to Safavian-Martinon (1998) and from various works, we have established a list of 25 items of beliefs about behaviors and characteristics that can influence career advancement or promotions. The intensity of the importance of each proposal or item was measured by a Likert scale with five answer choices: “not at all important”, “little important,” “moderately important”, “important” and “very important “.

We submitted our questionnaire to a population of “grandes écoles” graduates and university graduates who are currently employed. We have chosen to put it online for easy access and in order to reach a larger sample. We were able to get answers from 1370 individuals with 1023 “grandes écoles” graduates (engineering school or business school) and 347 university graduates (in science or management). With the concept of “perception of the factors influencing career advancement”, the objective is to generate a list of proposals for behavior or characteristic. We choose not to aggregate the characteristic into factor with a factor analysis in order to obtain a finer analysis of perceptions. Thus, any group of items taken independently will cover a maximum of perceptions of our population. Furthermore, our sample size allows us to keep each item individually. We tested the influence of the type of degree and sex on these perceptions by using variance analysis (ANOVA) which allows the study of the relationship between qualitative and quantitative variables and the influence of age using a regression that is used in the study of the relationship between two quantitative variables.

RESULTS

As detailed in Annex 1, our sample of 1370 persons contains 75% of “grandes écoles” graduates and 25% of university graduates, 75% of men and 25% women. When we look at the distribution by age, approximately 51.5% are under 35 years, 38.5% are between 35 and 50 years and 10% over 50 years.

Annex 2 presents the average score for each proposal in the total sample and in groups by gender, type of degree and the age group. It appears that in all categories of managers, dynamism, ambition, leadership skills, relational and communication ease, ability to show themselves or to make themselves known, the political sense, creativity

Table 1: Significant Results of variance and regression tests

	SEX	DEGREE	AGE
2. Ambition	Women > Men		
3. Leadership ability		University > « Grandes écoles »	**Positive influence**
4. Relational and communication ease	Women > Men	University > « Grandes écoles »	
5. To show off, to market themselves, to get known	Women > Men		
6. Political sense, acquisition and use of relationships	Women > Men	University > « Grandes écoles »	
7. Skills, knowledge, know-how	Women > Men	University > « Grandes écoles »	
9. Be creative, have initiative and be able to solve problems		University > « Grandes écoles »	
10. Work hard and work long hours		University > « Grandes écoles »	
12. Be different from the other, original			Negative influence
13. Support from a superior	Women > Men	University > « Grandes écoles »	Negative influence
14.Support from husband/ spouse / the entourage			Negative influence
16. Be appreciated, respected and listening to people under your responsibility and/or colleagues	Women > Men		Negative influence
17. Be cooperative, have the spirit of collaboration		University > « Grandes écoles »	
18. Accept criticism and admit its mistakes		University > « Grandes écoles »	Negative influence
20. Take risks			**Positive influence**
22. Be inclined to geographic mobility	**Men > Women**	**« Grandes écoles » > University**	**Positive influence**
24. Be a man	Women > Men	University > « Grandes écoles »	
25. Not having a foreign nationality or foreign origin	Women > Men	University > « Grandes écoles »	

and to be able to anticipate (items 1-6, item 9 and item 19) are among the first 10 items with the highest scores. The support of a supervisor is also part of the 10 most important factors in all groups except for managers of "more than 50 years". With categorization by sex, the item "skills, knowledge, know-how" appears in the top 10 factors scores in women and not in men, while the item "be inclined mobility geographic "appears in the top 10 scores of factors in men and not in women. With categorization by type of degree, among the 10 items with the highest scores, the item "skills, knowledge, know-how" appears in university graduates and not in "grandes écoles" graduates, while the items "inclined to a geographic mobility" and "being cooperative" are in the 10 best scores for "grandes écoles" graduates and not for university graduates. Finally, with the categorization by age, the age under 35 years and 35-50 years have the items "skills, knowledge, know-how "and" support a superior" among the 10 best scores in contrast to more 50 years. The individuals older than 50 years have the items "take risks" and "be inclined to a geographic mobility," which do not appear in the top 10 score factors in individuals under 50 years. Furthermore, in individuals aged 35-50 years, the item "achieve good results even exceptional ones" constitutes one of the 10 most important factors for promotions while this is not the case for the other two groups, i.e. less 35 years and over 50 years. Annexes 3, 4 and 5 present the results of ANOVA and regression testing.

The following table summarizes all significant results:

DISCUSSION AND CONCLUSION

This work aimed to determine the perception of a certain category of managers (such as "grandes écoles" graduates and university graduates) about the factors or behaviors that could influence promotions. We have seen that whatever the manager category, the variables with the 10 best scores are more or less the same. This suggests that the managerial characteristics such as dynamism, ambition, leadership, communication ease and ability market themselves are perceived in general as determining promotions. To retain and motivate its managers and stay competitive in an increasingly aggressive market, companies must be able to generate formations or situations to develop these characteristics.

It is interesting to see in more detail the variables for which the differences or links are significant by sex, degree or age group. Thus, in our analysis by sex, we found that for all significant mean differences, women still have a higher average than men with the exception for the variable "be inclined to a geographical mobility ". The average of this variable is not only higher in men but it is also part of their 10 best averages unlike women. Thus, men attach more importance to mobility than women. This result concurs with some studies which have shown that women are less willing to geographic mobility, especially international mobility. Some factors, such as age, sex, family situation and work experience internationally, have influences on the acceptance of an international assignment. Although, the influence of these factors on international mobility does not meet unanimity among researchers, we have noted some characteristics: the youth are more predisposed to mobility, women are more reluctant to accept mobility, the attitude of the spouse regarding mobility influences the decision of an international mobility (this would be more important for women than for men), having children (especially children under five years) and adolescents discourage international mobility, and finally, the highest paid managers would be more inclined to accept an international affection (their employment ensuring financial security) (Saba et Haines, 2002). But for international mobility, as recalled by Saba and Haines (2002), in the current context of globalization and international business development, mobility has become more important for executives. For the individual, the success of international mobility is seen as a career accelerator and success after the return is conceived by career progression with a promotion or increased responsibilities (Cerdin, 2004). According to Bournois (1991), the main reasons pushing executives to mobility in Europe would be "the hope of a future promotion or a better career development" (52%), "Personal and / or family experience in another culture" (21%), "the immediate promotion" (14%) and "compensation" (10%). This perception is more pronounced in men than in women and it could influence the differences in career success. In a context of international competition, companies should take into consideration that this mobility is less clear for women and should ensure better support to facilitate their mobility, positively influencing career success and also the satisfaction of these managers.

Moreover, in our analyses by age group, the item "be inclined to a geographical mobility" is significantly positively linked with age. Indeed, the average for this item is one of the 10 best averages in the people who are over 50 years unlike the under 35 and 35-50 years. Indeed, as stated by the survey of Saba and Haines (2002), older executives would more easily consider international mobility. This mobility is explained by the fact that they have less family responsibility and thus can find a way to escape from the career plateauing problems they often face. The other variable that marks the difference between the over 50 and under 50 years old is the item "take risks". This item is part of the 10 best averages for the manager over 50 years in contrast to less than 50 years. Indeed, as in the case of international mobility, it seems that older managers can easily envision taking risks notably due to less family responsibility, a need to prove themselves to fight against to possible career plateauing and / or a risk of failure more easily surmountable financially with higher work experience. It is also interesting to note that for all variables significantly linked to age, this relationship is negative except for items "leadership ability", "take risks" and "be inclined to a geographical mobility". The perception of originality, support from a superior, spousal support, appreciation by colleagues or people under his responsibility and acceptance of criticism is higher among younger than among older managers. Indeed with age, individuals would give less importance to the judgments of others and need less support in more advanced positions. Companies can therefore be more attentive to these factors with younger managers to motivate and retain them.

Finally, in our analyses by type of degree, we note that for any significant mean differences, university graduates still have a higher average than "grandes écoles" graduates except for items "leadership ability" and "be inclined to a geographical mobility ". These two items are also among the 10 best averages of factors perceived as important for promotions in "grandes écoles" graduates unlike the university graduates. During their initial education, "grandes écoles" graduates have an obligation to stay abroad. Moreover, these institutions recruit the brightest students who have often privileged backgrounds and who are dedicated to the most prestigious and remunerative careers (Bouffartigue and Gadea, 2000). Therefore, this socialization may encourage "the acquisition of habitus or forms of know-who" (Bouffartigue and Gadea, 2000) in keeping with the belief of the importance of a leader's profile for career development. Therefore, the perception of these variables as influencing the promotions seem more pronounced among "grandes écoles" graduates. Moreover, as with women compared to men, the item "skills, knowledge, know-how" has an average significantly higher among university graduates and one of the 10 best averages unlike "grandes écoles" graduates. So we can say that women and university graduates attach more importance to technical skills than their male counterparts and "grandes écoles" graduates.

Thus, in the light of these analyses, it is possible to better understand the perceptions of managers to understand the possible career differences, to act on their motivation, their involvement or their sense of recognition and allow their loyalty, which is one of the main issues of human resources and companies in a context of global competition

REFERENCES

1. Beehr, T. A and Taber, T. D (1993), « Perceived intra-organizational mobility: reliable versus exceptional performance as means to getting ahead », Journal of Organizational Behavior, vol.14, 579-594
2. Blevins, D.E, Pressley, M.M. and Henthorne, T. L. (1989), « Perceptions of ethical and career advancement pratices: business executives vs. business students », American Business Review, 6-14
3. Bouffartigue, P. and Gadea, C. (2000), Sociologie des cadres, La Découverte (ed), Paris
4. Bournois, F. (1991), La gestion des cadres en Europe, Eyrolles (ed), Paris
5. Daley, D. M (1996), « Paths of glory and the glass ceiling: differing patterns of career advancement among women and minority federal employees », Public Administration Quarterly, 143-162
6. Dubar, C. (1991), La socialisation: construction des identités sociales et professionnelles, Armand Colin (ed), Paris.
7. François-Philip Boisserolles De Saint Julien, D. (2005), Les survivants : vers une gestion différenciée des ressources humaines, l'Harmattan (ed), Paris
8. Hall, D. T. (1976), Careers in organizations, Jossey-Bass, San Francisco.
9. Heisler, W. J. and Gemmill, R. (1978), « Executive and MBA student views of corporate promotion practices : a structural comparison », The Academy of Management Journal, 21(4), 731-737
10. Plane, J-M. (2012), Théorie et management des organisations, 3rd edition, Dunod, Paris
11. Saba, T. and Haines, V. (2002), « Des cadres prêts Ã accepter une affectation internationale : une question de profil ou de pratiques incitatives? », Gestion, 2002/1, vol.27, 33-40.
12. Safavian Martinon, M. (1998), « Le lien entre diplôme et la logique d'acteur relative Ã la carrière : une explication du rôle

du diplôme dans la carrière des jeunes cadres issus des grandes écoles de gestion », Phd in Mangement, University Paris1-Panthéon-Sorbonne

13. Sturges, J., Guest, D., Conway, N. and Mackenzie Davey, K. (2002), « A longitudinal study of the relationship between commitment among graduates in the first ten years at work », Journal of Organizational Behavior, 23(6), 731-7 14. Vroom, V.H. (1964), Work and motivation, Jossey-Bass

7

CHAPTER

Analysis of the Level of Emotional Intelligence among Executives in Small and Medium Sized Enterprises

Susan Tee Suan Chin, R.N. Anantharaman and David Yoon Kin Tong

Multimedia University, Malacca, Malaysia

ABSTRACT

The purpose of this research is to study the level of emotional intelligence among executives in small and medium sized enterprises particularly from the manufacturing sector. SMEs have problems in attracting and retaining their employees. For the purpose of the study, the GENOS Emotional Intelligence questionnaire developed by Palmer and Stough (2001) has been used. A total of 96 employees from different manufacturing sectors took part in the survey. It was found that emotional intelligence did not have a significant relationship with organizational citizenship behaviour. Results from the study show that employees in the SMEs do experience some kind of experiences that affect their working attitudes. The initial study provides many insights especially to the areas where respondents show a low level of emotional intelligence. The low level of emotional intelligence is related to the nature of work involved especially when it involves a high level of stress.

Keywords: small and medium sized enterprises, emotional intelligence, organizational citizenship behavior

INTRODUCTION

The importance and contributions of small and medium sized enterprises (SMEs) or organizations to the country cannot be dismissed. SMEs represent a large percentage of establishments in Malaysia [SMIDEC 2009]. 99.2% of established organizations are from SMEs, while the remainder belongs to the larger organizations. SMEs contribute 32% to Gross Domestic Product (GDP) and they employ 56.4% of the total workforce of the country. SMEs represent an important backbone to the Malaysian economy especially on the unemployment issue [Che Rose, Kumar, and Lim, 2006]. Many studies have showed that only 10% of the SMEs survived beyond the 10 years mark [CCM 2002].

The services and manufacturing sector are expected to take in substantial amounts of people by the year 2010 [JobStreet 2009]. The manufacturing sector will remain as the vital engine to spur growth for the Malaysian economy, and SMEs are a major contributor to it. However, the challenges that SMEs face are focused towards the people. They have problems in attracting and retaining talented employees. They need to enhance the competencies and the innovativeness of the workforce so that they will be able to compete in the global market. However, this problem is not prevalent in Japan where the concept of "lifetime employment" is deeply rooted [DeloitteKassimChan 2009].

However, Cooper [1998] has showed that emotions when properly managed, drives trust, loyalty and commitment among the employees. Through this, there would be productivity gains, high level of innovations coupled with organisational accomplishments. Hence, the objectives of this research are:

1. To examine the relationship between emotional intelligence and organisational citizenship behaviour together with their dimensions.
2. To explore the relationship between the demographic variables and emotional intelligence in particular, age, length of employment and department.

By definition, SMEs in Malaysia would fall into the categories of those organizations having less than 150 employees. Abdul Hamid, Baharun and Hashim [2008] state that the most common problems faced by SMEs include recruiting and selecting good and dedicated employee. These account for 49.5% and 36.9% respectively.

Based on Cooper's [1998] findings on "managed emotions", human resources problems faced by SMEs can be resolved if there were some training programmes conducted for the employees. However, more importantly, there is a need to know the level of emotional intelligence that exists among executives in the SMEs as well as their relationship towards the expected behaviours.

Emotional Intelligence and Employee Engagement

Mayer and Salovey [1997] have defined emotional intelligence as "the ability to perceive emotions, to access and generate emotions so as to assist thought, to understand emotions and emotional knowledge and to effectively regulate emotions so as to promote emotional and intellectual growth. When applied to the workplace, Emotional Intelligence involves the capacity to effectively perceive, express, understand and manage emotions in a professional and effective manner at work [Palmer and Stough 2001]. According to the Genos EI developed by Palmer and Stough [2001] (previously named as Swinburne University Emotional Intelligence Unit), there are five key emotional competencies which are applicable to the workplace situation; these are Emotional Recognition and Expression, Understanding Others Emotions, Emotions Direct Cognition, Emotional Management and Emotional Control.

Emotional Intelligence and Organisational Citizenship Behaviour

Based on Watson Wyatt Malaysia [2009], employee engagement is important as part of the employee retention programme. Engaged employees will be better performers and will contribute positively to the company's financial performance. In this respect, employee engagement can be related to contextual performance. Results have showed that there is a strong link between employee engagement and rate of productivity [The Star 2009b]. Employee engagement can be related to organizational citizenship behaviour. Organisational citizenship behaviour includes all the extra-role, discretionary behaviour that helps other members in the organisation to perform their jobs. According to Podsakoff et al [1990], organizational citizenship behaviour has five elements that measures conscientiousness, sportsmanship, civic virtue, courtesy and altruism.

According to Abraham [2000], emotional intelligence enhances the altruistic behaviour of an individual. It enables employees to comprehend their fellow colleagues and to respond better than those with lower level of emotional intelligence. This is due to their ability to shift from negative moods to positive moods. Altruism refers to the act of helping others who have been absent or are behind in their work. It is sometimes called the wilful sacrifice of one's own interest or well-being for the sake of something that is non-self. Douglas, Frink and Ferris [2004] note that highly conscientious people with higher level of emotional intelligence performed better than those with a lower level of emotional intelligence. Deshpande and Joseph's [2005] study found that employees with a high level of emotional intelligence are able to counter negative behaviours. However, a study conducted by Sitter [30] disagrees with the results. Based on the research, the level of emotional intelligence has a positive but does not have a much significant factor to organizational citizenship behaviour. In a study conducted by Pasanen [2000], emotional intelligence was not found not to be a predictor of organizational citizenship behaviour. The differing results could be due to the nature and size of the sample. Hence, in this research, one of the objectives is to ascertain the relationship between emotional intelligence and organizational citizenship behaviour.

Emotional Intelligence and Demographic Variables

According to a study made by Boncher [2003], gender reveals a statistically significant interactional effect for Understanding Emotions. Based on Brooks [2002], management tenure does not have a significant impact of the level of emotional intelligence. Langhorn [2004] finds that experienced managers had a lower level of emotional intelligence than lesser experienced managers. Based on a research by Dolcos [2008], older people tend to be better at regulating and controlling their emotions than those who are younger. In terms of age and level of emotional intelligence, there seems to be some disagreement between the findings of Chipain [2003] and Langhorn in 2004. In Chipain's [2003] study, it is found that there is a positive and a significant correlation with the level of emotional intelligence and age. In Langhorn's [2004] study, age does not demonstrate any significance.

Similar findings were found by Lim [2004] based on his studies of 218 employees, age has no effect on the level of emotional intelligence. A study by Scott [2004] gives another insight: the level of emotional intelligence is said to have rose only after 40 years of age. Alloway [2004] finds that there are significant differences in the level of emotional intelligence among managers. Senior level managers scored a higher level of emotional intelligence in comparison with middle level managers. This gives an indication that the more experienced the employee, the higher would be his or her level of emotional intelligence. The differences in the results give ground for further research.

The manufacturing sector is famous for the "job-hopping illness" and this could be detrimental to the industry if it is not arrested [Mustapha and Abdullah 2005]. Job-hopping could be related to the type of occupation that the employee is involved with. If they typically deal with complaints lodged by customers, they would feel highly stressful [JobStreet 2009]. These occupations include: information technology, engineering, sales and marketing, finance and human resources, operations, production and clerical. If their stress levels are affected, then their level of emotional intelligence will be affected as well. Traumatic and significant events will have impacts on the behaviours of the employees [Mignonac and Herrbach 2004; Weiss and Cropanzano 1996]. Their attitudes would affect their performance at work. Based on a study by Rozell et. al. [2001], students majoring in accounting have a lower level of emotional intelligence in comparison with students majoring in management and finance. The second research objective is to examine the level of emotional intelligence among executives in small and medium sized industries.

RESEARCH DESIGN

Sample Selection and Population

Malaysian manufacturing industry has been chosen for the study because it represents one of the important driving forces and contributes to a sizeable portion to the Gross Domestic Product of Malaysian economy. In terms of the manufacturing sector, there has been a rise in job-hopping among employees [Mustapha and Abdullah 2005]. Melaka is one of four states in Malaysia which has attracted a considerable number of foreign investors.

There are about 469 manufacturing organisations in Melaka [MSDS 2007]. About 422 of them belong to small and medium sized organisations while the remaining have been categorised as large organisations. In this initial study, 8 companies have been randomly identified. A total of 96 executives from 8 different companies have taken part in the research study.

GENOS EI Framework

In terms of measuring the level of emotional intelligence, the GENOS Emotional Intelligence questionnaire developed by Palmer and Stough [1997] is used. The Genos EI model consists of five dimensions; recognising and expressing emotions, understanding emotions of others, making decisions, managing emotions and controlling emotions.

The Genos EI model compared with the other three models has a distinct edge. This is in terms of the original focus area and time taken. Although MSCEIT and Bar-On Eqi have been used by many researchers, they have some drawbacks. The questionnaires were initially developed not based on a workplace and were more clinically based. Goleman's ECI focuses on the workplace, but it has 117 items in the questionnaire. A person's focus level drops when the number of items is bigger and it takes a longer time [Palmer and Stough 2007]. MSCEIT has been peer reviewed more than 10 times but it takes 45-60 minutes to complete the questionnaire.The Genos EI has been peer reviewed 5 times, which adds to the evidence of reliability and validity of the construct.

The Genos EI is reliable with $\alpha = 0.88$ (Emotional Recognition and Expression : $\alpha = 0.73$, Understanding of Emotions : $\alpha = 0.83$, Emotions Direct Cognition : $\alpha = 0.63$, Emotional Management : $\alpha = 0.72$, Emotional Control : $\alpha = 0.72$) It has been also shown to have good internal consistency and test re-test reliability [Gardner and Stough 2002; Palmer 2003]. This test re-test reliability is an important aspect of the psychometric property of the emotional intelligence measurement. The test consists of 64 questions and takes about 12-15 minutes to complete. There are a balanced number of positively and negatively phrased items that will help to determine inconsistent patterns and also illogical responses by the respondents. There are 11 statements for Emotional Recognition and Expressions, 20 statements for Understanding Others Emotions, 12 statements for Emotions Direct Cognition, 12 statements for Emotional Management and 9 statements for Emotional Control.

According to the GENOS EI, there are five key emotional competencies which are applicable to the workplace situation:-

- **Emotional Recognition and Expression** – refers to the ability to identify one's own feelings and emotional states and the ability to express those inner feelings to others.
- **Understanding Others Emotions** – refers to the ability to identify and understand the emotions of others and those that are manifest in response to workplace environments and staff meetings.
- **Emotions Direct Cognition** – refers to the extent to which emotions and emotional knowledge are incorporated in decision-making and or problem solving situations.
- **Emotional Management** – refers to the ability to manage positive and negative emotions both within oneself and others
- **Emotional Control** – refers to the ability to effectively control strong emotional states experienced at work such as anger, stress, anxiety and frustration.

The questionnaire uses the five-point Likert scale (1 = strongly disagree, 2 = disagree, 3 = neutral, 4 = agree, 5 = strongly agree).

Organisational Citizenship Behaviour Scale

Organisational Citizenship Behaviour Scale developed by Podsakoff et al [1990] is used to measure contextual performance. The scale has five elements that measures conscientiousness, sportsmanship, civic virtue, courtesy and altruism.

- **Conscientiousness** – punctuality in attendance, use of work time and adherence to rules. It also refers to the trait of being painstaking and careful, or the quality of acting according to the dictates of one's conscience. It includes such elements as self-discipline, carefulness, thoroughness, organization, deliberation (the tendency to think carefully before acting) and need for achievement. It is an aspect of what was traditionally called character. Conscientiousness is related to emotional intelligence and impulse control.
- **Altruism** – helping others who have been absent or who have fallen behind in their work (any voluntary action that helps another person out at work) it is often referred to as the wilful sacrifice of one's own interests or well-being for the sake of something that is

non-self. It is also often defined as being the selfless concern for the welfare of others.

- **Sportsmanship** – putting up with minor inconveniences, or not always finding fault with the organisation.
- **Courtesy** – consulting people who may be affected by a decision or at the very least informing other people in advance of such actions.
- **Civic virtue** – keeping up with developments happening in the organisation (being constructively involved in the political process of the organisation).

Like the GENOS EI, this questionnaire also uses the five-point Likert scale.

Table 1 : Demographic Analysis of Respondents

Particulars	Items	Freq	%
Gender	Male	61	63.5
	Female	35	36.5
		96	
Age	Less than 25 years old	6	6.3
	More than 25 but less than 30	42	43.8
	More than 30 but less than 35	26	27.1
	More than 35 but less than 40	16	16.7
	More than 40 years old	6	6.3
		96	
Employment Length	Less than 2 years	17	17.7
	More than 2 years but less than 5 years	54	56.3
	More than 5 years but less than 10 years	15	15.6
	More than 10 years	10	10.4
		96	
Department	Administration	15	15.6
	Finance and Accounting	10	10.4
	Production	38	39.6
	Sales and Marketing	21	21.9
	Maintenance	2	2.1
	Engineering	5	5.2
	Others	5	5.2
		96	

EMPIRICAL ANALYSIS

Respondents Analysis

From Table 1, it can be noted that there are more male than female executives working in the manufacturing industry. A majority of them are aged between 25 to 35 years of age, this accounts for 70.9%. About fifty percent of them are working between 2 to 5 years. 10.4% of respondents have worked more than 10 years; this indicates that many of these employees are not willing to work longer in SMEs. 39.6% of the respondents are working in Production indicating that there are few personnel working in the offices.

Emotional Intelligence and Organisational Citizenship Behaviour

With reference to Table 2, it is found that emotional intelligence has no significant relationship with organizational citizenship behaviour. The present study agrees with the findings of Sitter [2004] and Pasanen [2000] who found that emotional intelligence does not have a much significant factor with organizational citizenship behaviour. This is contrary to the belief that having a high level of emotional intelligence would automatically result in a high level of organizational citizenship behaviour.

Table 2 : Relationship between the Level of Emotional Intelligence and Organizational Citizenship Behaviour

		Level of Emotional Intelligence	Level of Organisational Citizenship Behaviour
Level of Emotional Intelligence	Pearson Correlation	1	.114
	Sig. (1-tailed)	.	.135
	N	96	96

Table 3 : Relationship between the Dimensions of Emotional Intelligence and the Dimensions of Organizational Citizenship Behaviour

	Conscientiousness	Sports-manship	Civic Virtue	Courtesy	Altruism
ERE	r = -0.168 p=0.051	r = 0.009 p=0.464	r=0.071 p=0.246	r=0.250** p=0.007	r= -0.223* p=0.015
UOE	r=0.275** p=0.003	r=-0.182* p=0.038	r=0.369** p=0.000	r=0.117 p=0.128	r=0.171* p=0.048
EDC	r=0.566** p=0.000	r=-0.648** p=0.000	r=0.517** p=0.000	r=0.455** p=0.000	r=0.450** p=0.000
EM	r=0.150 p=0.072	r=-0.191* p=0.031	r=0.094 p=0.181	r=-0.028 p=0.394	r=0.202* p=0.024
EC	r=0.294** p=0.002	r=-0.346** p=0.000	r=0.097 p=0.174	r=0.313** p=0.001	r=0.268** p=0.004

* Correlation significant at the 0.05 level (1 tailed)
** Correlation significant at the 0.01 level (1 tailed)
ERE: Emotional Recognition and Expression
UOE: Understanding Others Emotions
EDC: Emotions Direct Cognition
EM: Emotional Management
EC: Emotional Control

In terms of the dimensions of emotional intelligence, Understanding Others Emotions, Emotions Direct Cognition and Emotional Control have a positive and significant relationship with Conscientiousness. It indicates that employees do take care in their work. This is shown in Table 3.

Having a high level of conscientiousness would help the organization in terms of its stability. However, in terms of Sportsmanship it has a negative and significant relationship with Understanding Others Emotions, Emotions Direct Cognition, Emotional Management and Emotional Control. Sportsmanship refers to putting up with minor inconveniences and not always finding fault with the organisation. Since it is negatively related, it indicates that the employees are not willing to put up with the minor inconveniences and they are always finding fault with the organisation. It could be that the situations that they have to put up with make them very uncomfortable. These situations that happened have a negative impact on their working attitudes [Mignonac and Herrbach 2004; Weiss and Cropanzano 1996]. These negative working attitudes would have an adverse effect on the work performance.

Civic Virtue has a positive and significant correlation with Understanding Others Emotions and Emotions Direct Cognition. It indicates that employees do care for their organisation's properties and they would not in any way harm these properties.

In terms of Courtesy, it has a positive and significant relationship with Emotional Recognition and Expression, Emotions Direct Cognition and Emotional Control. Courtesy refers to consulting people who would be affected by a decision or at the very least informing other people of such actions. In this case, it would seem that employees do care for their fellow colleagues and they will lend a helping hand as and when required. In terms of the organisation, this is a good indication. Altruism has a negative and significant relationship with Emotional Recognition and Expression but positive and significant relationship with the other dimensions of emotional intelligence. Altruism refers to the act of helping other fellow employees who are behind in their work. This help is voluntary. It can be interpreted that the employees are sometimes not aware of their fellow colleagues' needs especially in the times of problems. These colleagues of them could be trying to hide their difficulties or sometimes do not want help from their fellow colleagues. However, in general, it indicates that employees do care for their colleagues and would always lend a helping hand.

Emotional Intelligence and Demographic Variables

As shown in Table 4, the level of emotional intelligence has a positive and significant relationship with age. Dolcos [2008] and Chipain [2003] also report that older people have better control on their emotions and therefore have higher level of emotional intelligence. The findings disagree with Langhorn [2004] and Lim [2004] for they found that age did not have any impact on emotional intelligence.

Table 4 : Relationship between the Level of Emotional Intelligence and Age

		Age Group	Level of Emotional Intelligence
Age Group	Pearson Correlation	1	.280(**)
	Sig. (1-tailed)	.	.003
	N	96	96

** Correlation is significant at the 0.01 level (1-tailed).

The findings agree with Dolcos [2008] and Scott [2004]. Older people do have a higher level of emotional intelligence. Younger generations tend to be rash and are not in control of their emotions. They could be single adults. Single adults may have less emotional support and could therefore be having problems accommodating at the workplace [Dunn 2003]. Older people have better emotional management as they have undergone experiences. Experiences gave them better understanding. As defined by Mayer and Salovey [1997], emotional intelligence refers to an ability to perceive emotions. The perception relates to the person's understanding ability. Emotional intelligence has a positive and significant relationship with the length of employment. This is as seen in Table 5. The longer the employee works in the organisation, the more familiar he or she is with the environment and the situations that he or she will encounter. The findings agree with Alloway [2004] where it is found that senior managers had a higher level of emotional intelligence than junior managers, as seen in Table 6.

Table 5: Relationship between the Level of Emotional Intelligence and Length of Employment

		Employment Length	Level of Emotional Intelligence
Employment Length	Pearson Correlation	1	.186(*)
	Sig. (1-tailed)	.	.035
	N	96	96

* Correlation is significant at the 0.05 level (1-tailed).

.

Table 6: Level of Emotional Intelligence and the Different Lengths of Employment

Employment Length	Mean	N	Std. Deviation
Less than 2 years	203.4706	17	15.16624
More than 2 years but less than 5 years	202.6852	54	9.32196
More than 5 years but less than 10 years	201.2000	15	16.04102
More than 10 years	215.8000	10	21.01745
Total	203.9583	96	13.56149

The average length of employment is 2.19 years which indicates that the workforce is made up of people who have just joined the organisation. This also indicates a high level of turnover in the organisation as the majority of people are within the 2 to 5 years category. Having a high turnover would affect the productivity of the organisation. This could also be part of the reason why emotional intelligence did not have a significant relationship with organizational citizenship behaviour. Employees could be affected by the traumatic events that have impacted their behaviours [Mignonac and Herrbach 2004; Weiss and Cropanzano 1996]. Their inability to manage these events pushed them towards leaving the organisation. If they have stayed longer in the organisation, they would have benefited and so would the organisation. Hence, SMEs do have a problem in retaining their employees.

Based on Table 7, employees from the Administration department have the highest level of emotional intelligence in comparison with those from the Maintenance department having the lowest level of emotional intelligence. Employees from the Administration department deal with human resource issues and have to be very good in their interpersonal skills. This indicates that the events that take place in the maintenance section might be very stressful such as having a high level of complaints, workload and long hours.

TABLE 7: Level Of Emotional Intelligence And The Various Departments

Department	Mean	N	Std. Deviation
Administration	207.2000	15	16.94192
Finance and Accounting	204.2000	10	12.62977
Production	205.0263	38	11.11728
Sales and Marketing	201.9524	21	16.56042
Maintenance	192.0000	2	14.14214
Engineering	203.8000	5	14.30734
Others	199.0000	5	7.84219
Total	203.9583	96	13.56149

Table 7: Level Of Emotional Intelligence And The Various Departments

Events that impact the working attitude would result in the employee taking drastic actions such as leaving the organisation [Kuchinsky 2006, Mignonac and Herrbach 2004; Weiss and Cropanzano 1996]. Highly stressful jobs affect employees [JobStreet 2009]. Based on the study, it is found that employees from the Accounting department have a lower level of emotional intelligence than those from the Finance and Accounting department. The findings support the results by Rozell et. al [2001], where it is found that accounting students had lower level of emotional intelligence than those in management and finance. The level of emotional intelligence could be related to the nature of work involved. The higher the stress level, the lower the level of emotional intelligence. As indicated by Mignonac and Herrbach [2004], work events have an impact on the person's effective state and attitude. Respondents in the Accounting department are exposed to stressful working conditions in comparison with those in the Administrative department.

DISCUSSION

The first research objective is to examine the relationship between emotional intelligence and organizational citizenship behaviour. The second research objective was to investigate the relationship between emotional intelligence and the demographic variables particularly age, length of employment and department. It is found that emotional intelligence does not have a significant relationship with organizational citizenship behaviour. Age and length of employment has a positive and significant relationship with emotional intelligence. Employees from the Administration department have the highest level of emotional intelligence in comparison with those from the Maintenance department. Significant traumatic events that take place which severely impact the employee's feelings will have a serious effect on the working attitude [Kuchinsky 2006, Mignonac and Herrbach 2004; Weiss and Cropanzano 1996].

Results from the study show that employees in SMEs do experience some kind of experiences that have affected their working attitudes. A majority of them have not worked long in the organisation. The average length of work in the organisation is 2.19 years. As such they would not be able to give a more conclusive result. It would be helpful and beneficial for SMEs to take advantage of the Human Resource Development Fund organized by the Ministry of Human Resource,

Malaysia to train and develop their employees. Many of SMEs have not fully utilized their funds [The Star 2007]. The aim of the fund is to improve the organisation's level of productivity. Many SMEs shy away from training as they are afraid that these employees would leave for another organisation. In general, Malaysian graduates lack dynamism [The Star 2009a]. This can be seen in terms of the dimensions of emotional intelligence and organizational citizenship behaviour. The Malaysian government intends to increase the tertiary educated employees by 13% that is from 20% to 33% by 2010 [The Star 2008].

Conclusion and Area of Future Research

Results from the initial study provide many insights especially to the areas where respondents showed a low level of emotional intelligence. The low level of emotional intelligence is related to the nature of work involved especially when it involves a high level of stress. The higher the stress level, the lower the level of emotional intelligence. This is evident in the Maintenance department. Executives in the Maintenance department have to ensure that the machines in the production area are functioning well. If the machines malfunction, the production will be affected.Management can take heed from these findings by sending the executives for training on soft skills management. SMEs represent the backbone of the industry. Despite their contribution to the economy, SMEs problems are largely human resource related. They are unable to attract and retain employees. Hence, the purpose of the research is to explore the level of emotional intelligence among executives in SMEs particularly those from the manufacturing sector.

The present study has certain limitations. In terms of the sample size, the study only managed to get about 8 companies to participate in the survey and not all types of industries took part. One of the reasons is that some companies do not have many people working. For example, in terms of furniture manufacturing companies, they have about 5 people working in the office, 2 of them are the owners and the remaining 3 are the clerical employees. Some of the employees are family related. As such, these companies were not included as the employees' responses would be biased. Certain precaution needs to be taken in terms of the results especially in terms of the departments. Not many organisations have all the departments. For example, Maintenance had only 2 responses as compared with other departments like Production which has 38 responses.

Table 7: Level Of Emotional Intelligence And The Various Departments

Only 96 questionnaires were able to be used; others had to be discarded as employees gave partial answers. The study could be further improved by increasing the sample size. Having a longitudinal study to measure the increase in the level of emotional intelligence especially in the problem departments would also be helpful. Longitudinal study would enhance the research by having a before and after results in the levels of emotional intelligence. It could also shed more light in terms of the influencing effects of the environment that the employee works in.

ACKNOWLEDGMENT

Many thanks to those who were instrumental in the completion of this paper. You have provided the inspiration and also the determination to move on.

REFERENCES

1. Abdul Hamid, A. B., Baharun, R. & Hashim, N. H. (2008). 'Comparative Analysis of Managerial Practices in Small Medium Enterprises in Malaysia,' Retrieved 14 March 2009 from http://www.fppsm.utm.my/files/jurnal/JK08/804.pdf
2. Abraham, R. (2000). "The Role of Job Control as a Moderator of Emotional Dissonance and Emotional Intelligence – Outcome Relationships," Journal of Psychology, Vol. 134, pp 169-184
3. Alloway, B. M. (2004). "Emotional Intelligence and Extrinsic Career Success: A Comparison of Gender and Management," Gannon University
4. Boncher, M. K. (2003). 'The Relationship between Attachment Styles and Emotional Intelligence,' New York University.
5. Brooks, J. K. (2002). "Emotional Competencies of Leaders: A Comparison of Managers in Financial Organisation by Performance Level," (A Doctoral Dissertation) North Carolina State University
6. CCM (2002). 'Companies Commission of Malaysia, Statistics of Insolvency Completed,' Retrieved 13 March 2009 fromhttp://www.ssm.com.my

7. Chipain, G. C. (2003). 'Emotional Intelligence and Its Relationship with Sales Success,' (A Doctoral Dissertation) De Paul University

8. Cooper, R. (1998). "Sentimental Value," People Management 4(7) 48-51

9. Deloitte Kassim Chan (2009). 'Companies Urged to Identify the MNCs they Seek to Support,' [Retrieved 13 March 2009 from http://www.deloitte.com/dtt/press_release/0,1014,sid%253D 34169%

10. Deshpande, S. P. & Joseph, J. (2005). "The Impact of Emotional Intelligence on Counter-productive Behaviour in China,"Management Research News, Volume 28 Number 5 Pages 75 – 85

11. Dolcos, F. (2008). "Wisdom Comes with Age, at Least When it Comes to Emotions," ScienceDaily. University of Alberta, Faculty of Medicine and Dentistry. Retrieved 15 July 2008 from http://www.sciencedaily.com/releases/2008/06/0806121854 28.htm

12. Douglas, C., Frink, D. D., Ferris, G. R. (2004). "Emotional Intelligence as a Moderator of the Relationship between Conscientiousness and Performance," Journal of Leadership and Organisational Studies, Volume 10, No. 3

13. Dunn, S. (2003). "Demographic Trends, the Bottom Line, and the Case for Emotional Intelligence in the Workplace," Retrieved 20 March 2009 from http://www.webpronews.com/ node/2523/print]

14. Gardner, L. & Stough, C, (2002). "Examining the Relationship between Leadership and Emotional Intelligence in Senior Level Managers," The Leadership and Organization Development Journal, 23, 68-78

15. JobStreet (2009). "HR Corner: Miscellaneous," Retrieved 12 March 2009 from http://my.jobstreet.com/employers/ misc.htm

16. Kuchinsky, C. (2006). "The Most Stressful Jobs in America," Stress in the American Workplace. Retrieved 15 June 2008 fromhttp://www.associatedcontent.com/article/92667/the_m ost_stressful_jobs_in_america.html

17. Langhorn, S. (2004). "How Emotional Intelligence Can Improve Management Performance," International Journal of Contemporary Hospitality Management, Volume 16, No. 3, Pp 220-230

18. Lim, H. H. (2004). 'Significance of Knowledge Worker's Emotional Intelligence in Organisations,' Multimedia University

19. Mayer, J. D. & Salovey, P. (1997). 'What is Emotional Intelligence?,' In P. Salovey and D. Sluyter (Eds.), Emotional development and emotional intelligence (pp3-31) New York: Basic Books.

20. Mignonac, K., Herrbach, O. (2004). "Linking Work Events, Affective States, and Attitudes: An Empirical Study of Managers' Emotions," Journal of Business and Psychology, Vol. 19 No.2, pp.221-40.

21. MSDC (2007). 'Malacca State Development Corporation,' List of Name and Addresses of Companies in the Industrial Estates.

22. Mustapha, R. & Abdullah, A. (2005). 'Malaysia Transition Towards a Knowledge-Based Economy,' Journal of Technology Studies, pp 51-61

23. Palmer, B. (2003). 'Measures of Emotional Intelligence in the Workplace – A Comparative Analysis,' Swinburne University, Australia

24. Palmer, B. & Stough, C. (2001). 'Swinburne University Emotional Intelligence Test,' Interim Technical Manual. Organistional Psychology Research Unit.

25. Pasanen, S. E. (2000). 'Emotional Intelligence, Conscientiousness and Integrity as Predictors of Organisational Citizenship Behaviour,' Doctoral Dissertation. California State University, Long Beach

26. Podsakoff, P. M., Mackenzie, S. B., Moorman, R. H. & Fetter, R. (1990). "Transformational Leaders Behaviour and their Effects on Followers' Trust in Leader, Satisfaction and Organizational Citizenship Behaviours," Leadership Quarterly 1, 107-142

27. Rose, R. C., Kumar, N. &Yen, L. L. (2006). "Entrepreneurs Success Factors and Escalation of Small and Medium-sized Enterprises in Malaysia," Journal of Social Sciences, 2(3): 74-80

28. Rozell, E. J., Pettijohn, C. E. & Parker, R. S. (2001). "An Empirical Evaluation of Emotional Intelligence: The Impact on Management Development," Journal of Management Development, Volume 21, No.4

29. Scott, B. S. (2004). 'The Relationship between EI and Ethical Decision Making,' A PhD Dissertation, Union University

30. Sitter, V. L. (2004). 'The Effects of a Leadership Emotional Intelligence on Employees' Trust in Their Leader and Employee Organisational Citizenship Behaviours,' Doctoral Dissertation. Regent University SMIDEC (2009) Profile of SMEs in the Manufacturing Sector, Retrieved 12 March 2009 from

31. http://www.smidec.gov.my/detailpage.jsp?page=statistic

32. The Star (2007). "Training One's Employees Is Worth the Investment," September 9, 2007.

33. The Star (2008). "Graduates to form 33% of Workforce by 2010," April 22, 2008.

34. The Star (2009a). "Subra: Graduates Lack Dynamism and Edge," February 16, 2009.

35. The Star (2009b). "Crucial to Engage Staff," March 10, 2009

36. Watson Wyatt Malaysia (2009). 'Asia-Pacific Leads in Pay Hikes,' Retrieved 16 March 2009 from http://www.watsonwyatt.com/asia-pacific/localsites/malaysia/news/press.asp?ID=18981

37. Weiss, H. M. & Cropanzano, R. (1996). "Affective Events Theory: A Theoretical Discussion of the Structure, Causes and Consequences of Affective Experiences at Work," in Cummings, L.L. (Eds), Research in Organizational Behavior, JAI Press, Greenwich, CT, Vol. Vol. 19 pp.1-74.

8

CHAPTER

A Case Study of Employees' Performance at Prime Group Vietnam

PhanThi Phuong Hoa[1] and Nguyen Bao Thoa[2]

[1] Hanoi University of Natural Resources and Environment, Vietnam

[2] Vietnam Rural Industries Research and Development Institute,Vietnam

ABSTRACT

Improving performance is an important goal of modern management. The quality of the workforce is a deciding factor behind organizations' success because employee performance has proven to have a significantly positive effect on their performance (Collis and Montgomery, 1995 pp. 118-128). There is a growing recognition that the primary source of competitive advantage is derived from an organization's human resources (Brewster and Carey et al., 2003). This case study of Prime Group, the leading group in producing construction materials in Vietnam with 10 factories nationwide and one of the top five in the world in this field, examines the correlation between employees' performance and the overall performance and productivity of the company. The aim of the study was to find solutions to improve the company's productivity through improving its employees' performance. The research used a combination of qualitative and quantitative methods to analyze data. Quantitative data were collected through a survey of 500 Prime employees, divided into three groups: managers, office staff and manufacturing workers and analyzed with the help of SPSS software. Qualitative data were collected through in-depth interviews of the same groups. Through the analysis, the study proposes possible solutions to address the company's current problems and increase its employees' performance.

Keywords: employee performance, human resource management, work outcomes, competitive advantage.

INTRODUCTION

Prime Group Co., Ltd was founded in 1999 in Hanoi. Originally named Vinh Phuc Co.,

Ltd, the company had an annual capacity of two million sqm of ceramics. By the end of 2006, Prime Group had become one of the leading companies in Vietnam in ceramic tile production as well as a multi-functional group with five main areas of business: construction material, mining, transportation, real estate and trade.

As of 2013, Prime Group has become the leading group in producing construction materials in Vietnam (Tran, 2013). The company now employs 5,000 employees and has 10 factories in Vietnam that manufactures a broad variety of ceramics, granite, porcelain wall and floor tiles, decorative tiles, border tiles and also German clay roof tiles. Prime Group products are sold in many domestic markets and regions throughout the world.

Prime Group is committed to unceasing innovation in technology and improving human resource quality so as to continually launch new lines of products with high standards and maintain the leading position in the construction material industry in Vietnam. The company also invests in sustainable development and contributes to the development of the community.

ACHIEVEMENTS

Prime Group's thirteen-year path to its current position of a leading construction material manufacturing group in Vietnam owes itself to the company's strategic focus on human resources. With an entrepreneurial and collaborative culture, Prime Group combined its internal strength derived from a united, well-trained workforce with external help from an expansive network of organizations and unions. This approach resulted in a stable path to success for the company and a healthy business environment for the Vietnamese economy in general. Thanks to this strategy, Prime Group is now positioned as the top company producing construction materials in Vietnam (Tran, 2013).

Awards (since 2007)

In 2010:

- Awarded the Banner in 2010 by the Prime Minister for being the leader of the emulation movement for business achievements.
- Awarded the Merit for achievements obtained from the emulation movement of good working and the establishment of a solid and strong labor union in 2010 by the Vietnam General Confederation of Labor (Decision No. 28/QÄ□-TLÄ□LÄ□VN dated 10/01/2011).
- Awarded the Merit for outstanding results of organization and performance of local cultural, sport and tourism in 2010 by the Ministry of Culture, Sport and Tourism (Decision No. 198/QÄ□-BVHTTDL dated 20/01/2011).

In 2009:

- Officially recognized for outstanding achievements of production and business and its active contribution to the development of the Vietnamese enterprise community by the Vietnam Chamber of Commerce and Industry (Decision No. 2840/PTM-TÄ□KT dated 29/09/2009).

In 2008:

- Awarded by the Government with the banner for being the leader in the emulation movement in 2008.
- Awarded by the Central Committee of Young Entrepreneurs Association of Vietnam with the Vietnam Gold Star Cup.

In 2007:

- Awarded the third labor medal by the President (Decision No. 1287/QÄ□-CTN dated 08/11/2007).
- Awarded a merit from the Ministry of Industry and Trade dated 06/01/2008.

- Awarded a merit for the company's compliance with the tax policy by the General Director of Directorate of Taxation with the (Decision No. 827/QÄ⍰-TCT dated 26/06/2008).
- Awarded a merit for excellent results in establishing, developing brand name and participating in the global economic integration by the National Committee of International Economic Cooperation (Decision No. 68/QÄ⍰-UBQG dated 01/09/2008).

Basic Economic Targets Achieved

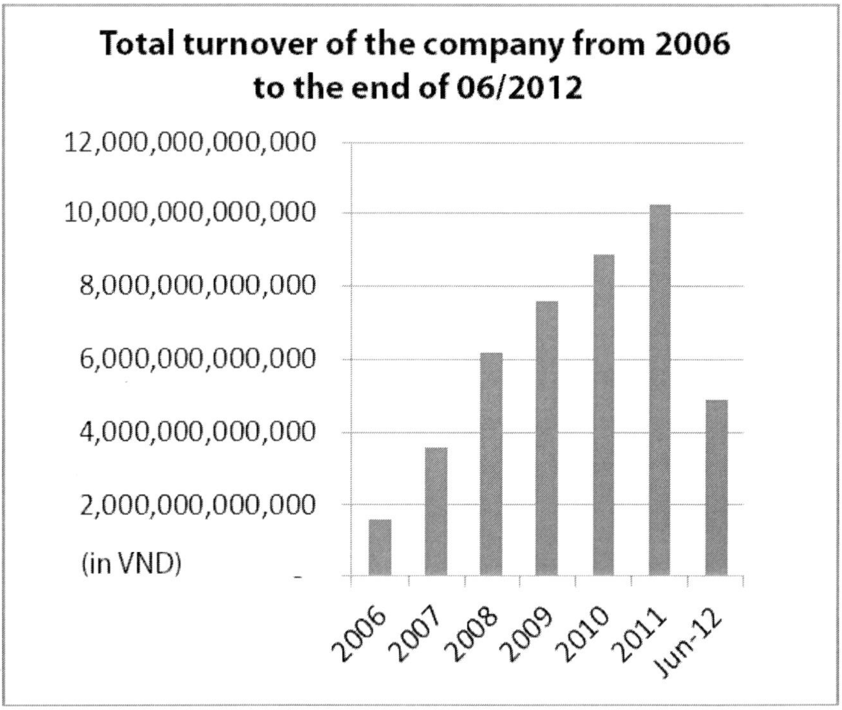

Figure 1: Total Turnover of the Company from 2006 to the End of 06/2012

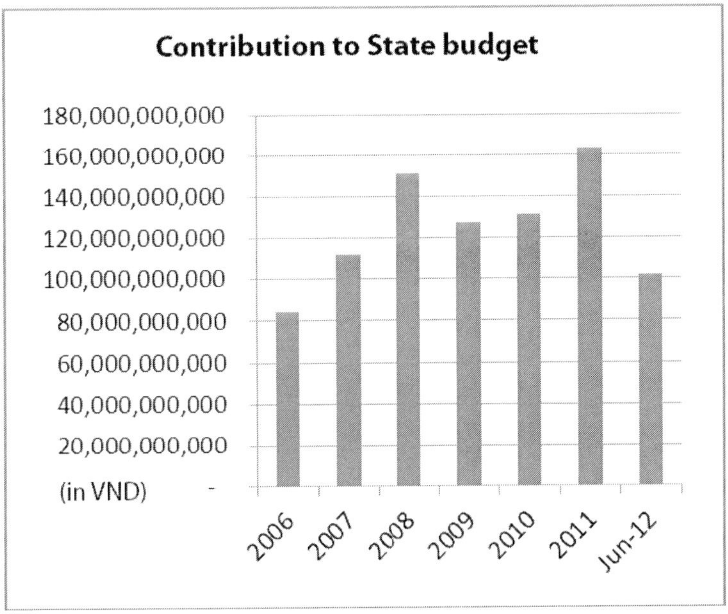

Figure 2: Total Amount of Tax Payment from 2006 to the End of 06/2012

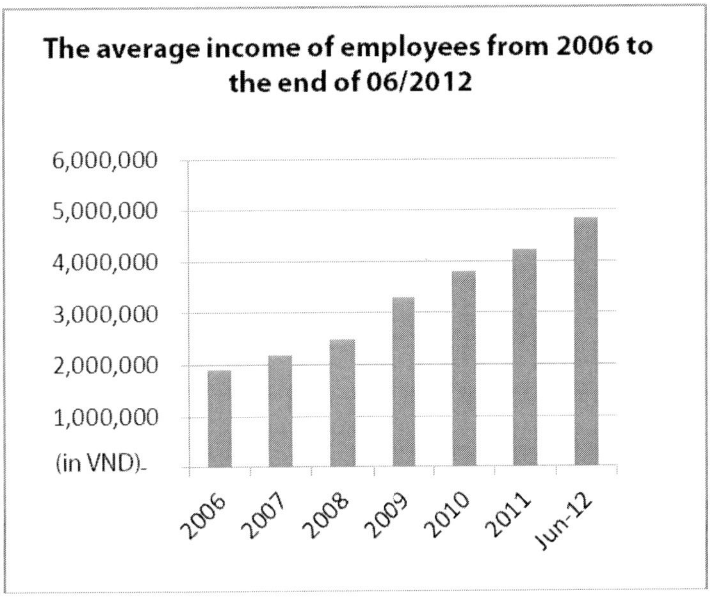

Figure 3: The Average Income of Employees from 2006 to the End of 06/2012

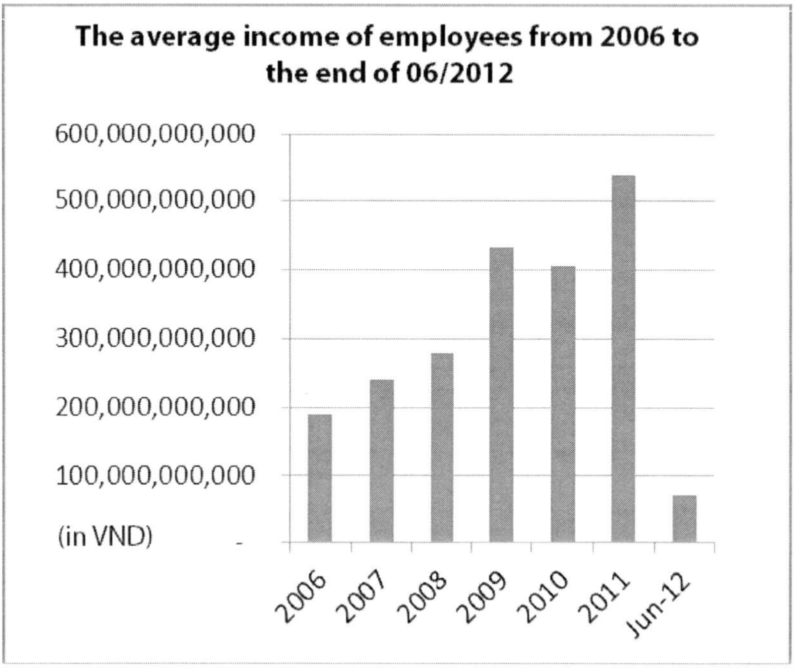

Figure 4: Profit before Tax from 2006 to the End of 06/2012

Management System

Prime Group has adopted a centralized management model that integrated a unified matrix to control and manage multiple aspects of operations such as Finance – Accounting, Procurement and Supply, Sales and Marketing, Production, Technology, Human Resource and Administration. The model includes:

- Standardized system: Plan, policy, regulation, procedure, rules, standards and production norms are harmonized among Prime Group's activities
- Planning system, policy and management system at company-level complies with the ISO 9000:2008 standard.
- Prime Group applies Enterprise Resource Planning (ERP) in which real-time data are gathered in one place.

In general, Prime's management system covers every aspect of business and renders a useful impact on the fulfillment of leadership, checks, assessment, and internal review. The system is continually and properly amended, supplemented and updated in order to meet the legal requirements, management system standards and leadership improvement.

However, the management system of Prime Group is still facing some shortcomings and there is room for improvement:

- The unavailability of an orthodox, comprehensive and independently-verified system.
- The unavailability of an official definition of validity and its scope between Prime Group and its member companies;
- Although the promulgation and amendment is maintained, the control and internal audit process has been underperforming, which reduced the effectiveness of the system during its implementation;
- The online E-doc system is still limited while the update is not as expected; being only properly done at Prime Group level;
- The completion of ISO system for the member units is still under operation, to be finished at the end of September 2012;
- The decentralized system of the two relatively independent levels led to overlapping and inconsistency within the policy.

HUMAN RESOURCES

Systematic Organization

Prime Group directly manages the operation of its member companies, making decisions regarding recruitment, appointment, rewards, discipline and treatment of the board of directors as well as every management position of its member companies.

The scope of Prime Group's management enables a unified solution to human resource cultivation, maximization and capability development as well as effective control of operation activities and fair treatment of employees at all levels.

Human Resource Plan

By clearly defining current working demands and investment plans for the near future, Prime Group and its member companies are able to maintain and control an effective human resource plan. For example, every position is analyzed from the beginning to the end to determine the pay rate. This approach helps optimize the time spent on the job, prevent strikes, enhance productivity and foster fair treatment.

To ensure harmonious human resource management throughout the entire group, Prime also utilizes a standardized analysis table, which serves as the basis for job description and procedures across its member companies.

The company establishes a unified system in order to define the human resources' plan, recruitment, training and treatment plan as well as labor costs. This analysis table is the basis for the completion of job description and procedures as well as management norms. Besides, the company also implements thorough welfare and treatment policies which cover income, reward and welfare.

Prime Group's capability improvement program for management and employees focuses on three aspects: specialized knowledge, working skills and working attitude; and includes training courses together with communication and coaching programs. The company also has an appropriate policy on Environment, Health and Safety, and Labor Relations.

Nonetheless, problems in employees' performance are still prevalent, such as (1) The compliance of management in member companies being not good enough, (2) The overall attitude and responsibility towards the company's goals being rather low, (3) Working results being at modest levels, (4) Pro-activity towards self-improvement among employees falling behind external requirements of change, (5) Employees' contribution to the human resource plan being not as high as expected, and (6) The effectiveness of work being rather low.

LITERATURE REVIEW

This empirical research proposes a framework to identify the relationship between employees' performance and compliance, work attitude, work outcome, self-improvement and contribution of employees in Prime Group.

Every organization has to utilize all resources at their disposal to overcome challenges and achieve strategic goals. Resources available for an organization include but are not limited to fixed assets, current asset, and intangibles such as social capital and human capital. In a time of cut-throat competition in the market and unstable environmental conditions worldwide, it is essential for companies and organizations to utilize all of their resources to gain competitive advantage, especially human resource as it has been proven to be a sustainable factor that is possible to improve through proper management. It is important for management to find a system to develop employees' capacity and motivate them to improve. Companies should also set up a feedback system to assess their employee performance and adjust strategy accordingly.

Indeed, review of employee performance records is an important part of operations in modern businesses. The most common form is annual reviews of individual employees done by managers. The feedback gathered from those reviews will then be discussed between managers and employees before being signed off. Some aspects of performance management include assessing employees' effectiveness on the job, aligning the goals of the organization with individual goals and addressing the needs of employees in order to retain talents in the company. The purpose of performance management is to ensure that most of the human capital is utilized and directed towards business success. Despite its importance, in many cases, managers fail to comprehend the role of this process in driving greater performance. It is crucial that a business owner or manager understands the foundation of "performance" and how to assess employees from a performance-oriented perspective.

Theory of Compliance

Compliance is the linchpin of modern society. From urban planning to business running, every aspect of life in the modern day needs certain regulations that are complied with by the people to maintain the order of society. Similar to the case of residential zoning ordinances, it is necessary for businesses to build a compliance program, educate employees about what they can or cannot do, and set consequences for violation. In both cases, the active participation and abidance of individual members is mandatory to make the program work. This concept was recognized by the United States Office of Inspector General (OIG) under "compliance as an element of employee performance" (Nicole, 2000). The implication is that understanding, participating in and adhering to the requirements of the company's compliance program should be factored into the employee's performance assessment. The question of what aspects that "compliance" covers yields diverse answers. Overall, compliance can cover rules, regulations, policies, processes and procedures. Johnson & Johnson is an example of a multinational company whose policies and regulations work well towards the business success. In their Policy Business Conduct, the company clearly draws the line of what is acceptable and what is not on multiple fronts — antitrust laws, environmental regulations, healthcare, labor policies, and security laws, among others.

The need for compliance in the workplace is, first and foremost, to reduce risks especially in companies where employees are exposed to tasks with high rates of injuries. The most commonly found area where strict compliance is present is in construction companies where workers are trained in safe procedures to reduce industrial accidents. In those companies, employees' understanding of and compliance with procedures are utmost important. As a construction material company, Prime Group is not an exception. Diaz and Resnick (2000) identified several factors that may affect employees' willingness to comply, such as incentive system to reward compliance, managerial commitment to safety, primary goals set forth by managers and individual perception of safety.

Theory of Work Attitude

Economists have been hesitant to acknowledge the link between attitude and performance, as the former is deemed a subjective variable. However, employee attitude can have significant economical impacts on a company, as argued by Freeman in his National Longitudinal Survey (1966-71) and Michigan Quality of Work Survey (1972-73). Since Freeman laid the foundation for a change in the way we view attitude as a factor in performance, numerous empirical studies have established a connection between attitude and performance.

In a time when human capital is considered one of the most important resources for business success, the link between employee attitude and workplace performance has been the topic of much research in organizational behavior (Weiss and Cropanzano, 1996). While attitude is a broad psychological concept, in this paper we will mainly focus on the job satisfaction aspect of work attitude.

Organizational behavior studies on job satisfaction emerged and developed rapidly in the late twentieth century. In his Range of Affect Theory, Locke (1976) coined the most-used definition of job satisfaction as "a pleasurable or positive emotional state resulting from the appraisal of one's job or job experiences" (Locke, 1976, p. 1300). He recognized the two interconnected elements that comprised job satisfaction: affect (emotions) and cognition (thoughts). The implication of Locke's finding is that our thoughts influence our emotions and the way we feel influences the way we think. Both sides of this interlocking relationship are important for performance improvement. This is a progressive move from the traditional managerial approach which only focuses on controlling external factors such as working environment and rewards system, etc. Organizational behavior research since the early twentieth century has recognized that personal factors, such as cultural background and emotional state also affect an employee's job satisfaction. Indeed, Staw and Ross (1985) were among the first to argue that the level of satisfaction of a person is stable over time regardless of situational changes in position, job and company. Hofstede (1980, 1985) found the importance of culture in shaping employee attitudes. According to Hofstede, the main dimensions of culture that affect attitudes are (1) individualism — collectivism; (2) uncertainty avoidance versus risk taking; (3) power distance and (4) masculinity / femininity. This was among a large body of research done in the last twenty years that emphasizes the dispositional source of job satisfaction (Arvey and Bouchard et al., 1989, pp. 359â˜383; House and Shane et al., 1996, pp. 203â˜224). Some researchers have attempted to explain the dispositional causes of job satisfaction by looking into the psychological factors behind them (Erez, 1994, Weiss &Cropanzano, 1996). A series of studies by Judge and his colleagues found that the personality trait that has the most influence on job satisfaction, core self-evaluation, is linked to the employee's own perception of the job itself (Judge & Bono, 2001, p. 80). The limitation of those studies is that they mostly demonstrate correlations instead of causation relations and thus, are lacking of explanatory value as to how personal factors influence performance in future cases. Nonetheless, they draw our attention to not only situational factors but also dispositional or personal factors when assessing job satisfaction.

The question worth pondering here is how companies can influence personal elements to increase job satisfaction. Saari and Judge (2004) pointed out that selecting the right people and placing them in the right positions is one way to improve satisfaction. This is not to say that we should dismiss situational influence altogether. To the contrary, the nature of the work plays an important role in affecting employee satisfaction (Judge and Church, 2000, pp. 166â˜198, Jurgensen, 1978, pp. 267â˜276). Thus, the adjustment of work-attitude-oriented management needs to start with modifying situational factors by making the work more interesting, challenging and rewarding.

Job Satisfaction and Withdrawal Behaviors

When assessing the performance of a company, two measurable economical elements that can be used are employee turnover rate and absenteeism, both of which exemplify withdrawal behaviors. High employee turnover rate and absenteeism are unfavorable because they cause delays and disruptions in workflow, thus increasing labor cost. Multiple studies conducted in the United States and other countries in Europe confirm the negative relationship between employee satisfaction and employee turnover rate (Akerlof and Rose et al., 1988, pp. 495â˜594; Clark and Georgellis et al., 1998). Likewise, dissatisfied employees are more likely to quit or be absent, as proven by Hacket&Guion (1985) and Kohler & Mathieu (1993), among others. However, not all sources of dissatisfaction result in decisions to quit. Clark, Georgellis and Sanfey (1998) found that (dis)satisfaction with the type of work has more influence on quitting decision than (dis)satisfaction with job security. Frijters, Shields and Wheatley-Price (2007) found that monetary reward is less effective than immaterial improvement in reducing quitting decisions due to dissatisfaction. In the same vein, Vroom (1964) found that low satisfaction results in high absenteeism. The implication of those studies is that the unwanted economical consequences of employee turnover and absenteeism are directly linked with employee attitude. In this way, we can measure the financial value of attitude through studying the relationship between a subjective element like satisfaction and withdrawal behaviors such as quitting and being absent which bear economic consequences.

Theory of Work Outcome

There have been many studies that sought to establish a theoretical framework for assessing work outcomes. Dyer and Reeves (1995) identified three types of outcomes — financial, organizational and human-resource-related (HR-related). Financial outcomes include revenues, profits, return on investment; organizational outcomes include product and service quality, innovation, and effectiveness; and HR-related outcomes include positive attitude and behavior from employees. Collins, Ericksen and Allen (2005) examined multiple theories regarding how Human Resource Management (HRM) influences employee outcomes, which, in turn, affects operational and/or financial performance. They identified five types of employee outcomes and their impacts on business performance:

- Commitment to supervisor
- Trust in management
- Cooperation with others and being cooperative
- Effort and involvement
- Turnover intentions

The study found that companies that have good financial growth tend to have high employee effort and involvement and low employee turnover rates. The latter was also proven to be a competitive edge. Another important group of stakeholders are the customers. The study found that companies with high customer satisfaction display common characteristics in their labor force, such as high commitment to superiors, firm trust in management and a cooperative mindset. Moreover, high trust in management also correlates with good product/service quality and new product development.

It is crucial to address employee-supervisor relationship because it stands behind two of the five employee outcomes that Collins, Ericksen and Allen (2005) pointed out in their study — commitment to supervisor and trust in management. Since this is a mutually beneficial relationship with a hierarchy, we can utilize the power dependence theory by Emerson (1962) to explain its nature. The basis of Emerson's theory is that power resides on one party's ability to control what the other party values. When applied in business, this theory means that employees are dependent on their supervisor when the supervisor has the power to provide what their employees desire, such as tangible and intangible rewards (Emerson, 1976, pp. 335â˘'362; Casciaro and Piskorski, 2005, pp. 167â˘'199). When the employees perceive the rewards to be a proper acknowledgement of and a fair compensation for their good performance, they will be motivated to continue their efforts as a means to obtain more rewards. Indeed, many studies have found a positive correlation between supervisor rewards and employee productivity, performance and satisfaction (Simon, 1976; Hunt and Osborn et al., 1981).

Theory of Motivation

The question of how to motivate employees has become one of the foremost concerns for managers because a motivated workforce has been proven to drive an organization's productivity and profitability (Carlsen, 2013, pp. 14â˘15). Motivation can be defined as the psychological force that drives a person's behaviors. In his influential paper, "A Theory of Human Motivation," Maslow (1943) set the framework for assessing motivation based on a hierarchy of needs. According to Maslow, humans have five basic needs as followed, arranged in the order of importance to human life: physiological, safety, love and belonging, esteem, and self-actualization.

Lewin (1951) acknowledged the role of both personal drive and the environment on motivating desired behaviors. Likewise, Herzberg's Two Factor Theory (1959) pointed out that there are two separate sets of factors in the workplace that cause job satisfaction and job dissatisfaction respectively. He broke down motivation into intrinsic and extrinsic. Intrinsic motivation refers to internal, personal sources of motivation such as an employee's own interest in the job whereas extrinsic motivation refers to external sources of motivation such as rewards and recognition from management.

Theory of Competitive Advantage

In the context of increasingly cut-throat competition on both a domestic and global scale, the pressing question for every organization is how to create and maintain competitive advantage. Creating sustainable competitive advantage boils down to developing valuable and scarce resources and capabilities (Collis and Montgomery, 1995; Prahalad and Hamel, 1990). In the scope of this project, the question we need to address is what role human resource management plays in creating and maintaining competitive advantage?

Given the two most important qualities of competitive advantage — value generating and not being imitable (Barney, 1991, pp. 99â˘120), human resource management can work to recruit and retain exceptional human capital that contributes significantly to the firm's competitiveness. In order to achieve this goal, management should make sure that employees are carefully selected and trained to have proper skills, motivated to deliver exceptional products and services to customers, and encouraged to contribute to a unique corporate culture. Indeed, not all employees can be recruited and trained to become a source of competitive advantage for a company. Barney & Wright (1997) pointed out the importance of having unique and valuable employees as opposed to those that perform repetitive tasks and thus, do not add value to the firm (Barney and Wright, 1997). Moreover, effective human resource management for competitiveness is as much about recruiting exceptional talents as it is about fitting them in proper positions and managing them so that their strengths play out to benefit the organization. Previous studies have also proven the connection between social capital, corporate culture and the development of organizational capabilities (Barney, 1991, pp. 99âˆ’120; Reed and Defillippi, 1990, pp. 88âˆ’102).

Theory of Productivity

Productivity is another key component of business success. Bartel, Freeman, Ichniowski and Kleiner (2003) found a positive correlation between satisfaction and productivity. Some empirical studies looked into the source of satisfaction that impact upon productivity and found mixed answers. Vanek (1970) argued that giving employees active ownership of the work would motivate them to improve productivity. Contrary to Vanek's finding, Jones (2007) compared Italian construction firms that operate with a co-operative (co-op) model with those that follow the traditional top-down management style. The productivity level at the co-op companies where employees are given higher ownership of the job does not prove to be higher than that at the traditional companies. The relationship is not as straightforward in reality. Kruse and Blasi (1995) found that ownership could have a positive or negative impact on employee attitude. Their study demonstrated that employee ownership only works if the extra responsibility brings tangible and intangible benefits to the employee. Otherwise, once the ownership is perceived by the employee to be a burden, their productivity may even decrease.

Research Methodology

This section justifies the choice of the combined quantitative and qualitative method used in this study. All necessary checks and balances were considered to ensure the results would be valid, reliable, practical and generalizable. The main criteria underlying the choice of using both a qualitative case study and quantitative survey instrument were construct validity, reliability and the ability to generalize results.

The researcher has stated the main problems that have been affecting employees' productivity in Prime Group. These problems were then considered to be factors that, if they were changed, then the Prime

Group employees' productivity would change accordingly. They were identified as independent variables in this research.

This research seeks to provide an empirical framework to identify the relationship between employees' performance and employees'; compliance, work attitude, work outcome, self-improvement and contribution in Prime Group. All these five independent variables are potential determinants in increasing employees' performance at Prime Group. There are some determinants that have significant and obvious effects on an employee's performance while there are others with impacts that still need to be studied.

In this study, a consideration of variables associated with the problem are under review, thus this becomes a study of correlation

Research Hypotheses

Based on the research framework (fig. 5) and research questions, five research hypotheses have been developed to test the relationship between employees' performance and the following factors:

H1: There is a relationship between compliance and employees' performance.

H2: There is a relationship between work attitude and employees' performance.

H3: There is a relationship between work outcome and employees' performance.

H4: There is a relationship between self-improvement and employees' performance.

H5: There is a relationship between contribution and employees' performance.

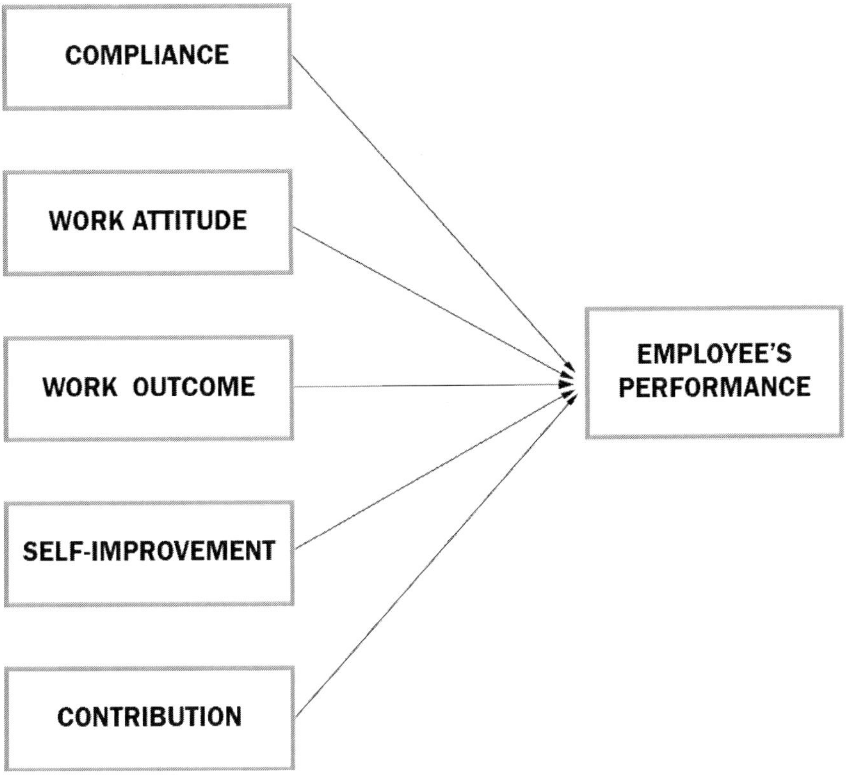

Figure 5: Research Framework

Sampling and Selection of Participants

In order to ensure that the final results of the research are valid, reliable and relevant, it is necessary to develop a sampling strategy to select a good cross-section from the employees of Prime Group.

In this research, the sample for the evaluation of employee performance was selected randomly from several factories and departments within Prime Group and divided into three groups including manufacturing workers, office staff and managers. The researcher contacted the Human Resource department and representatives from each of these sample groups for confirmation of participation. One of the key criteria that helped the survey to be successful and ensure its precision was that participants were randomly selected from throughout Prime Group.

This section discusses the types and methods of data collection used for research.

The selected participants are divided based on age (20â˜30 years old, 30â˜40 years old), level of position (intermediate, high), position (60% worker, 30% staff, and 10% manager), salaries ($200, $400, $1,000 to $2,000), This study uses a combined quantitative and qualitative methodology with questionnaires and in-depth surveys. The survey was designed so that all the active variables were covered.

Data Collection

In this study, collected data came from employees as a result of combined quantitative and qualitative studies and the product was analyzed together with information from secondary data to offer a qualitative conclusion. Data collection: primary: interview, secondary: For this research, it was possible to approach data not fully exploited by original collectors of the data and from a different aspect as this is a private own source of data which can be exploited by only people in Prime Group. Experiential: observation of the researcher.

The questionnaire includes sections as followed. It was designed according to the independent variables so as all research hypotheses can be tested easily based on items per section.

Section A: Demography

Section B: The employees' compliance

Section C: The employees' attitude

Section D: The employees' outcome

Section E: The employees' self- improvement

Section F: The employees' contribution

Section G: The employees' performance

The survey consists of two parts. The first part of the survey is interviews with Prime Group managers, seeking a general picture of department type, background of employees including experience, education, and work content. And the second part is for employees whose answers would help determine the research results.

The researcher personally collected all data and was involved in every instance, thus while the names and personal information of the participants were kept anonymous and confidential, everyone was surveyed personally in order to have the highest percentage of respondents completing the survey.

In this research, individual answers or scores had no relevance, for the unit of analysis was an event rather than a firm or an individual, and the researcher ensured the anonymous nature of the surveys, thus ensuring that there were no ethical considerations to consider. In addition, participants had the rationale of the survey explained and were able to cease their participation at any time without reason

Data Analysis

A multivariate analysis design, which allows the simultaneous investigation of more than two variables (Zikmund, 1997, p 657), was chosen to analyze the data.

Data analysis: SPSS was chosen to analyze data for this research survey. However, whilst the SPSS program was used to seek patterns within the data, as there were only a relatively small number of cases, in order for the richness and depth of meaning to be extrapolated, additional software was not considered necessary.

Data Analysis

This chapter provides a thorough analysis of the research problem and seeks answers to the research questions through different research approaches. The triangulation of the analysis helps narrow the gap in increasing employees' performance in a manufacturing group in Vietnam. This triangulation of the data analysis is necessary to include all of the factors that might have had impacts on employees' performance in Prime Group.

The survey began with preliminary interviews with managers and some manufacturing workers in several factories in order to have an overall picture of the employees' performance as well as to listen to their objective opinions regarding performance-based promotions within the company. The elaborated answers provided through in-depth conversations were very helpful in providing a multilayered picture and opened up different possible explanations for the situation. These interviews will be the source for the qualitative analysis phase.

Also, through this series of preliminary interviews did the researcher recognize the drawbacks of face-to-face interviews and decide on the quantitative approach. Because the researcher tapped into both manager and worker levels, regardless of the strict confidentiality standards that the research process followed, many interviewees were hesitant to express their real thoughts due to concerns of the potential consequences of publicly disclosing what they thought. Thus, the researcher also conducted anonymous questionnaires to allow the groups under study to express their opinions more comfortably.

The second and final phase of this analysis applied a quantitative approach where the researcher distributed 500 questionnaires to the randomly selected sample group. The data collected from these questionnaires were analyzed using non-parametric analysis techniques. Factor analysis was applied. The findings of this phase complemented the qualitative phase, where five factors were addressed and only two of them were influencing factors to employees' performance.

QUALITATIVE AND QUANTITATIVE RESEARCH

Multicollinearity

According to Sekaran (2003), multicollinearity refers to "the successive inclusion of additional variables that lift the collinearity of the full set of explanatory variables to a 'harmful' level". This is when additional variables closely correlate with other variables in the model and contribute relatively little to the prediction. The most common measure of multicollinearity is the variance inflation factor (VIF). In quantitative research, a VIF level exceeding 10 means that multicollinearity may cause estimation problems. Table 12 shows the VIF values for the five independent variables in this study. The values of the independent variables are in the range of 1.101 and 2.632, which is much lower than 10. Therefore, multicollinearity issues do not exist.

Employee Compliance

There were five issues mentioned in measuring employee compliance among Prime Group — compliance training, compliance policies, compliance is easy, violate and trouble. Most participants answered straightforwardly about the policies related to compliance to workplace regulations and whether they would be in any trouble if they did not comply precisely with the regulations of the corporation.

Table 1: Test of Collinearity

Independent Variables	Tolerance	VIF
Compliance	0.380	2.632
Work Attitude	0.577	1.732
Work Outcome	0.909	1.101
Self-improvement	0.461	2.171
Contribution	0.856	1.168

Table 2: Employee Compliance in Prime Group (%)

	Compliance training	Compliance policies	Compliance is easy	Violate	Trouble
Manufacturing workers	60	68	34	32	92
Office Staff	44	78	64	88	48
Manager	94	90	72	90	40

As regulations are the tool for managers to manage their staff and control work processes, most managers being asked felt that complying with corporate regulations was obvious and not many of them saw any trouble if someone was caught violating a regulation and reported to the management level. However, the response was very different among manufacturing workers. Most of them understood that memorizing all of the company's regulations and keeping them handy were important to their daily work, yet they admitted that, in reality, it was not easy to strictly comply with the regulations due to their positions or work characteristics. They also tended not to think of reporting any violations as sometimes the people who violated the regulations were their peers or a higher manager.

"All of us can make mistakes sometimes due to personal reasons or objective reasons, we should have sympathy for each other rather than reporting the mistakes to managers", said an interviewed manufacturing worker. They thought that ignoring rather than reporting violations of company regulations would be good for their peers and for themselves. However, they failed to grasp the overall effects on the company level as well as the long-term damage to the regulation of the company.

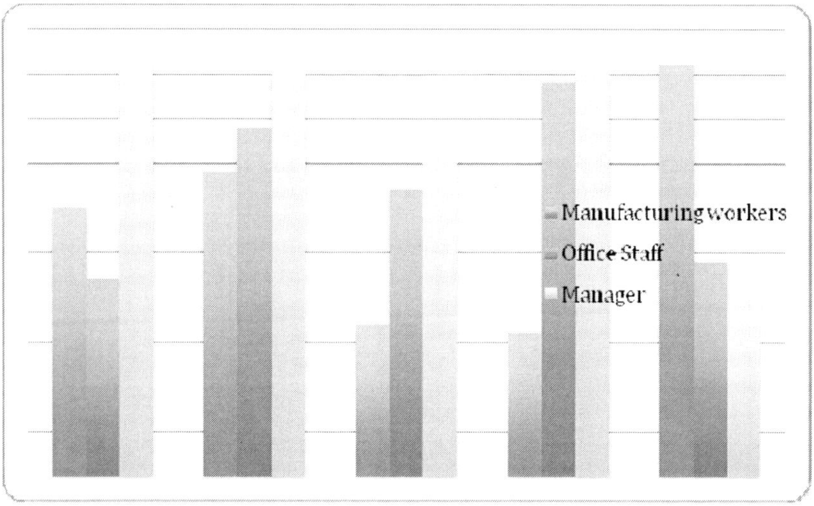

Figure 6: Complance Percentages among Three Groups of Population in Prime Group

Office staff often falls in between managers and manufacturing workers in their responses. They agreed with the managerial group that regulations must be complied with; 64% of them thought that regulations were easy to comply with. However, they were mostly medium ranking staff; their responses were similar to those of manufacturing workers who thought that it was not always true and necessary to report someone who violated the company's regulations. A staggering 48% of the office staff interviewed said that they might be in trouble if they reported any violation. Office staff was the group that received the least compliance training in the corporation, with only 44% of them having participated in a company compliance-training program. One of the reasons for the low participation rate in the compliance training program among office staff was that most of them worked on positions that, according to the corporate management, did not have many regulations.

Employee Attitude

Employees' attitude is a very important matter to all corporations because they are closely related to productivity and performance. In fact, productive and loyal workers play a crucial role in the success of a company. It is reasonable to assume that satisfaction is the most desirable employee attitude. Yet a common mistake that many managers tend to make is to assume that high performing workers have the kind of attitude that is favorable for the company's performance and development. This is not always the case. There are productive, high performing workers who are willing to switch to a new company once a better opportunity comes up and there are workers who stay with the company for many years who are not the most effective problem solvers. Above all, it is not correct to assume that an employee's performance reflects the whole picture of his or her satisfaction towards the job and the company.

Table 3: Employees' Attitude (%)

	Work hard	Loyal	Effectively and efficiently	Highly productive	Responsible
Manufacturing workers	96	60	76	84	94
Office Staff	90	78	72	82	88
Manager	94	100	96	90	96

The survey revealed that, in general, most participants perceived that they had a good attitude towards their jobs. More than 90% of manufacturing workers and managers assessed themselves as hard working and responsible. However, when it came to effectiveness and efficiency, only 76% of manufacturing workers were confident that they possess this quality, compared to 96% among managers. There was also a very big difference between workers and managers in loyalty assessment. A remarkable number of 100% of managers confirmed that they possessed this quality while only 60% of workers acknowledged this quality among themselves. While it is expected that workers, especially those in labor-intensive industries like the construction material industry that Prime operates in, are more prone to changing jobs due to better salary and benefits, forty percent of employees not perceiving themselves as loyal to the company is an alarming number that management should pay attention to and find ways to improve upon.

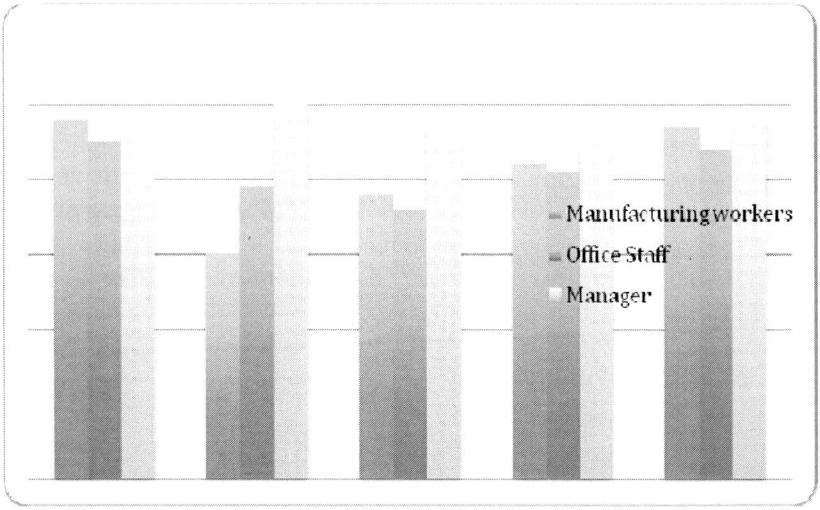

Figure 7: Employees' Attitude Percentages among Prime Group Staff

Office staff scored relatively low compared to the rest of the company in all aspects being surveyed, especially in self-perception of loyalty and effectiveness and efficiency. Only 72% of office staff thought that they were working efficiently and effectively. A potential reason for this low level of confidence in effectiveness and efficiency is because most of the office staff works in operational divisions where their main duties are to support the overall system and provide administrative work. The immediate results of their work may not be as discernible as those of the workers and managers, whose work results reflect immediately on indicators such as sales, performance and product quality, among others. Office staff also admitted a pretty low level of loyalty to the company. Only 78% of them reported to be loyal to the company. This is an area that needs management attention in order to find a proper solution to improve loyalty because, all other things being equal, it is more expensive to recruit and train new employees than retaining those who are already used to the job.

Everything a person does must provide some joy to him/her for a feeling of contentment from their performance. This joy should not be sought in the outcome of the job but in its performance from beginning to end. This requires that either the person does what he/she loves to do, or he/she seeks joy in everything he/she does.

Employee Outcomes

According to prior literature in the field of organizational behavior, employee outcomes might include a broad range of indicators, including commitment to the company, trust in management, higher levels of cooperation, higher levels of effort and involvement, and a lower inclination for employees to leave the company. These positive individual outcomes will lead to higher levels of operational and financial performance. However, for the purpose of this research, employee outcomes were measured based on the opportunities through which employees could grow and develop their talent.

Table 4: Employee Outcomes (%)

	Opportunity	Work well	Recognition or praise	Use talent well	Do job better
Manufacturing workers	42	60	58	46	90
Office Staff	54	60	62	82	88
Manager	90	92	84	90	96

Following the same patterns in attitude assessment, compared to their subordinates, the manager group was more satisfied with their outcomes as they had more opportunities to grow and develop in their job. Their overall perception of the company was more positive; they found a stronger attachment to the company's performance. Likewise, more than 90% of managers reported that they could use their talent on the job and do their job better. This positive feeling of self-worth and ownership of the job would, in turn, serve as an intrinsic motivation for them to contribute to the overall performance of the company.

However, up to 16% of surveyed managers complained that they were not recognized reasonably for their contribution to the company. This is a point worth noticing for the company's leadership. As previous studies have pointed out, a mismatch between the employees' perception of what they deserve in exchange for their efforts at work and actual compensation they receive from the company could act as a de-motivation force that, in the long run, causes dissatisfaction and reduce work results among employees.

In contrast to the managers' assessment, manufacturing workers were quite pessimistic about their opportunities to grow and prove themselves in the workplace. Only 42% of workers saw that they had opportunities to learn and grow at work — an alarming number for a corporation like Prime. Some said that they did have chances to learn from colleagues and training courses but they had to strive hard to gain a promotion opportunity or develop their skills. "I attended some training courses when I began to work for the factory and during my probation, sometimes I also learn a new skill or technique from my colleagues but I don't think I have any chance of utilizing my skills or being promoted in the short or medium term", a manufacturing worker shared in the in-depth interview.

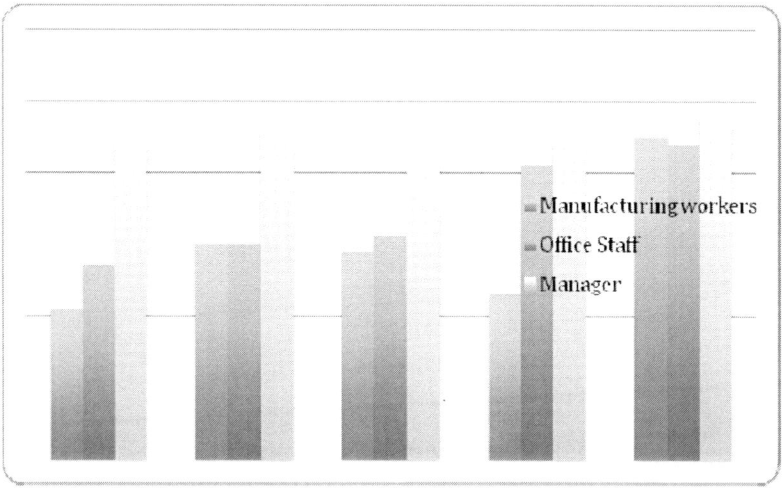

Figure 8: Percentages of Employees' Outcomes in Prime Group

Manufacturing workers shared that they also tried to do better in their jobs but their talents were not utilized appropriately. Only 46% of surveyed manufacturing workers said that they could make full use of their talent in their jobs. Given that human resources are an important factor in creating competitive advantages and improving the overall performance of the company, such a low level of talent utilization is unacceptable, especially in a large organization like Prime. If this resource is discovered and utilized, the benefits for the company could be remarkable.

Office staff and manufacturing workers at Prime also thought that they were not appropriately recognized or praised for their job, only 62% and 58% respectively. When staffs perceive that their efforts have not been recognized and rewarded properly, they will be hesitant to devote themselves to their work in the long term. In fact, immediate benefits such as recognition and rewards could have a profound impact on the long-term working attitude of staff, which would successively influence the final outcomes of the company. Although rewards and recognition as a source of motivation is very common in modern organizations, not many business owners are able to apply a reasonable system of recognizing proper employee achievements to their company, hence the high rate of job-hopping among low ranking staff.

Self-improvement among Employees

Self-improvement at work is doable for many employees. Many just need some guidance in areas where they are deficient in skills and often, just a hint that they might be more efficient or in line for a promotion if they had a particular skill set, is enough motivation. An employer who provides on-site training from outside trainers or in-house developed programs, or provides access to on-line training programs or sponsors local training providers or schools, coupled with rewards for completed certificates or degrees, will benefit from an increasingly better-trained workforce.

In the case of Prime Group, "self-improvement" is determined by what an individual has to and should do to improve his or herself and overcome barriers to improve.

Table 5: Self-improvement among Employees (%)

	Improve myself	Know what to do	Make commitment	Overcome barriers	Know what strategies
Manufacturing workers	68	58	86	46	48
Office Staff	82	76	90	78	68
Manager	84	90	98	84	72

The results summarized in table 4.8 demonstrated that the willingness to make commitment to self-improvement among Prime employees was remarkably high — up to 98% among managers. Again, we saw a lower level of commitment among staff and workers compared to managers — 90% among staff and 86% among manufacturing workers. Nevertheless, having the willingness to self-improve is a positive starting point for people at Prime to further advance their selves and skills.

Overall, there still existed a wide gap between managers and employees' perception of self-improvement, especially when it comes to knowledge of what to do to overcome barriers and an ability to come up with a strategy for self-advancement. Despite their strong willingness to improve, manufacturing workers struggled to turn their will into executable, actionable plans. Only half of the manufacturing workers being surveyed admitted that they knew what to do, how to overcome barriers and how to build a strategy to improve. In Prime Group, the percentage of employees who were confident in their ability to overcome performance barriers was not high, especially among manufacturing workers. Only 46% of them thought that they could improve themselves enough to overcome these barriers. Even only 84% of the manager group thought that these barriers could be addressed when their skills and knowledge were improved. To overcome potential barriers to self-development besides efforts from him or herself, an employee also needs significant support from the company. This is an area that management should pay attention to in order to help employees develop, as their improvement will contribute to the long-term health of the company.

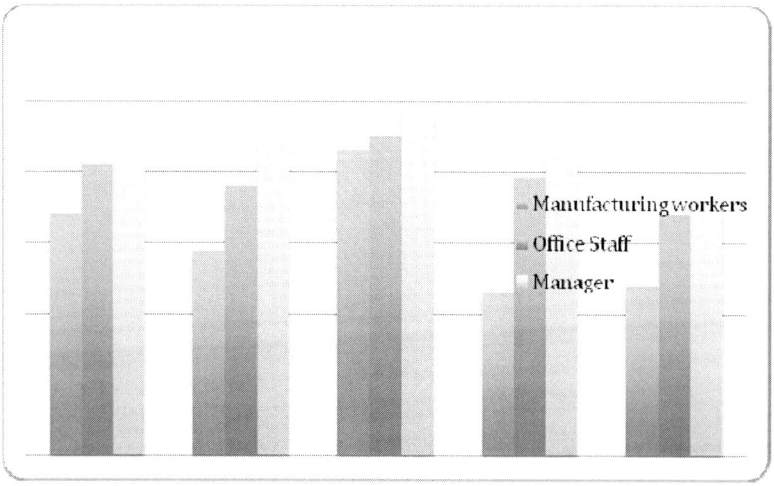

Figure 9: Employee Self Improvement

Employee Contribution to the Group

Since contribution from employees is an important factor underlying a company's success, human resource management comes down to the proper management of employee contribution. Human capital is the main source of competitive advantage today and Human Resources is responsible for the design of the HR tools to develop, nurture and utilize the human capital of an organization. In this research, the researcher focused mainly on the willingness of participants to contribute to the company in the forms of sharing skills/knowledge and improving their own performance based on the feedback received.

Table 6: Employee Contribution (%)

	Share knowledge	Share skills	Contribute time	Contribute efforts	Work better
Manufacturing workers	100	86	60	62	60
Office Staff	80	80	70	72	78
Manager	90	92	88	100	96

The level of commitment to give back to the company is exceptional among managers. All of the managers interviewed for the study said that they would contribute all their efforts to the development of the company. They were also willing to improve on their work and share their knowledge and skills with others. This is very important to the success of a company as the manager group has not only a broad skill set but also a thorough understanding of the systems. The fact that they are open to sharing their skills is very important for Prime to design training programs where the internal exchange of training and self-advancement information is fostered. Besides, all manufacturing workers under study were also willing to share knowledge with others. The company should cultivate this spirit and utilize it in its training program for newcomers.

More office staff was willing to share skills and knowledge than contribute extra time and effort and to improve their work based on feedback. Unlike in the case of managers and manufacturing workers, in all five aspects of contribution under evaluation, there was no aspect that received total agreement from office staff. There was always 20 to 30% of staff that were not willing to put in extra contributions in any form. When being asked about the reason behind their absolute unwillingness to contribute beyond what is expected of them, most of this particular group of staff reflected three reasons. The first reason is the reward system that does not tend to recognize the efforts of office workers as much as factory workers. This resulted from the nature of business at the company. Because Prime is a manufacturing group with a heavy focus on the productivity of the factory, there is not a thorough and comprehensive system to measure the improvement in performance of the office staff. The second reason is related to the first reason – 10% of the staff expressed dissatisfaction with their current salary and believed that should a better paid job opportunity arise they would take it into consideration. The third reason that was cited by half of the staff is that they have low expectations and motivation because they believe their day-to-day tasks are repetitive and without much new, challenging problems to solve. This same group also expressed low expectation in career advancement within the office segment of the organization. Therefore, even though the office staff is generally contempt with the working conditions, a third of the group under studied does not show any intention to contribute further to the organization.

While they were very willing to share skills and knowledge, manufacturing workers were reluctant to contribute their time and efforts to the corporation. Only 60% of them said they would contribute their time and 62% of them would contribute their effort to the company. When being asked about the reason, some said that they only worked for the salary and they understood that at their position, with low salary and not many opportunities to develop, there was no use to devote too much to the company. Besides, according to them, the recognition system of the company was not reliable and they were not confident in being appropriately appraised when putting in extra time and efforts for the company. Most manufacturing workers thought that devotion was not a joy or a personal choice to them; they should be paid for their contribution. It is expectable for employees to match their performance to compensation, especially for low-level workers. However, there is potential for a breakthrough in performance if Prime found a way to motivate their workforce beyond monetary rewards.

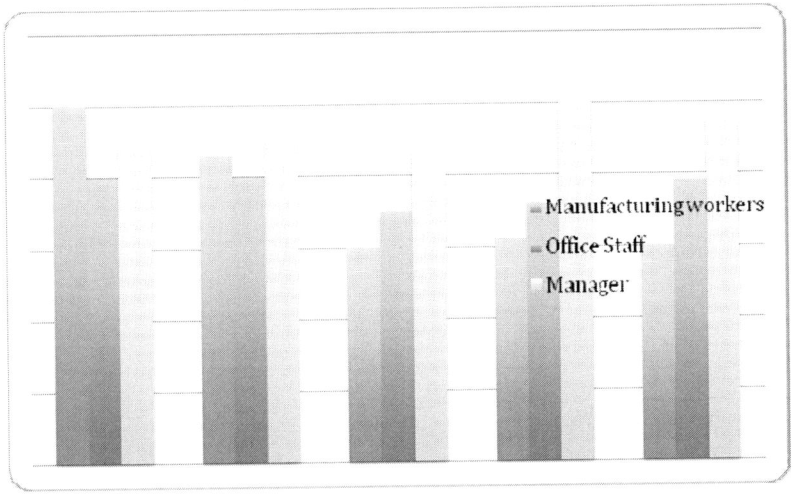

Figure 10: Employees' Contribution to the Corporation

The willingness to improve based on feedback is relatively low among manufacturing workers — 60% of manufacturing workers agreed that they would be willing to receive feedback and improve themselves based on that feedback. However, in-depth interviews revealed that some manufacturing workers believed that not all kinds of feedback were reasonable and suitable as sometimes the feedback came from people who did not understand the workers' jobs well.

Employee Performance

This research looked at factors that might have impacts on employees' performance, including compliance to job regulations, attitude to the company and their job, outcomes when working for Prime Group, self-improvement, and contribution to the development of the corporation.

Participants were also asked to assess their work performance and the factors that might affect their performance. Most employees thought that they would be willing to receive feedback from others to improve their work. They believed that they could work even better if the organization helped balance their work and life. This is an important issue in the modern working environment. The quality of life outside of work deserves managerial attention as it influences an employee's attitudes and productivity. Organizations that are able to support good qualities of work life relationships among their employees will have better productivity and happier employees. Respect from the organization is also crucial to employees. When they are respected and feel confident in their job, the employees tend to demonstrate more dedication and better performance. Cooperation among employees would also help employees improve their performance.

Table 7: Employee Performance

Variable names	Receive feedback	Do my best	work balance	Respect	Cooperation
Manufacturing workers	92	86	94	90	88
Office Staff	92	88	94	90	94
Manager	96	94	88	90	96

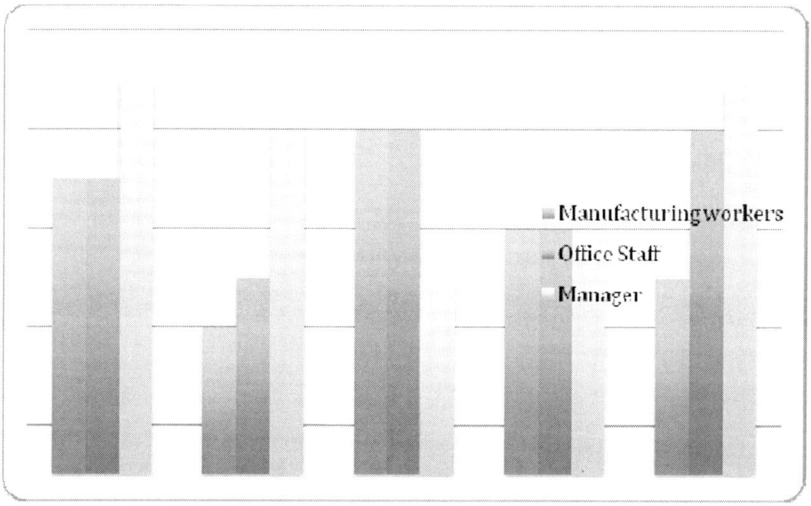

Figure 11: Percentages of Staff Agreeing about Factors to Improve Employee Performance

QUANTITATIVE ANALYSIS

Reliability of Factors Test

All variables have high Cronbach's Alpha values which are above 0.6 (Malhotra, 2013) except for variable B which is 0.562. In other words, all variables are reliable to proceed for inferential analysis.

Table 8: Reliability Statistics

	Reliability Statistics	
Variable	Cronbach's Alpha	No. of Items
Compliance	0.562	5
Work attitude	0.832	5
Work outcome	0.819	5
Self-improvement	0.803	5
Contribution	0.817	5
Employees' productivity	0.822	5

Factors Analysis

To determine the appropriateness of factor analysis, examining the correlation among all of the questionnaire items is essential. This can be obtained through the Bartlett test of sphericity which tests the presence of nonzero correlations among the variables. Kaiser-Meyer-Olkin (KMO), the measure of sampling adequacy (MSA), is another indicator of factor analysis appropriateness that uses a range from 0 to 1 to determine appropriateness. According to Tabachnick and Fidell (2007) and Pallant (2010), factor analysis is acceptable if the value of KMO is greater than 0.5. As Table 4.12 indicates, it has been verified that factor analysis in this study is appropriate as the Kaiser-Meyer-Olkin measure of sampling adequacy = 0.918, Bartlett's test of sphericity is highly significant with a Chi-Square value = 5.073E3, at p value = 0.000. Hence, all the data are useful for the research.

Table 9: KMO and Bartlett's Test

KMO and Bartlett's Test		
Kaiser-Meyer-Olkin Measure of Sampling Adequacy.		.918
Bartlett's Test of Sphericity	Approx. Chi-Square	5.073E3
	df	300
	Sig.	.000

The extracted Eigenvalues indicate that 5 variables can be extracted. Together, they account for almost 58% of the variability in the original variables. This suggests that five latent influences are associated with employees' performance, but there remains room for a lot of unexplained variation.

The R-Square shows that 48.2% of variation in DV can be explained by the five IVs.

The F-value is high and significantly (p<0.05) indicates that the research model is robust.

Table 10: Model Summary

Model	R	R Square	Adjusted R Square	Std. Error of the Estimate
1	.694a	.482	.477	.33208
a. Predictors: (Constant), AVGIVF, AVGIVB, AVGIVC, AVGIVE, AVGIVD				

The table below shows that that AVGIVE and AVGIVF are significantly and positively related to DV (p<0.05). AVGIVB, AVGIVC and AVGIVD are not significantly related to DV.

The research formula can be shown as below:

DV = 1.263 + (-0.011) AVGIVB + (0.034) AVGIVC + (-0.006) AVGIVD + (0.224) AVGIVE + (0.529) AVGIVF

Table 11: Coefficients

Model		Unstandardized Coefficients		Standardized Coefficients	t	Sig.
		B	Std. Error	Beta		
1	(Constant)	1.263	.203		6.207	.000
	AVGIVB	-.011	.025	-.016	-.438	.661
	AVGIVC	.034	.037	.038	.907	.365
	AVGIVD	-.006	.040	-.007	-.141	.888
	AVGIVE	.224	.045	.234	5.024	.000
	AVGIVF	.529	.046	.512	11.426	.000
a. Dependent Variable: AVGDVG						

Summary of Hypotheses

After proposing the hypotheses, the researcher conducted statistical hypothesis testing which began with selecting and evaluating a sample group. Null and alternative hypotheses were set for each corresponding hypothesis under evaluation.

There are 5 hypotheses in this study. Statistics are generated accordingly based on SPSS in order to assess all the hypotheses.

Table 12: Summary of Hypotheses

No	Independent variables	Results
1	Employee compliance	Not Supported
2	Employee attitude	Not Supported
3	Employee outcomes	Not Supported
4	Employee improvement	Supported
5	Employee contributions	Supported

DISCUSSIONS AND CONCLUSIONS

Implications for Corporations

This case analysis of Prime Group reveals issues and lessons learned that are applicable for other corporations to improve their overall performance through improving employee performance. Due to the differences in culture, industry and nature of the work at different companies, there is no one-size-fits-all answer to the complicated question of workforce management for better corporate performance. However, the research could serve as a guideline for management or leaders to identify problems in employee performance management and determine parameters to set up an assessment system that accounts for factors that exert strong influences on performance. Overall, it is important to ensure strict yet practically flexible compliance, create a cooperative working environment, and apply discipline with regards to the background and interests of different groups of employees in mind.

Objective 1: To enhance employee compliance

As analyzed in Chapter 4, while managers thought that company regulations were easy to understand and follow, and they were the ones who always complied with those regulations, most manufacturing workers, although they agreed that all their company's regulations were reasonable, could not always follow them due to their job characteristics and other objective reasons that were out of their control. In general, despite the managerial acknowledgement of the importance of compliance, the level of compliance among manufacturing workers in Prime Group is not very high. However, it is too early to assume that obedience will guarantee productivity. In many cases, flexible workers can adjust quickly to changes in the working environment or solve problems instantaneously.

Indeed, with the global economic instability and the emergence of a decentralized organizational structure where employees can take an active part in the decision-making processes at the company level, there is a growing trend in modern organizations to favor quick problem solving and adaptability over obedience among employees. However, in order to sustain an organization that follows the aforementioned structure, it is important to set up a very clear and strong set of regulations that also allow a room for freedom to take action when needed. In other words, management at Prime Group should find an approach to improve compliance not by imposing stricter policies but rather by examining and improving the current regulations. A good practice could be conducting a company-wide survey to collect thoughts and opinions about how to make the regulations "better" for each individual and group. Based on the results of this survey, management can rebuild a set of regulations that can both serve as the backbone of the company structure and reflect the voice of employees.

Objective 2: To improve employee work attitude

The results of the analysis indicate that the work attitude in Prime Group is not the factor that influences employees' performance — or at least in the perception of their employees. A very high percentage of surveyed employees thought that once working for the company, they would always be loyal and work as hard as possible. They also believed that they were working efficiently, effectively and responsibly. Such a positive and dedicated mentality shared by the majority of the employees is an ideal starting point to improve employee performance.

However, two potential shortcomings of this conclusion are 1) possibility of response bias and 2) the mismatch between positive attitude and good performance. Due to the data collection method that relies mainly on self-reflection, the responses on which the research based its conclusions are prone to personal bias. Future research should look into ways to crosscheck the assessments given by employees for a more accurate picture of the situation. The research also reveals that while work attitude is very favorable among employees, it does not translate well into performance. In the long term, Prime Group management should maintain and reinforce this spirit while figuring out a way to convert positive working spirit to positive performance.

Objective 3: To increase employee work outcomes

The results derived from Prime Group's manufacturing workers contradicted the general belief that on-the-job opportunities, recognition and praise, and talent promotion will help increase employee performance. The hypothesis that work outcomes correlate with performance is not supported by the data collected, which means this relationship is weak at the point of the research. According to Prime Group manufacturing workers, they did not have many opportunities to develop in their jobs and the recognition and praise systems in the corporation were not satisfactory. Surprisingly, this factor did not seem to have altered their productivity, at least in the timeframe the study was conducted. Yet it is irrefutable that rewards and recognition can serve as an important source of motivation for desired behavior among employees. Thus, in the long run, it is strongly advised that Prime Group continues examining this relationship in the future and increases employee performance through simple solutions such as promoting a better recognition system or creating more job opportunities for their staff or making use of the talent being wasted among their staff.

Objective 4: To stimulate the employees' self-improvement

Self-improvement is one of the two factors whose influence on employee performance in Prime Group is supported by the data analysis results. Overall, employees of Prime Group demonstrated a strong willingness to improve, yet many of them struggle to find a proper strategy to achieve this goal, especially among low-level workers. This is where the organization should step in and help their staff build an effective action plan. Indeed, self-learning and self-improvement are important qualities that a lot of modern organizations look for in their employees, as these qualities add values to the human resources and help the entire company become a better workplace in the long term.

Objective 5: To encourage employees to contribute more to the company

When being asked to assess their own willingness to contribute, most employees of Prime Group thought that they have contributed enough for the company, with a disparity between the responses of managers and manufacturing workers. The results from questionnaires and interviews showed that while managers were willing to devote extra time and efforts to the job, many employees at a lower ranking level thought that it was no use for them to devote more than what they were compensated for. This is understandable from the point of view of this group of employees, especially when the recognition and praise system is still not sufficient. Even if managers deem the current productivity and commitment level among employees satisfactory, their reluctance to put in extra effort when needed is not very favorable. This raises an issue for the management of Prime Group; that they have to make their staff see the value of devoting to the company through reasonable encouragement and mindset changing strategies.

The case of office staff is also worth the attention of management. With 20-30% of the staff expressed unwillingness to contribute extra time and efforts in any forms due to reasons of rewards and recognitions, salary, and career advancement, it is important that the management at Prime pays more attention to the office segment inside the company. The rewards and recognition system needs to have a better way to measure improvements made by office workers. Compensation is also an important motivational factor. However, due to the scope of this study, the author cannot examine in further details the amount of salary that would be optimum for the office staff at Prime. The management at Prime should conduct an internal examination of their current compensation level, with comparison among individuals within the company as well as between the Prime and other companies in the same segment, and the expectations of their staff. A structural review is also recommended so that more career advancement opportunities for office staffs become available and transparent. Only when the staff knows that their extra contribution goes towards the overall advancement of the company and of their own career path in particular, does the management expect a motivated contribution from this group of employees.

Implications for Policy Makers

Even though increasing employee performance seems to be the internal concern of individual corporations, if the government plays an active role in supporting enterprises to improve their performance through reasonable and immediate policies, it might help improve the performance of the whole economy and even the whole society. The Government can support enterprises from a macro perspective such as implementing policies and strategies related to labor training and labor management. Besides, from a labor perspective, the Government can help organizations to improve their capacities by setting standards in the fields of working environment, payment and recognition policies for laborers or loyalty requirements.

Limitations of Study

A number of limitations were identified in the course of the research process. They are listed below for improvements in future studies.

Prime Group Member Limitations

Whilst the sample group of participants was randomly selected from three groups, including managers, office staff and manufacturing workers, only some factories and branches of Prime Group were selected for the survey due to location and time limitations. Although some representatives of participating factories or branches were prepared to point out the faults of branches and factories, on the whole, participants were reluctant to offer hard criticism. However, when it came to personal assessment, participants appeared to be open and honest regarding the factors that might have had an impact on their performance.

Participant Number Limitations

The size of sample group could be a limitation for the research. For this study, the number of managers selected was 100, office staff was 100 and manufacturing workers were 300. These numbers were quite small compared with the size of the labor force of Prime Group. This relatively small number may restrict to some extent the ability to generalize results based on statistical convention.

REFERENCES

1. Akerlof, G. A., Rose, A. K., Yellen, J. L., Ball, L. & Hall, R. L. (1988). "Job Switching and Job Satisfaction in the US Labor Market," Brookings Papers on Economic Activity, 1988 (2), 495â˘'594.
2. Arvey, R. D., Bouchard, T. J., Segal, N. L. & Abraham, L. M. (1989). "Job Satisfaction: Environmental and Genetic Components," Journal of Applied Psychology, 6, 359â˘'383.
3. Barney, J. (1991). "Firm Resources and Sustained Competitive Advantage," Journal of Management, 17 (1), 99â˘'120.
4. Barney, J. & Wright, P. (1997). "On becoming a Strategic Partner: The Role of Human Resources in Gaining Competitive Advantage,"
5. Bartel, A., Freeman, R., Ichniowski, C. & Kleiner, M. (2003). "Can a Work Organization Have an Attitude Problem? The Impact of Workplaces on Employee Attitudes and Economic Outcomes,"
6. Brewster, C., Carey, L., Dowling, P., Grobler, P., Holland, P. & Warnich, S. (2003). "Contemporary Issues In Human Resource Management: Gaining a Competitive Advantage," Cape Town: Oxford University Press.
7. Carlsen, K. (2013). "Sales Motivation: One Size Does Not Fit All," Selling, (October), 14â˘'15.
8. Casciaro, T. & Piskorski, M. (2005). "Power Imbalance, Mutual Dependence, and Constraint Absorption: A Closer Look at Resource Dependence Theory," Administrative Science Quarterly 50 (2), 167â˘'199.

9. Clark, A., Georgellis, Y. & Sanfey, P. (1998). "Job Satisfaction, Wage Changes and Quits: Evidence from Germany,"Research in Labor Economics, 17.

10. Collins, C., Ericksen, J. & Allen, M. (2005). "Human Resource Management Practices, Workforce Alignment, and Firm Performance,"

11. Collis, D. & Montgomery, C. (1995). 'Competing on Resources: Strategy in the 1990s,' Harvard Business Review, 73 (July-August), 118â^'128.

12. Diaz, Y. & Resnick, M. (2000). "A Model to Predict Employee Compliance with Employee Coporate's Safety Regulations Factoring Risk Perception," paper presented at Human Factors and Ergonomics Society Annual Meeting,

13. Florida, July 2000. Miami: Florida International University Miami.

14. Dyer, L. & Reeves, T. (1995). "HR Strategies and Firm Performance: What Do Weknow and Where Do We Need to Go," International Journal of Human Resource Management, 6 (3), 656â^'670.

15. Emerson, R. (1962). "Power-dependence Relations," American Sociological Review, 31â^'41.

16. Emerson, R. (1976). "Social Exchange theory," Annual review of sociology, 2, 335â^'362.

17. Erez, M. (1994). 'Toward a Model of Cross-Cultural Industrial and Organizational Psychology,' Handbook of industrial and organizational psychology, 4, 559â^'608. [Accessed: 5 Nov 2013].

18. Freeman, R. (1977), "Job Satisfaction as an Economic variable," Cambridge: Harvard University. [E-book], Available through: National Bureau ofEconomic Research., [Accessed: 5 Sep 2013],http://citeseerx.ist.psu.edu/viewdoc/download?doi=10.1.1.333.6783&rep=rep1&type=pdf

19. Freeman, R. & Medoff, J. (1982). "Why Does the Rate of Youth Labor Force Activity Differ across Surveys?,"Chicago: University of Chicago Press. [E-book], Available through: National Bureau of Economic Research., [Accessed: 5 Aug 2013],http://www.nber.org/chapters/c7872.pdf.

20. Frijters, P., Shields, M. & Price, S. (2007). "Investigating the Quitting Decision of Nurses: Panel Data Evidence from the British National Health Service,"Health Economics, 16 (1), 57â"73.

21. Hackett, R. & Guion, R. (1985). "A Re-Evaluation of the Absenteeism —Job Satisfaction Relationship," Organizational Behavior and Human Decision Processes, 35, 340â"381.

22. Herzberg, F., Mausner, B. & Snyderman, B. (1959). 'The Motivation to Work. Second Edition,' [By] F. Herzberg, Bernard Mausner, Barbara Bloch Snyderman, xv, 157, John Wiley & Sons: New York; Chapman & Hall: London; printed in the U.S.A.

23. Hofstede, G. (1980). 'Culture's Consequences,' Beverly Hills, Calif.:Sage Publications.

24. Hofstede, G. (1985). "The Interaction Between National And Organizational Value Systems," Journal of Management Studies, 22 (4), 347â"357.

25. House, R., Shane, S. & Herold, D. (1996). "Rumors of the Death of Dispositional Research Are Vastly Exaggerated,"Academy of Management Review, 21 (1), 203â"224.

26. Hunt, J., Osborn, R. & Martin, H. (1981). "A Multiple Influence Model of Leadership,"

27. Jones, D. C. (2007). "The Productive Efficiency of Italian Producer Cooperatives: Evidence from Conventional and Cooperative Firms,"

28. Judge, T. & Bono, J. (2001). "Relationship of Core Self-Evaluations Traits–Self-Esteem, Generalized Self-Efficacy, Locus of Control, and Emotional Stability–with Job Satisfaction and Job Performance: A Meta-Analysis," Journal of Applied Psychology, 86 (1), 80.

29. Judge, T. & Church, A. (2000). 'Job Satisfaction: Research and Practice,' In: Cooper, C. and Locke, E. eds. 2000. Industrial and organizationalpsychology: Linking theory with practice. Oxford, UK: Blackwell, 166â"198.

30. Judge, T., Locke, E., Durham, C. & Krugger, A. (1998). "Dispositional effects on Job and Life Satisfaction: The Role of Core Evaluations," Journal of Applied Psychology, 83, 17â"34. [Accessed: 5 Nov 2013].

31. Jurgensen, C. (1978). "Job Preference (What Makes a Jobgood or Bad)," Journal of Applied Psychology, 63 pp. 267â˜'276.

32. Kohler, S. & Mathieu, J. (1993). "Individual Characteristics, Work Perceptions, and Affective Reactions Influences on Differentiated Absence Criteria," Journal of Organizational Behavior, 14 (6), 515â˜'530.

33. Kruse, D. & Blasi, J. (1995). "Employee Ownership, Employee Attitudes, and Firm Performance,"

34. Lewin, K. (1951). 'Field Theory in Social Science,' New York: Harpe.

35. Locke, E. (1976). 'Range of Affect Theory,'

36. Malhotra, N., Baalbaki, I. & Nasr, N. (2013). 'Marketing Research,' Harlow, Essex: Pearson Education.

37. Maslow, A. (1943). "A Theory of Human Motivation," Psychological Review, 50 (4), 370.

38. Nicole, H. (2000). "Publication of the OIG Compliance Program Guidance for Nursing Facilities," [E-book], 14299, Available through: Office of Inspector General [Accessed: 5 Aug 2013], http://oig.hhs.gov/authorities/docs/cpgnf.pdf

39. Pallant, J. (2010). "SPSS Survival Manual," Maidenhead: Open University Press/McGraw-Hill.

40. Prahalad, C. & Hamel, G. (1990). 'The Core Competence of the Corporation,' Boston (MA).

41. Reed, R. &5 Defillippi, R. (1990). "Causal Ambiguity, Barriersto Imitation, and Sustainable Competitive Advantage,"Academy of Management Review, 15 (1), 88â˜'102.

42. Saari, L. & Judge, T. (2004). "Employee Attitudes and Job Satisfaction," Human Resource Management, 43 (4), pp. 395â˜'407.

43. Sekaran, U. (2003). 'Research Method for Business: A Skill Building Approach,' John Wiley & Sons. (4th ed)

44. Simon, H. (1976). 'Administrative Behavior,' New York: Free Press.

45. Staw, B. & Ross, J. (1985). "Stability in the Midst of Change: A Dispositional Approach to Job Attitudes," Journal of Applied Psychology, 70 (3), 469.

46. Tabachnick, B. & Fidell, L. (2007). 'Using MultiVariate Statistics,' Boston: Pearson/Allyn& Bacon.

47. Tran, H. (2013). '5th Shape the World Conference in Vietnam,' Consulus, [blog] 14 June 2013, [Accessed: 5 Nov 2013], Available at: http://www.consulus.com/2013/06/5th-shape-the-world-conference-in-vietnam/.

48. Vanek, J. (1970). 'The General Theory of Labor-Managed Market Economies,' Ithaca: Cornell University Press.

49. Vroom, V. (1964). 'Work and Motivation,' New York: Wiley.

50. Weiss, H. & Cropanzano, R. (1996). "Affective Events Theory: A Theoretical Discussion of the Structure, Causes and Consequences of Affective Experiences at Work," Elsevier Science/JAI Press.

9

CHAPTER

Review on The Research of Dynamic Competition Theory

Jianbin Zhang, Dan Gao

Management School, Jinan University, Guangzhou, China

ABSTRACT

In the 1980s, dynamic competition theory originated in the field of strategic management abroad. It focused on the behaviors of attacks and counterattacks interaction among the enterprises. But Chinese researchers paid attention to the dynamic research a long time later. On the basis of the existing research, this article summarized the theoretical background research object and the research methods, and analyzed the limitations and future research direction of dynamic competition.

Keywords: Dynamic competitive, Action/Response, Competitive interaction

1. INTRODUCTION

Study on dynamic competition began in the early 80s. The research of Edwards on confrontation between enterprises can be traced back to the mid 50s. They proposed the opinion that we could explore the competitive strategy from the perspective of enterprise competitive behavior. In the late 90s, Chinese scholars began to introduce the methods and conclusions of dynamic competition [1] -[3] . In the western literature, it was generally called dynamic competition. The object of study generally refers to specific behaviors in the process of enterprises competition.

In the 1980s, MacMillan, McCaffrey and Van Wijk (1985) provided a reference for empirical research of dynamic competition in response to the innovation behavior of a bank of small sample study [4] . Bettis and Weeks (1987) studied the stock market for Polaroid and Kodak imaging products in a competitive field of interactive response [5] ; Smith, Grimm, Chen, and Gannon (1989) used the data of high-tech enterprises, researching on attack behavior features which could arise rapid counterattack [6] .

In the 90's, Chen, Smith and Grimm (1992) took the competition behaviors of American aviation industry as an example, studying on the relationship between the company competitive response and competitive behavior features. They found different competitive action traits combination including competitive influence, attack strength, executive condition, and action which had different effects on response rate, and time competitors [7] ; taking software producers as the object of the research, Young, Smith and Grimm (1996) found that if the enterprises could attack more fiercely and frequently, it could gain better performance [8] ; Xie Hongming and Lan Hailin (2003) carried out an empirical research on dynamic competition of the Chinese color TV market [2] .

This article aims to summarize the background, research conclusions, and possible development direction of the dynamic competition theory in the future.

2. THE THEORY OF DYNAMIC COMPETITION BACKGROUND

Dynamic competition theory from Schumpeter's (1950) "creative destruction" [9] theory is used to explain the dynamic market, every enterprise how to use in a dynamic market for action and response to pursue market opportunities. May also be defined as the process of experience in competitive action and response, the company decided how the ups and downs.

"Austria school" to the market competition as a dynamic process, rather than a static market situation, for profit action will break the stable status, so the market will never reach equilibrium, except in the absence of competition. For an explanation of the "destruction", the Austria school put forward the concept of "entrepreneurial discovery", that is when the market opportunities have emerged, the enterprise can successfully guide and the allocation of resources, to meet customer demand action. From the dynamic point of view to explain the competition, the scholars began to focus on the competition behavior of innovation, such as the first dynamic action or radical action [10] .

Play an important role in Schumpeter's "creative destruction" theory and the Austria school "entrepreneurial discovery" plays a very important role in the dynamic competitive field. Action is the core of the research unit of the two theories, starting from the two theories, the research of dynamic competition more and more scholars focus on the competitive supply and counter attack.

3. THE BASIC MODE AND KEY FACTORS OF DYNAMIC COMPETITION

3.1. The basic mode

Study on the key factors of dynamic competition is competition among enterprises, it will be the competition behavior understood as interactive competitive action and response [11] . The manufacturer's own relative competitive position for defensive or improvement, through the analysis of the market, integrate its own resources, to reduce the use of the product price, new product introduction and other ways to gain market share and additional benefits. Obviously, this process may be by the market of other manufacturers counterattack, obtain additional benefits, to defend the attacker to occupy the market share. Through the cycle back and forth such attack and counterattack, to allow the market to achieve a temporary equilibrium process. According to the behavior of the process of dynamic competition, can be obtained as shown in figure 1 [11] .

3.2. The key factors of dynamic competition

Competitive interaction: Competition among enterprises is the key to the research of dynamic competition among enterprises, usually will process this attack and response is called competitive interaction. As shown in figure 2 [7] .

Competitors and competitive action: Competitors generally refers to the initiator competition, it is the primary sponsor attacks, is also the result of the action of beneficiaries [12] . How the dynamic competition theories concerned competitor characteristics influence the attack action decision. Different research to find the organization characteristics, there are three kinds of recessive and key influence strategic action that is Awareness-Motiva- tion-Capability, AMC [13] .

Awareness: How firms cognitive competitors, the driving force and competitive environment of the overall intra industry competition. To observe the influence to the enterprise to understand the result of the action, so it is very important to [13] .

Motivation: Associated with gains or losses can be felt, actions taken or not taken action depends on the gain from action possible advantage or no action possible loss.

Capability: Action is the result of the resource allocation process and enterprise decision. When the enterprise to take action, the rest of the organizational resources (the flow of financial resources), and characteristics of top management team will affect the attack and counter thinking form or execution, so the ability to organize action execution is important influence [13] .

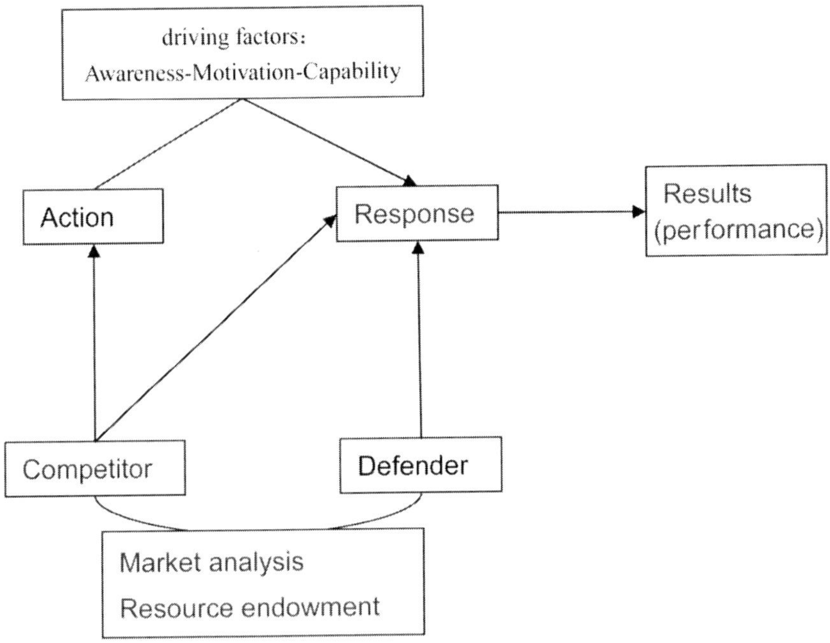

Figure 1. dynamic competition model.

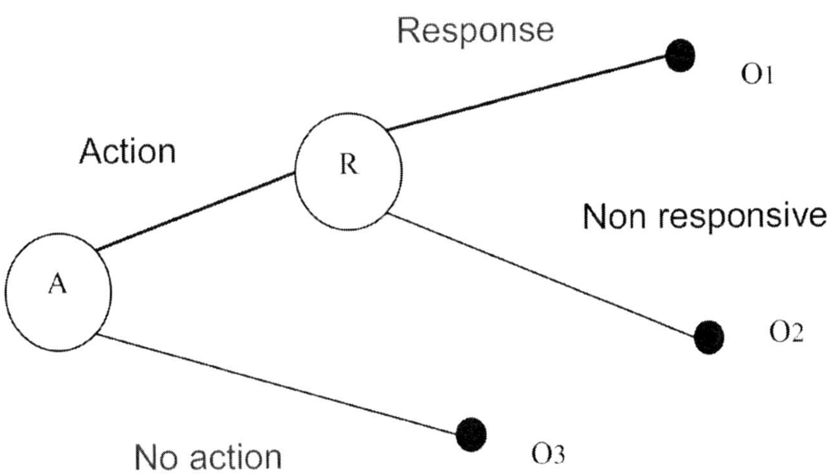

Figure 2. Game decision tree. Game decision tree is shown, when firms a planning competitive action, competitor r there are two types of action: response (o1) or no response (o2). Usually will process this attack and response is called competitive interaction.

Competitive action is a basic concept of dynamic competition. For the performance of work or do new things in a new way. Smith, K.G., Grimm (1991) definition of competitive action as "manufacturers in order to enhance or defending the relative competitive position, instigated a certain cut can be clearly aware of the competitive behavior" [7] , Chen, Smith, K.G. and Grimm (1992) summarizes the competitive action characteristics: competitive impact: a action against competitors affect or influence degree; attract intensity: the degree of influence of an action on a major competitor market; implementation requirement: the level of effort to take action manufacturers perform the action of inputs required; type of action: strategic or tactical. Confirm the competitive action traits will affect different for defense of competition response has different effects [7] .

Competitive response: When the competitive action won the excess earnings or the attack effect to rival station, competitors will produce a response to its competitive action. Smith, K.G., Grimm (1991) defined competitive response to "manufacturers in order to defense or improve their relative competitive position, the one that can be observed and can be identified in response to action" [7] . Chen, Smith, K.G. and Grimm (1992) from "a potential response will affect the competitive action again to create and sustain competitive advantage on the effect of" starting, summarizes the competitive response traits:

Number of responses: the number of competitive response caused by the manufacturer.

Response lag: that competitive action occurred to the defender execute the response time of action [7] .

Characteristics of competitive response are vital to take competitive action by competitors, can predict the competitive action of competitors and success.

Competitive interaction results: To achieve the desired results through competition interaction, the general use of performance to assess the competitive interaction effect. Including the change of market share, sales growth to increase shareholder returns and other financial variables measure of profitability. The empirical study shows that attack, counterattack, combination of actions and action sequences characteristics will affect the performance of the organization (Smith, 1991; Smith and Young, 1996; Ferrier, 1999; Miller and Chen, 1995) [12] [14] .

Relationship between competitive action and response: Dynamic competition theory is in a dynamic environment, interaction between firms competitive focus. Companies take the lead in action after the success, will inevitably lead to competitors to imitate or counter (Schumpeter, 1950). Through a large number of empirical studies has been consistent conclusion, namely the use of the characteristic of enterprise forecast attack can competitor on the counterattack. Competitive action can predict the number and frequency response. Competitive action can also predict the response speed. Different types of competitive actions have different influence on the response speed (Smith, 1992; Chen, 1992) [15] [16] .

4. EMPIRICAL RESEARCH METHOD OF DYNAMIC COMPETITION

4.1. field research method

Based on the small sample enterprises and meticulous observation and monitoring, identification of the enterprise of attack and counterattack action, thus the relationship between organizational characteristics and competitive action verification. The earliest studies including Bettis and Weeks (1987) studied the stock market on the Polaroid and Kodak competitive interaction in imaging products in the fields of reaction [17] .

4.2. Structured content analysis method

Structured content analysis is based on a formal decoding procedure, a tool such as newspapers, magazines and other published data secondary data analysis. Enables researchers to develop a large sample, analyze the competition action from more data. Chen Smith, Ken's and Grimm (1992) by the method of competitive behavior of American aviation industry manufacturers to do the research [17] .

5. ANALYSIS OF DYNAMIC COMPETITION

The core research of dynamic competition theory is an important competitive element around the strategic management research, free from the traditional static analysis, the dynamic process of inter enterprise competition behavior as the research object, to in-depth understanding of enterprise competition behavior of competition must be changing trend and the influence to carry on the analysis, the study also shows that the enterprise competitive advantage has not can be maintained, to maintain the competitive advantage they need to constantly create new advantages.

Dynamic competitive enterprises through the competitive interaction among enterprises can change the allocation of resources and industrial structure has. Due to the difference of the degree of response to different types of competitive behavior, is advantageous for the enterprise to subsequent predictions for the competitors in the competitive interaction behavior, the promotion enterprise competitive advantage [18] .

Combining with the important concepts in different fields and theoretical research around the manufacturer will be a series of competitive behavior into research and development of dynamic competition, but also brought some new theory system, made a great contribution to such as first mover advantage, irreversibility, multipoint competition and competition network, super strong competition for strategic management theory to further improve the. At the same time analysis method based on the level of action, so that the dynamic competition theory to establish a detailed analysis of the structure to compensate for the lack of competition orientation and group orientation, strategic researchers and practitioners from the basic perspective, to understand the competition and effectively participate in the competition [19] .

Dynamic competition theory also has certain limitation, pay attention to the research on the content of the manufacturer in competition market level, but between enterprises compete not only exist in the market also exist with deeper. Such as the value chain of enterprises, organizational ability, human resources and other aspects. So for the competition behavior of attention should expand the range and depth of. At present the research methods of scholars use basic including early field research and content analysis method. But the two methods all have limitations, the field study is confined to the study and review of small sample, validity, effectiveness is not strong. Structured content analysis using secondary data, because of the competition behavior is not easy to define and measure, the credibility of the data have some limitations, the research methods need to be further perfected. Scholars in the research field of the current are too single, limit the scope to study the dynamic competition theory. Need to exaggerate the new industry, enhance the applicable scope of the theory.

6. CONCLUSION

Jianbin Zhang, Dan Gao Many foreign scholars believe that the research of dynamic competition has a certain relationship with Chinese Sun Tzu art of war. China is still in the initial stage of development at present, so the research of dynamic competition in china will make sense. If we can combine the dynamic competitive strategy theory and the development status of China, it will contribute to the competitiveness and management level of Chinese enterprises.

REFERENCES

1. Chen, X. (2000) Dynamic Competitive Strategy and Chinese Enterprises. Chemical Technical Economy, 1, 36-39.
2. Lan, H.L. and Huang, Z.F. (2000) The Attack and Counter—Dynamic Competition from TV "Price War". Enterprise Management, 3, 27-29.
3. Lan, H.L. (2001) World Class Enterprise Strategic Management of Chinese Enterprises Research. Enterprise Management Press, China.
4. Van Wijk, M. (1985) Competitors' Responses to Easily Imitated New Products-Exploring Commercial Banking Product Introductions. Strategic Management Journal, 6, 75-86.
5. Bettis, R.A. and Weeks, D. (1987) Financial Returns and Strategic Interaction: The Case of Instant Photography. Strategic Management Journal, 8, 549-563.
6. Smith, K.G., Grimm, C.M., Chen, M.-J. and Gannon, M.J. (1989) Predictors of Response Time to Competitive Strategic Actions: Preliminary Theory and Evidence. Journal of Business Research, 18, 245-258.
7. Ming-Jar, C., Smith, K.G. and Grimm, C.M. (1992) Action Characteristics as Predictors of Competitive Responses. Management Science, 38, 439-455.

8. Smith, Y. (1996) "Austrian" and Industrial Organization Perspectives on Firm-Level Competitive Activity and Performance. Organization Science, 7, 243-254.

9. Liu, B.M., Sun, J.G. and Tan, R.H. (2011) Innovation Theory Overview. Science and Technology Management Research Damage, 24, 9-12.

10. Chen, M. (2007) Competitive Dynamics Research: An Insider's Odyssey. Asia Pacific Journal of Management, 26, 5-25.

11. Smith, K.G., Grimm, C.M., Gannon, M.J., et al. (1991) Organizational Information-Processing, Competitive Responses and Performance in the US Domestic Airline Industry. Academy of Management Journal, 34, 60-85.

12. Chen, M. and Macmillan, I.C. (1992) No Response and Delayed Response to Competitive Moves: The Roles of Competitor Dependence and Action Irreversibility. Academy of Management Journal, 35, 539-570.

13. Chen, M. (1996) Competitor Analysis and Interim Rivalry: Toward a Theoretical Integration. Academy of Management Review, 21, 100-134.

14. Qin, J. and Wang, Y.J. (2008) Dynamic Competition: A Conceptual Framework and Research Proposals Reviewed. Journal of Xi'an Institute of Finance and Economics, 2, 83-87.

15. Liu, Y. and Li, T. (2005) The Research of Enterprise Competition Behavior and the Theory of Dynamic Competition Environment. Journal of Information, 7, 64-66.

16. Wu, H.S. (2007) The Development and the Dynamic Competitive Advantage Creation of Strategic Management Theory. Journal of Shogun University, 1, 128-131.

17. Zhang, Y. and Chang, Y.S. (2008) The Research Perspective and Analysis of Dynamic Competition Theory Framework. The Productivity Research, 2, 11-12.

18. Xie, W.H. and Lan, H.L. (2001) Flexible Organization: Choice of Enterprise under the Condition of Dynamic Competition. The Soft Science, 3, 90-92.

19. Xie, H.M., Lan, H.L., Ye, G.Y., et al. (2003) Dynamic Competition: An Empirical Study of China's Main Color TV Enterprises. Management World, 4, 77-86.

10
CHAPTER

Does Downsizing Strategy affect the Retained Employees Performance?

Robert Kinanga and Anne Cherono Cheruiyot

Maasai Mara University, Narok, Kenya

ABSTRACT

Reduction of employees has become a potentially valuable way of securing a competitive advantage and improving organizational performance, downsizing has been in existence for a while now however, its effect on employee or organizational performance has brought mixed reactions in both developed and developing countries. This quagmire has led to a lot of uncertainty while considering downsizing as a tool of enhancing employee performance. Therefore, this study sought to find out the effect reduction of employees as a downsizing strategy on performance of employees of Barclays bank hypothesized as there is no relationship between reduction of employees and employee performance. The study adopted a survey research design. Data for the study were collected from a sample 183 employees of Barclays Bank South Rift Hub, Kenya. Questionnaires were used as the sole data collection instrument. The data that was collected from the field was analyzed using both descriptive and inferential statistics. The findings established that there was a strong positive correlation of 0.982 between reduction of employees and the dependent variable employee performance. The results indicated that higher levels of effective employee reduction leads to effective performance of commercial banks hence they need to consider applying downsizing. The results of this study shall therefore benefit the management of commercial banks to understand the effects of downsizing and put in place appropriate strategies to ensure that only the positive effects leading to improved performance are emphasized.

Keywords: Downsizing, Employee Performance, Barclays Bank

INTRODUCTION

In many companies, a lot of effort goes into separation packages and support for the employees who are leaving the organization as a result of downsizing with very little or even no attention given to the employees who are remaining. However, it is argued that what creates a high level of distrust in organizations is that leaders fail to acknowledge the impact of restructuring and downsizing on the people who are staying. This paper therefore aimed at finding out the effect of reduction of employees as a downsizing strategy on the performance of employees. It was guided by research objective which was to examine how reduction of employees during downsizing affects the performance of the employees of the Bank and the hypothesis that there is no relationship between reduction of employees and employee performance.

Related Studies

In the book by Bloise, Cook & Hunsaker, 2003, restructuring has been a major trend in developing countries as most companies have undergone restructuring with the aim of improving the organizations' effectiveness and efficiency, hence improving profits in the organisation. According to Kang (1999) downsizing began as the strategy of sickly corporations shedding workers in the face of weak demand, but soon strong firms looking to boost shareholder value even further adopted the policy. Downsizing is the conscious use of permanent personnel reductions in an attempt to improve efficiency and effectiveness of the organisation. Downsizing is regarded by management as one of the preferred routes to turning around declining organizations, cutting costs, and improving organizational performance most often as a cost-cutting measure. Vrooman, 2009 noted that the labour market is more flexible, and employers can more easily respond than in the past to reduced demand for their products or services by lying off employees

According to Greenberg & Baron, (2000), downsizing is likely to lead to disruptions in the workplace. Greenberg & Baron also noted that many companies consider the organization's profits by cutting down costs with all the attention firmly fixed on the need for change, the leaders are often blind to the impact of downsizing on people and their relationships and hence on the performance of the people. Greenberg & Baron, (2000), further noted that organizations focus more on taking care of the people who are leaving rather than those who are remaining. In many companies, a lot of effort goes into separation packages and support for the employees who are leaving the organization as a result of downsizing with very little or even no attention given to the employees who are remaining. Winkler, 2002 on the other hand noted that what creates a high level of distrust in organizations is that leaders fail to acknowledge the impact of restructuring and downsizing on the people who are staying.

According to Cappelli (2000) "Downsizing" is a term that was introduced to describe the contemporary development of permanent job cuts motivated by an effort to improve operating efficiency, not necessarily because of declines in business. Downsizing has received a great deal of attention, especially in the business press, in part because it appears to represent something of an enigma. Baumol s, Blinder and Worlf (2003) in his study on American firms found out that since the 1980's through the present time, around ten million jobs have been eliminated in the U.S. Munoz-Bullon and Sanchez-Bueno (2008) also noted that despite the growth of downsizing, the practice has been prominent in developed countries such as United States. Chen et al., (2001), identified that the practice of downsizing has recently become relevant in other contexts such as Canada, Japan, or Korea, the controversy surrounding its benefits still persists. This is due to the fact that downsizing eliminates redundancies and reduces employment costs, many executives believe that this practice helps firms to compete efficiently and improve profitability. Cascio (2003) indicate that, the objective of downsizing is to improve the organizational efficiency, productivity and/or competitiveness. The works by Espahbodi, R, T, A, John, G, Vasudevan, 2000; and Chen et al. (2001) show that profitability of American firms improved subsequently due to downsizing announcements. Likewise, empirical evidence in other countries supports the same conclusion according to the findings of Yu and Park, (2006) on Korean firms.

This study rests on the idea that the effects of job insecurity on performance are neither purely negative nor purely positive. Instead, job insecurity is both a hindrance and a challenge stressor. Job insecurity can be perceived as a stressful discrepancy between what employees hope for (job security) and what employers offer (job insecurity) that leads to effort withdrawal and thus to a reduction of job performance. At the same (but to a lesser degree), job insecurity can also motivate people to increase the effort because high performance might be perceived as a safeguard against being laid off. Both effects are captured by our integrated model that was supported by our data. Consequently, managers who believe that increasing job insecurity is a feasible motivation strategy should be warned not to overlook that the effects of job insecurity are predominantly negative.

De Meuse et al., (2004) and Yu and Park, (2006) on the other hand, have noted that, downsizing may not result in improved profitability of firms. According to the two studies, it is noted that downsizing is not enough to influence the performance of an organization. It is noted that though the reduction of staff can slim down a firm, it doesn't necessarily make it healthier and hence profitable. Munoz-Bullon and Sanchez-Bueno (2008)support this conclusion that employee reduction does not necessarily have a positive impact on organizational performance. According to Munoz-Bullon and Sanchez-Bueno a study carried out in the United States found that downsizing practices carried out along the 1980s and early 1990s were unable to reflect corporate profitability. In another related study Cascio (2003) found that companies which had implemented downsizing between 1981 and 1990 did not enjoy larger financial performance. In an extension of this research it was noted that since 2000 downsizers enjoyed lower profitability than stable employers or upsize in the two years subsequent to the announcement of layoffs. Other studies on American corporations also showed that downsizing did not lead to improved financial performance (De Meuse et al, 2004). It was further noted that financial performance of companies which downsized did not significantly differ from non-downsizers. Similarly, found that downsizing was not associated with better corporate performance among Canadian firms.

Djordjevic (2007) considered the effects of downsizing on establishment performance; the analyses from this study are broadly consistent with the common-sense view that job cuts make more sense when establishments experience excess capacity than when they do not. Even in such situations, however, the benefits of improvements in sales per employee must overcome increases in labor costs per employee. Djordjevic (2007) looked at downsizing as job cuts when operating at or above capacity, appears to hurt sales per employee. In the context of this model, it is clearer why downsizing may hurt performance, because it is difficult to cut without doing damage to organizational capabilities when there is no slack to cut. In most cases, labor costs per employee move in the opposite direction from changes in sales per employee: When job cuts make sales per employee rise, so do labor costs per employee, and when the former fall, so do the latter. This relationship may mitigate some of the gains from cutting employees as well as the losses and lead to an overall moderating effect in relations with performance outcomes.

An explanation for these findings is that downsizing may not be managed effectively. Indeed, learning how to downsize effectively is important not only for companies experiencing difficulties, but also as a proactive strategy for healthy organizations. Djordjevic (2007) further noted that embarking on downsizing without learning how to do it well leads to several kinds of problems. The loss of vital organizational memory is one of the negative and expensive effects firms have suffered in downsizing. If managers do not think and plan ahead, their companies risk losing key skills and experiences as well as valuable knowledge when employees are moved out of their working units or leave the organization entirely.

Cappelli (2000) in his study on examining the incidence of downsizing and its effect on the establishment performance, noted that academic research and casual observation before the early 1980s suggested that employment levels, and reductions in jobs, were derived in a straightforward way from the demand for a firm's product or services. Cappelli further noted that most layoffs were seen as driven by business cycles; they were temporary in that employees were rehired when product demand returned, and they concentrated on production workers. The exceptions were typically limited to industry-specific market changes; the long-term decline of an industry, such as coal mining, or the movement of industries overseas, such as textiles. Virtually all of the public policy attention given to unemployment centered on the view that job losses are driven by cyclical or structural declines in product demand.

Goesaerty andHeinzz, (2012), studied downsizing and firm performance, considering the banking industry in early 2005, the bank reported highest profits for years after the downsizing was done. With downsizing, the company reorganizes its structure by undertaking 6,400 layoffs in order to achieve higher profitability in the future. In the same period, another company 'Opel' announced a record loss and decided to shed 12,000 jobs to decrease their production capacities and to rescue the company. Both CEOs stated that there was no alternative to the downsizing. These two firms faced a different financial situation, but shared one common goal: to increase their performance through downsizing. The fact that these two firms recorded higher profits after downsizing may assist the current study in establishing whether the case is similar in organizations operating in Kenya.

According to Cappelli (2000) it is noted that despite the popular attention given to downsizing and the continuing stream of studies about job security for individual workers, there has been essentially no research directed at the causes of downsizing. A growing body of research on the consequences of downsizing developed to address the perception that firms could improve their financial performance by downsizing. Although Cappelli's study does not relate to the central question being addressed in the current study, the study may shed light on how to conceptualize and measure downsizing. Cappellis study established that financial performance was measured by stock prices seems to decline following downsizing. A similar view was held by Gunderson, Verma, and Verma (1997) who studied the effect of downsizing among Canadian firms, in this study it was noted that at least some in some cases downsizing was noted to have a negative performance of the firms as a result of the adverse effects on the workforce.

Ahmadjian and Robinson, (2001) noted that downsizing has a negative effect where by in their study they reported that it can foster an organization so preoccupied with bean counting, so anxious about where the ax will fall next, that employees become narrow minded, self-absorbed, and risk averse. It was noted that the ability of employees to continue to work well is likely to be severely curtailed in such stressful situations and they tend to be even less able to innovate and learn. Therefore, the most significant conclusion drawn by studies of experiences in U.S. corporations is that downsizing must be regarded as something firms have to actively learn how to do well. Instead of conceiving downsizing to be "a one-time, quick-fix solution" (De Meuse et al., 2004).), a comprehensive framework is required, a whole process of grappling with the underlying problems and developing a range of activities to both restructure the organization and enable employees to make the transition to different jobs within or outside the organization (Greenberg, J. & Baron, R.A. (2000).

RESEARCH METHODOLOGY

The study adopted a descriptive survey. This design was most suitable because it provides appropriate basis for descriptive analysis of characteristics of a sample from the population (Mugenda and Mugenda, 2008). The target population of the study included all the employees of Barclays Bank of Kenya, South Rift Hub. The study used stratified, simple random and purposive sampling techniques in selection of the sample. Stratified sampling technique was used to select the six branches from within the South Rift Hub while simple random sampling technique was used to select the employees from each of the selected branches. Purposive sampling was used to select all employees from the management level who included area managers, accessible branch managers, the accessible operations managers and the sales managers. The researcher used the sample size formula according to Bartlett, Kotrlik, & Higgins (2001) was to determine the sample for the study. The researcher used a sample size of 183 employees from the South Rift Hub of Barclays Bank that were accessible at the time of the study. Of which 17 were managers at the management level while the rest 166 were from the middle level employees. This represented a total percentage of 52.2 % which is above the sample of above 20% as recommended (Mugenda and Mugenda, 2003). Data was collected using a questionnaire; the method was selected because the sample population is literate.
The data was analyzed using both descriptive and inferential statistics, descriptive statistics, frequencies and percentages were used to give summary of the results. Inferential statistics where correlation and regression were used in order to establish-the relationship between the dependent variable and the independent variable as described in the objectives.

Research Findings and Discussions

The respondents were asked to indicate their opinion on the following questions related to employee reduction and their effect on employee performance as stipulated in table 4.1 below.

Table 4.1: Respondents Opinion on Reduction of Employees as Downsizing Strategy

To what extent do you agree with the following statements on the change in job roles on employee performance (mark on a scale of 1-5) 1- Strongly Agree, 2- Agree 3- Not Sure, 4- Disagree, 5- Strongly Disagree						
		1	2	3	4	5
1	The organization recognizes the need of relationship among its staff.	9 (7.14%)	100 (85.7%)	8 (7.1%)	0 (0%)	0 (0%)
2	Reduction of employees leads to fear and job insecurity	83 (71.4%)	17 (14.2%)	17 (14.2%)	0 (0%)	0 (0%)
3	Reduction of employees in the bank leads to negative public image.	25 (21.4%)	59 (50%)	17 (14.2%)	8 (7.1%)	8 (7.1%)
4	Reduction of employees increases employee workload	109 (92.9)	8 (7.1%)	0 (0%)	0 (0%)	0 (0%)
5	Reduction of employees reduces the efficiency and effectiveness of the remaining employees in the organisation	33 (28.6)	25 (21.4)	8 (7.1%)	50 (42.9%)	0 (0%)
6	Reduction of employees improves the financial validity of the organisation.	91 (78.2%)	17 (14.2%)	8 (7.1)	0 (0%)	0 (0%)
7	Reduction of employees improves the customer satisfaction in the organisation	17 (14.2%)	25 (21.4%)	75 (64.3%)	0 (0%)	0(0%)

The study sought to recognize the relationship existing among its staff during reduction of employees so as to enhance performance,8(7.1%) strongly agree while the remaining 8(7.1%) employees were not sure. On whether Reduction of employees leads to fear and job insecurity 83(71.4%) of the employees strongly agreed, 17(14.2%) agreed that Reduction of employees leads to fear and job insecurity and the remaining 17(14.2%) were not sure. On whether Reduction of employees in the bank leads to negative public image only 25(21.4%) agreed to this statement, 59(50%) agreed, on the other hand 17(14.2%)of the respondents were note sure, 8(7.1%) respondents disagree, the remaining 8(7.1%) emloyees strongly disagreed.

Majority of the respondents 109(92.9) of employees in BBK South Rift Hub strongly agreed to the statement Reduction of employees increases employee workload, the remaining 8(7.1%) agreed. On whether Reduction of employees reduces the efficiency and effectiveness of the remaining employees in the organisation a majority of the respondents 50(42.9%) of employees in BBK South Rift Hub disagreed to this statement, another 33(28.6) strongly agreed to the very statement 25(21.4) agreed and the remaining 8(7.1%) were not sure.

On whether Reduction of employees improves the financial validity of the organisation, a majority of 91(78.2%) of the employees of BBK South Rift Hub strongly agreed to the statement,another 17(14.2%) agreed to the stament, while the remaining8(7.1)were not sure of the same statement. Finally on whether Reduction of employees improves the customer satisfaction in the organisation, 17(14.2%) strongly agreed to the statement, majority of 75(64.3%) of the respondents were not sure, while the remaining 25(21.4%) agreed.

In regard to correlation analysis the results shows that using Pearson's correlation coefficient there was a strong positive relationship r = 0.960, which was highly significant at p value =0.000 between the reduction of employees and the performance during the downsizing exercise in the organization. On the basis of these results the study establishes that similar results existed from other scholars who considered whether reduction of employees and the performance of employees though they studied different organizations. Chen et al., (2001) for instance it was noted that if the survivors in any change leading to employee reduction don't believe that it was legitimate, their commitment to the organization may get adversely impacted. But if they believed that the change was going to be beneficial to them then their performance will not be affected. Similarly Cascio (2002) and Spreitzer & Mishra, (2002) indicated that the way employees perceive the reduction whether it is fair or not will have a strong influence on their performance to the organization in a downsizing context

Regression analysis indicated that there is no linear relationship between reduction of employees and employee performance. In testing whether there is a relationship between the reduction of employees and employees' performance and the effect of the relationship. The result shows that there is a positive and significant relationship between reduction of employees and the employee's performance during the downsizing process in the organization. The results revealed that the Pearson's correlation coefficient R = 0.96 which is positive and indicating a very strong correlation and highly significant p value = 0.000 between reduction of employees and the employee's performance. This indicates that the effect of downsizing on the performance of the employees at Barclays bank can be explained by 92.2 % of reduction of employees.

CONCLUSION AND RECOMMENDATIONS

Throughout the study, majority of the respondents agreed with the statement; the organization recognizes the need of relationship among its staff in its reduction of employees so as to enhance performance. Majority of the employees strongly agreed that reduction of employees leads to fear and to job insecurity and only a slight majority agreed that reduction of employees in the bank leads to negative public image.On the other hand majority of the respondent employees in BBK South Rift Hub strongly agreed to the statement Reduction of employees increases employee workload.

However, Majority of the respondent employees in BBK South Rift Hub disagreed on whether Reduction of employees reduces the efficiency and effectiveness of the remaining employees . a majority of the employees of BBK South Rift Hub. strongly agreed that reduction of employees improves the financial validity of the organisation. Finally, majority of BBK employees South Rift Hub were not sure on whether Reduction of employees improves the customer satisfaction in the organisation.

The study findings appear to agree with scholars who are in support of the positive effects of reduction of employees since if it is properly undertaken the employees who remain behind tend to be more effective and efficient in their duties, this translates to better organisational performance.
The study therefore recommends proper structuring of the process of reduction of employees as a downsizing strategy . In addition since Reduction of Employees is a key process in employee Performance the ratio of employees to the workload should be equal so as to maximize the available revenue with the best possible skills, hence maximum output.

The study recommends that the same study should be duplicated to cover a wider area, not just the South Rift Hub and establish whether similar results can be established. There is need to have further study to compare the performance of the different hubs in BBK in line with the effects of downsizing on the performance of employees cited in this study.

REFERENCES

1. Ahmadjian, C. L. And P. Robinson (2001). "Safety in Numbers: Downsizing And The Deinstitutionalization Of Permanent Employment In Japan." Administrative Science Quarterly 46: 622-654.

2. Armstrong, M. (1999). Human Resources Management Practice. London: Kogan Press Ltd.

3. Bartlett, J.E.; Kotrlik, J.W.; Higgins, C.C. (2001). Organizational Research: Determining Appropriate Sample Size In Survey Research. Information Technology, Learning and Performance Journal, 19:43-50.Causes, And Consequences, New York, NY: Russell Sage Foundation Press

4. Baumol, J.W., Blinder, S.A. And Wolff, N.E. (2003). Downsizing In America: Reality,

5. Bloisi, W., Cook, C.W. & Hunsaker, P.L. (2003). Management And Organisational Behaviour. London: Mcgraw-Hill.

6. Cascio, W. F. (2002). Strategies for Responsible Restructuring. Academy Of Management Executive, 16(3): 80—91.

7. Cascio, W.F. (2002). Responsible Restructuring: Creative and Profitable Alternatives To Layoffs. San Francisco: Berrett-Koehler.

8. De Meuse K.P., Bergmann T.J., Vanderheiden P.A. and Roraff C.E (2004). New Evidence Regarding Organizational Downsizing and a Firm's Financial Performance: A Long Term Analysis, Journal of Managerial Issues 16 (2), 155-177 (2004).

9. Djordjevic B.:(2007)."Managing Human Resource during Downsizing Process", Doctoral Thesis, The Economic Faculty Of Belgrade.

10. Espahbodi, R.T, John A., Vasudevan G (2000).The Effects of Downsizing on Operating Performance. Rev. Quant. Finance Accounting (15) pp. 107-126.

11. G. Yu And J. Park (2006). The Effect of Downsizing on the Financial Performance and Employee Productivity Of Korean Firms. International Journal of Manpower, 27 (3), 230-250.

12. Greenberg, J. & Baron, R.A. (2000). Behavior in Organisations: Understanding And Managing The Human Side Of Work. 7th Edition. New Jersey: Prentice Hall.

13. Gyu Chang Yu, Jong Sung Park, (2006). "The Effect of Downsizing on the Financial Performance and Employee Productivity Of Korean Firms", International Journal Of Manpower, Vol. 27 Issue: 3, Pp.230 — 250

14. Mishra, K., Spreitzer, G., & Mishra, A. (2002). Preserving Employee Morale during Downsizing. Sloan Management Review, 39, 83-95.

15. Mugenda And Mugenda (1999). Research Methods Qualitative and Quantitative Approach. Nairobi. Act Press

16. Mugenda O.M and Mugenda A.G (2003). Research Methods: Qualitative and Quantitative Techniques, Nairobi Act Press.

17. Peter Cappelli & Neumark, David (2000). On The Job: Is Long-Term Employment a Thing Of The Past? New York: Russell Sage.

11

CHAPTER

E-generation, What's New?

Franck Brillet, Annabelle Hulin, Julie Leroy and Stéphane Bourliataux-Lajoinie

Institut d'Administration des Entreprises, Centre d'études et de Recherches en Management de Touraine

ABSTRACT

This article discusses the "e-generation's" characteristics and the management tools and methods capable of handling them. In particular, we take a look at how to get a better grip on this generation's values when faced with the issues of being attractive, recruitment, and employee loyalty that many enterprises have to deal with. Much food for thought is offered on these topics: establishing a new style of management (giving more meaning, handling the individualism/collective paradox, fostering intergenerational management, etc) and adapting existing tools (recruitment through social networks for instance);

Keywords: generation, internet, values, HRM.

INTRODUCTION

To consider the values and behavior of young employees or students today, means taking an interest in the concerns peculiar to the different generations and the needs and expectations they express. By generation, is meant a group of individuals in a given context together who share the same history and relatively similar experiences. More precisely, a generation designates a sub-category of the population whose members have almost the same age or have lived in the same historical period. They share a certain number of practices and representations owing to having the same age and belonging to the same epoch.

Sociologists have always been interested in the generations as they traverse time. Five types of generations have been distinguished since the Second World War (Bourhis, 2006): the seniors born before 1946; the baby boomers born between 1947 and 1963; generation X born between 1964 and 1977; and generation Y born between 1978 and 1992. This last generation is described as a population of young students or young graduates at the start of their careers. Also known as the Internet or "E" generation they have developed skills in this field while modifying their relations not just to society but also to the professional world; and lastly, generation Z born after 1993.

The purpose of this article is to look more precisely at one of these generations – the generation Y. In France, the expression "Generation Y" means persons born between 1978 and 1992. Invented in 1993 by the magazine Advertising Age, the expression "Generation Y" designates the generation following "Generation X". Other expressions are commonly used to refer to this generation. In particular, they are called "Echo Boomers" as many of them are the children of baby-boomers or "Children of the millennium" ("Millennials" in English) linked to their date of birth. Americans also use the expression "Digital Natives" to underline the fact that these children were born with a computer or quite simply the diminutives "GenY" or "Yers".

In France the generation Y comprises about 13 million persons, i.e. nearly 21% of the population (INSEE – Institut national de la stastique et des études économiques – National Institute for Statistics and Economic Studies). It is the most numerous generation since that of the baby-boomers. As a comparison, the Generation Y totals about 70 million persons in the United States and 200 million in China[i].

i http://lagenerationy.com/2009/03/21/la-generation-y-vue-par-les-drh/.

In a context of retirement age population replacement, studying the generation Y has become essential for business. A labor shortage is foreseen and organizations will increasingly come face to face with recruitment, intergenerational management (Bourhis, 2006), and employee loyalty problems: "highly informed and naturally prepared for the new technologies this generation Y is also an opportunity for enterprises. Faced with the challenge to renew their workforce – which in France will come to a head from 2010-2015 – recruiters are racking their brains working out how to hire them and keep their loyalty" (Relinger, 2008).

The advantage of categorizing by generation type is to enquire into the diversity and differences of each generation's relations with information and communication technologies (ICT). Thus, generation Y is recognized as being seriously predisposed for everything concerning ICT; that is why in taking an interest in generation Y we place these ICT and e-management issues at the forefront of the enterprises' concerns. Following the studies of Jacob and Harvey (2005), it is discernable that adaptations are necessary for taking into account the differences potentially existing between generations from the point of view both of managing induction, the work itself, and productivity and of managing commitment, professional development, and conflict management. Hence, our study tends to show e-management tools and methods can be elements organizations can use to manage this new generation.

All the same, there are no settled opinions on the subject and some say the generation is not as different as may be thought. So what about this generation Y? What are its main characteristics that enable it to be described and how do its members behave within organizations? What relations does this generation have with all the ICTs and how may "e-management" be involved? The answers to these various questions will thus make it possible to put a finger on the specificities of this generation's relationship with the ICTs – if they exist – and so on the principal managerial issues revealed as far as e-management tools and methods are concerned. In short, the question this article discusses may be formulated as follows: **what are the characteristics of this "E-Generation" and how can the management tools and methods used in organizations be adapted to them?**

The answer to this question means accomplishing two objectives: to define the e-generation's main characteristics and its behavior at work and to present the implications this may have in terms of administrative and management tools and methods. Accordingly, an exploratory empirical study has been carried out. It consisted of a qualitative survey to determine the profiles of this generation and the working and management methods it would be useful to develop in the light of these profiles. 30 focused interviews were administered to a population of young employees and students and 10 to line-managers and heads of human resources. Totally re-transcribed, these interviews underwent both a computer assisted qualitative data analysis and a manual contents analysis. Thus, it will be possible to use verbatim extracts from the interviews to illustrate the conclusions and analyses of our study[ii] .

[ii] Each verbatim will refer to extracts from interviews numbered from 1 to 30 (number of sample interrogated): INTER.1 will concern for example extracts from the report for interview No.1

Taken as a whole, the results of these surveys will throw a light on why the e-generation is such a topical theme and on the principal managerial issues dealing with this generation entails. Indications and solutions to prefer when managing this population are also suggested; since many human resources managers admit to having difficulties in implementing HR practices for young people (Laize, Pougnet, 2007).

We search, therefore, to describe this generation by putting in perspective all the aspects connected to using information and communication technologies and what this implies for organizations (1). Thus, we show that management tools and practices seem more suitable for this e-generation (2).

1. The Generation Y: The Generation of the "E" and the Issues It Represents

In France, the expression "Generation Y" designates the persons born between 1978 and 1992. It is the most numerous generation since the baby-boom (Pouget, 2008). It represents about 21% of the French population (Pouget, 2008).

This generation is mainly characterized "by the fact it was born in contact with the new communication technologies, around which a whole communitarian ideology has developed in which the individual and his community take back their rights, thereby short-circuiting the traditional systems of legitimacy" (Gleyen et al., 2003).

After a presentation of the various characteristics of this generation (1.1) we insist on its representations (1.2) as seen from how it understands the "e" (via the web especially) before identifying the various relations this generation has with work and the Enterprise (1.3) and, lastly, revealing their major issues (1.4).

1.1.The Characteristics of the Generation Y

The aim of this first part is to understand the personal characteristics of the individual members of generation Y. Here we analyze the generation's essential traits, based on the results of our exploratory survey, through several key queries: who are the new entrants onto the labor market? What are they looking for? What are their needs?

Globally, the members of generation Y have individualistic, consumer, and zapping behaviors (Laize, Pougnet, 2007). As Benjamin Chaminade underlines, on his blog dedicated to the subject, the principal characteristics of Y culture are: individualism, interconnection, impatience, and inventivity. Nevertheless, "the diagnostic is not as obvious as all that. Certain enterprises attribute the same values of enthusiasm and dynamism to the young as before. Others refer to different values" (Rose, 2006: 14).

In this way, two points will be discussed in this first part: the Ys' new ways of life (1.1.1) and the relations they have with change (1.1.2).

1.1.1. New Ways of Life

Generation Y has changed its way of life fundamentally. Whereas the baby boomers lived to work, the Ys work to live. They seek the best possible balance between professional and private life, being quite prepared – if need be – to change work and region to keep this balance.

"As for me, what counts is work of course but my personal life too. I couldn't care less about working where I studied so long as I can find this balance". INTER.2

This is one of generation Y's characteristics: they are avid for novelty; they are also called the discoverers.

"What I want is to get around – something new – and I don't want to be bored by my work or else I'll leave." INTER.5

Whether in their professional or private sphere they fight against routine and search for new things to feed their adaptive capacities. They are also open to the world and take an interest in different cultures – which makes them more tolerant than generation X. This open-mindedness also holds good for new ways of life: flat-sharing, rent-sharing, etc.

"We must look at generation Y differently – it is magic; it is full of potential". "They need to work in groups; they are innovative. They produce and love it". Gino Andreetta, head of HR GO Club Méditerranée [iii]

[iii] http://lagenerationy.com/2009/03/21/la-generation-y-vue-par-les-drh/.

These various elements of ways of life concern the sphere of both private and professional life – which constitutes a major issue for the necessary administrative and management practices.

1.1.2. Change

Generation Y is the generation of change: it has no fear of the uncertainty inherent in it. Consequently, it is difficult to keep this generation's loyalty, both in the enterprise and its consumption habits.

"We were born with change and we young people love it when it moves. You can never tell, you say, but that's what makes it interesting, you can't know everything and that adds a pinch of spice to everyday life." INTER.30

Change is a particular feature of this generation; which is explainable by the economic and social context the generation evolves in: "digitalization" (Internet) and development of family ruptures:

"Those said to belong to this generation are as comfortable with change as fish in water. They create change, going from one brand or job to another. They flourish in ambiguity and uncertainty – environments in which many baby-boomers are not at home at all. Of course, this is an attribute of youth but generation Y aspires to change the world like their parents. Except that this time they hope not to toe the line" (Chaminade, 2007).

The new ways of life this generation favors, as well as, the search for permanent changes is also accompanied by noticeable evolutions in the social representations this population expresses.

1.2. New Kinds of Social Representations

Generation Y perceives human relationships, especially, through computing and digital tools such as Web 2.0. So it is interesting to realize that these tools are not without effects on the perceptions young people may have and the expectations they formulate in both their private and professional life.

1.2.1. Definition of the Web 2.0

Three phases are to be noted in the network's evolution (Bourliataux-Lajoinie, 2007):

- **The Web 0 (~1965-1995)**: the network establishes itself; not much content exists; access is reserved to the initiated – researchers, the military. The network is supplied by and for its users. The network's "philosophy" is born: liberty (of exchanges and ideas), gratuity, knowledge pooling;
- **The Web 1.0 (1996-2002)**: the network is stabilized technically; the graphic layer is in place; it is the end of CLI for ordinary members of the public who discover the power of this collaborative tool. Businesses develop communication strategies by searching to make site content profitable, and the notion of pay-for information becomes more important. The dominant logic tends towards site profitability (subscription payment, financing through advertising) and site content control. Businesses use the web as a new institutional or brand communication medium;
- **The Web 2.0 (~2003)**: the profitability based economic model has reached its limits; it is not abandoned but it is obvious it cannot have the network all to itself. The enterprises structure and make available contents generated by net-users for net-users (www.youtube.com). Profits come from functions ancillary to the core of the enterprise's business. The network is taken in hand by its users. Pooling gives users the whip hand as against the enterprises; blogs and forums serve as public tribunes for consumers' experiences who become consumer-players on the web.

> Technically, the break between Web1 and Web2.0 is characterized by the emergence of new languages (in particular flash and ajax) that allow great interactivity by favoring personalization between site and user.

Generation Y has grown up using the Internet and this substantially influences the expectations and needs it expresses – potentially having powerful effects at the managerial level.

1.2.2. Consequences and Effects on Generation Y Representations

The medium's intrinsic characteristics were quickly adopted by this population: liberty, gratuity and pooling. On this topic, two examples illustrate this adaptation to the web's fundamental values: illegal downloading of music, and using digital social networks (DSN). The latter is not without influence on how to envisage the management of this population, who paradoxically are individualists but want to belong to communities.

The example of digital social networks is more complicated to analyze – generation Y having begun its professional career and – to a certain extent – its social life with this tool. In his study Cardon (2008) proposes a cartography of digital identity on the DSNs. Two dimensions have been chosen to map the behaviors: self-exteriorization and self-stimulation. Within this framework, both these elements are essential in the management practices businesses will implement for this population; the businesses that will be able to foster these two values through their management practices, tools, and systems and be able to make it known, will best be able to attract this generation and keep it loyal.

The first of these dimensions is directly comparable to studies on perceived image and intended image in marketing; presence on the DSNs is measured here through the exteriorization – indeed the exhibition – of the values in the members' profiles. This touches on the issue of the image this generation wishes to give of itself through their presence in these DSNs (number of photos registered, tagged, number of friends, etc.). The second dimension is self-simulation; Cardon (2008) defines it as "self-simulation characterizes the tension between the traits that refer to the person in his real life (everyday, professional, with friends) and those referring to a projection or a simulation of the self, virtual in the basic meaning of the term, which allows people to express a part of or a potentiality within themselves.". The interactions between private and professional life are, therefore, essential for understanding this generation and its effects is important on what the latter express what they expect from enterprises.

With these two dimensions, a typology is presented that makes five segments appear: "The screen, chiaroscuro, the lighthouse, the post-it, and the magic lantern":

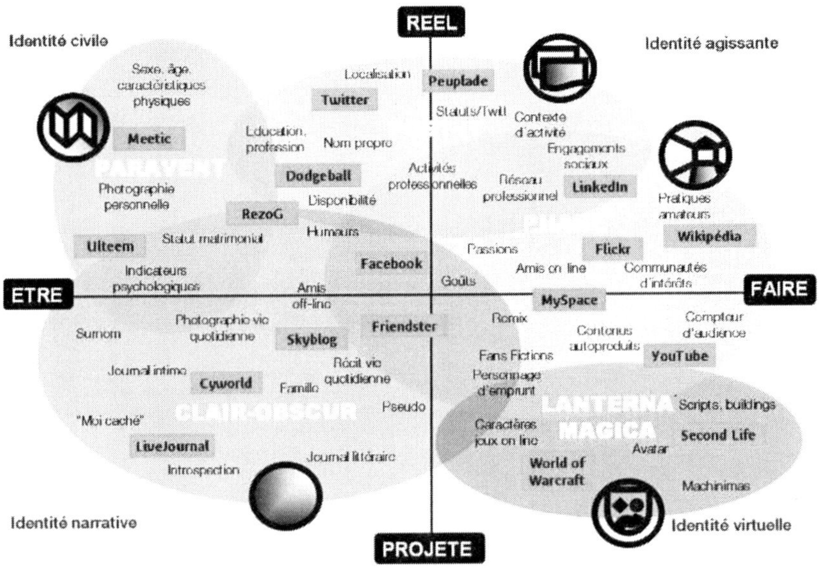

Fig 1. Digital Identity and Digital Social Networks (source: Cardon, 2008).

The detail of these types is interesting in so far as it helps to understand those who belong to them and enable the enterprises to respond to the generation Y's needs and expectations better. In this way, the management systems can be directed towards suitable methods and tools by taking into account the different values of each of the types according to their principal characteristics:

- The screen: they use the DSNs offering a filter before contact: the typical case is a meetic type network where the adherents pre-select one another through a very complete data sheet ;

- Chiaroscuro: for them the DSNs are an extension of close family and friendly relationships. They only share information with a close circle; they have no desire to exteriorize their life via internet;
- The lighthouse: they exteriorize on the network a lot, show, and display the size of their network of friends, their creations (texts, photos, etc...) and express the wish to share and defend their tastes (Flickr, Myspace, Youtube);
- The post-it: They make their presence on the network very visible but only for their "friends"; they create for themselves a bubble of intimacy (the mutual circle of friends). A strong idea of territory exists – whether physical (via geo-tracking applications such as latitude) or conceptual (a tacit recognition of the individual's abilities);
- The magic lantern: the most symbolic form of using the DSNs: the user creates his avatar while ignoring all real-life considerations; he becomes what he wants to be. This kind of behavior is very common in Second Life type virtual worlds or Wow [iv] .type MMORPG [v]

[iv] Wow is the acronym for World of Warcraft, this on-line role-play grouped together about 12 million players at the start of 2010.

[v] MMORPG is the acronym of Massively Multiplayer Online Role-Playing Game, these are on-line games involving thousands of users.

If these different types can orient the enterprises' management systems (see part 2.), they also strongly affect the relations this generation can have with work and the enterprise.

1.3. Generation Y in its Relations to Work and the Enterprise: Presence of Strong Values

Generation Y's behavior at work is often summed up as follows: "they want an interesting, evolving, formative job, but reject routine, boredom, and restrictions" (Laize, Pougnet, 2007: 3). According to a study by the APEC (Association pour l'Emploi des Cadres – Association for Managers' Employment) in 2009 work is a value supporting personal fulfillment for the under 30s.

"Of course, I want to have an interesting job – it's important for my well-being and those who believe that we young people couldn't care less are wrong." INTER.18

"I shall never choose a job that bores me, it must change and move." INTER.26

In other words, thinking about what this generation expects and needs entails the issue of renewing the human resources management systems inside the enterprise: rethinking how a business is to recruit, integrate, keep loyal, remunerate, and plan the careers of members of this type of population becomes essential.

This generation Y, thus, has many characteristics and values that allow a better grasp and understanding of how it relates to work and the enterprise.

1.3.1. The Strong Presence of Technologies

Prensky (2001) introduces the term "Digital Natives" to speak of this generation for whom the Internet is not a mere tool for information but essentially a means of communication, expression, and encounter for creating social connections. As progress advances, people are attracted by the Internet at an ever more precocious age. These individuals have grown up with the popularization of the personal computer (APEC, 2009).

As a whole, the communication media match the generation Y's need for instant expression. Members of the generation can use them to say what they feel without worrying about crossing the "t"s and dotting the "i"s. The desire to express overrides the manner – as certain exchanges by SMS or MMS prove.

Furthermore, generation Y has a strong sense of community identity, comparable to tribes. They strengthen this identity as they meet one another; as they go through life these young people keep contact with the people they have met.

"Thanks to facebook or Twitter you never lose anybody. You end up communicating with everyone, everywhere, and whenever; in fact, you travel all over the world with a few clicks." INTER.22

In order to reach this goal, they take advantage of the social networks arriving on the Internet -Facebook, Myspace, Twitter, etc. The web 2.0 has entailed new practices in communication (APEC, 2009). The Ys say what they think more directly and spontaneously than their elders. These factors are not without effect on the emergence of professional discussion forums and employee blogs that are sometimes taken over by the enterprises themselves.

"When we have something to say we can say it through forums and blogs. We need to say it the way it is – it's more transparent. And we share the information too." INTER.17

The rise of the Internet also materializes generation Y's need to be free:

in a "click" it is where it wants. This need for liberty also makes for harsher relations with parents – though the individuals of this generation stay living with their parents for longer and longer.

"All these digital tools are our way to get away from it all, and what's more avoid our parents' authority. It's our world." INTER.05

The development in ICTs also inverts the balance of power within the enterprise. Before – "the enterprise trained its workers on the technologies that would later become familiar to the general public. Now, it is often the employees who introduce mobility tools into the firm" (Vincent, 2010: 28).

1.3.2. The Importance of Individualism and Self-Fulfillment

Individualism is one of the "4i" used by Benjamin Chaminade on his blog to define the generation Y:

"individualism appears as a 'tidal wave' in contemporary society enveloping key values such as individual freedom, moral autonomy in relation to traditional standards, self-knowledge, and valuing personal well-being" (APEC, 2009: 20). Nevertheless, Rose (2006: 14) nuances these factors: "young people's individualism stems from society's increasing demand for strong individual responsibility. Young people tell us how our society has changed".

Besides, often from single-parent families (phenomenon of break-down in family structure) these only children are used to getting what they want, of being considered, being listened to, and having their needs and desires rapidly and systematically responded to. So the individual is at the centre of attention even if this individual paradoxically needs to become part of Facebook or Linkedin type virtual communities.

A primacy of the personal sphere is also evident, resulting in a strong search for fulfillment. This means trying to achieve a balance between professional and private life, as well as, reconciling individual and collective rhythms. This point is not unrelated to the search for strong sociability at work and close peer relationships in the professional sphere.

"Thanks to the networks, whatever they may be, you can at least say what you do. True, it's a bit self-centered but at least you can sometimes show you're different and that you do and say things that aren't too stupid." INTER.02

"As for me, work isn't my life; it's important, of course, but do you think someone who isn't happy can be happy in his work? The time when only work counted is over." INTER.10

All these factors relating to individualism and self-fulfillment explain why this generation has a certain conception of life and relation to work. Work, in fact, is not the only reference in their universe and the sole reference value; one is quite prepared to accept work is not the only source of fulfillment and well-being.

"Generation Y is a paradoxical generation nourishing both a strong desire for autonomy and a refusal to enter adulthood, which manifests strong individualism and ends up in sometimes improbable communities" "This generation imposes its conditions and expects a lot in terms of recognition and quality of life. It wants the enterprise to give it individual solutions, especially as concerns career development". Yves Desjacques, head of HR, Casino [vi] group.

[vi] http://lagenerationy.com/2009/03/21/la-generation-y-vue-par-les-drh/.

1.3.3. The Relation to Time and Space

Despite the reputation for constant fickleness they often have in both their professional and personal life a study by the CEGOS (Commission d'Étude Générale d'Organisation Scientifique) in 2009, reports nearly ¾ of generation Y young people will not leave their enterprise if it meets their expectations and lets them develop.

"It is said we aren't stable, but that depends because I don't see why I should change if I'm happy with my firm. If I can combine my personal with my professional life I'll stay, as soon as I can't I'll go." INTER.19

"So long as the enterprise has things to offer me and takes what I want into account I'll stay loyal." INTER.02

The influence of the context of instability must certainly be taken into account (APEC, 2009). They are very much affected by the current insecurity and unemployment (Laize, Pougnet, 2007). The young employees favor internal mobility: changing job within the same sector or enterprise (CEGOS, 2009).

"Even if I'm aware unemployment affects young people I still want to move around. So I'm looking for a firm big enough to be able to get around and not stay in the same job. I'd like to move between different firms but I'm aware circumstances aren't very favorable." INTER.13

1.3.4. The Relation to Power

In relations with power and line-management the elements are also quite characteristic. Generation Y is aware of the importance of making a commitment in professional life, especially at its beginning.

"People think we don't have our feet on the ground, but believe it or not we know we have to work. We're aware of the importance of putting a lot into our work – our first job especially. Besides, I'm sure we do so more than some others: forget about the clichés." INTER. 08

Accordingly, they generally express deep respect for their superiors, not for their hierarchical position but for their skills and expertise; attachment to the manager and respect for the hierarchy develop on these bases.

"You know a line-manager is important but for me he has to be competent and then I'll respect him. I do not see why I shouldn't ask him for an explanation and point out my disagreement. The relationship should be two-way." INTER.16

Thus, it is not rare to observe that this generation can openly and directly express its criticisms of line-management. It will obey the more easily if it considers the decision just and relevant. So it is thought that this generation's respect for their hierarchy is not a given but acquired throughout their experience in the enterprise in so far as it allows them to consider this hierarchy is legitimate.

"I just wait and see – of course he's my superior but I'll recognize him as such when I've seen him at work. If he's competent I'll obey him." INTER.13

1.4. The Social and Managerial Issues

Various issues arise in the light of the questions expressed and are connected to the enterprises' HRM systems. Thus, the questions of recruiting and attractiveness are still essential but those relating to career management, training policies or again remuneration are also present. These points confirm the results of surveys such as those by CEGOS (2009) and APEC (2009: 26): "the anticipation of professional or geographic mobility by young graduates and under 30 managers entails less emotional commitment to the enterprise".

Faced with the recruiting problems many enterprises encounter, it becomes essential to favor new communication and information methods aimed at this generation and oriented towards the ICTs. Thalès' experience gives pride of place to issues of diversity that are most important for this new generation:

"Our project consists of convoking managers and HRs to raise their awareness to the anti-discrimination rules and the risks of "cloning" due to narrow recruiting sources (about 15 colleges in France). Talking about career and origins diversity has enabled us to draw their attention to the importance of recruiting skills and not just qualifications from one college rather than another. We have trained each of our managers and both internally and externally the effect has been important for creating a link." Vincent Mattéi, Head of Recruitment Sourcing[vii].

[vii] Intervention during a round-table at the 6ths Journées internationales de la diversité of Corté on 30 September 2010.

This example shows that enterprises use themes when they communicate so as to give prominence to values matching what the individuals of this generation are looking for.

The traditional recruiting tools have proved to be rather ineffective and the arrival of human resources platforms, blogs, and employee forums is becoming one of the key factors for attracting and recruiting this generation. To attract these potential candidates and new talents and keep them loyal are two objectives that lead to favoring new ways of recruiting. Using information and communication technologies has become one of the key factors in these recruiting practices (recruiting via the web, social networks, etc.). To attract them the recruiter must give a precise job description: explain what is expected in terms of activities and missions, whom they are going to work with, and the consequences flowing from their career development. The objectives and values this generation looks for require the development of collaborative interfaces that can, for example, be useful to organizations. They are potent tools that are capable of giving a precise idea of how the professions work and how it is perceived they evolve, and of the social climate inside the organizations. The employer's capacity to be attractive will be enhanced by transcending thought on qualifications, positions or jobs; in this way, a more attractive approach to the professions must be favored.

More globally, attractiveness is also reinforced by all the actions undertaken to improve the enterprises' image with this generation. These various communication actions are, thus, designed to transmit values corresponding to those sought by this generation but they also develop more modern management tools and practices.

2. Management Tools and Practices: towards More "E"

Present-day research in managerial sciences shows that management must evolve towards a new style (2.1) inducing the adoption of new management tools (2.2).

2.1. Towards the Search for a New Style of Management

2.1.1.Towards More Meaning

The style of management that favorizes autonomy and taking initiatives can give new entrants a proactive attitude (Lacaze, 2005). On this subject, in academic circles, the emergence in management sciences can be observed of a new managerial tendency that favors benevolent intra-organizational management responding to the expectations expressed by employees of every generation. This element is interesting in so far as it matches the aspirations of generation Y concerning the desire to integrate with and trust colleagues and the enterprise.

"For me the enterprise is like in my personal life, I must establish reliable relationships and I have to be able to trust the others and have others trust me." INTER.21

"The links you make in professional life are important as they allow conviviality and favor a better atmosphere." INTER.20

The members of the generation Y need to have a global vision of the enterprise's personalities and processes or management systems as understood by De Vaujany (2006): "who are the other employees?", "what do they do?", what are the management processes in the enterprises, etc. All these questions are formulated so as to know and be able to judge by oneself whom to address and with what processes and tools. This point accords with what this generation looks for: autonomy and being treated as responsible. To do this, it is necessary to have a thorough knowledge of the organization – of its key figures and how it works.

Thus, this search for meaning through a better grasp of information – a search for trust and social connections – is sought by this generation, and the style of management must take an interest in it.

2.1.2. Towards Managing the Individual/Collective Paradox

Generation Y puts a lot into group projects to develop its skills and bring change to the enterprise. It wishes to devote time to achieving objectives fixed autonomously and with certain responsibilities. But it does not lose sight of another objective – having enough free time for itself. Generation Y's work-style gives pride of place to the project mode. One of the motivations for team work lies in the fact that a Y gives great importance to being able to learn constantly, which can materialize during project group exchanges. The generation wishes to take part in projects to develop new skills. As a result this generation no longer has a job for life outlook like generation X but rather:

"I'll leave my firm when I think I have done or contributed all I can or because I'm no longer learning anything". INTER.06

If it is accepted that managing young generation Y people is rather difficult, then it is because they are more receptive to change; in fact, they seek it as a stimulant for their professional life. Used to a changing world they are on the look rather for constant learning, and offering varied training to a Y is a way of meeting his expectations. Thus, compared to previous generations these individuals are characterized as a generation that consumes training; training is, therefore, perceived as a "real everyday consumption product" for these internal customers.

This generation is also very demanding when it comes to career progress and quality of working life, and does not hesitate to have multiple professional experiences to acquire new skills and broaden its network. In the same way, it will be advisable to offer them the chance to look about and make a career move at the European or international level. For this generation, mobility is a vital need.

Members of generation Y often demand a management adapted to each of them; for department heads this means knowing each of their subordinates, taking the time to become acquainted with the culture, values, and personality of each one so as to be sure of a high level of performance. This often involves a more personalized management style.

"Giving value to personal skills and adaptability are part and parcel of good team work. Individualism in such a case is not seen as selfishly damaging to the team of co-workers" (APEC, 2009: 27).

2.1.3. Towards a Recognition of Generation Y's Commitment

It should be noted that the generation of under 30 managers arrived on the jobs market after the 35-hour week law was passed (APEC, 2009). Training is central to the systems for integrating young people (Charles-Pauvers, Peyrat-Guillard, 2005).

This generation is often seen as less committed or less motivated by work. But looking at things differently means accepting the idea this generation is motivated in another way. Of course, seeking a balance between private and professional life is important and explains the sacrifices they can make in earning less, but this implies that the sacrifice is compensated for by an interesting extra-professional activity. Thus, those who think they are less committed are mistaken. The generation is looking for a more flexible organization of their working time and timetable. Working in a framework of fixed hours is considered a constraint. The relation they make between work and free time is calculated so as to profit all parties:

"I'm ready to work a lot but that way I also know I'll have more time free. It's quid pro quo." NTER.19

2.1.4. Towards Inter-Generational Management

Managing generation Y imposes inter-generational management on enterprises. Both generations X and Y are in the enterprises – a point that begs the question of managing the seniors. Thus, the issues managers face tend to be how to prevent conflicts that may arise between generations and the feelings of unfair treatment that may be perceived between these generations.Therefore, management systems must be oriented towards managing knowledge and especially the issues connected to its transmission. Mentorial or tutorial practices will enable enterprises to assure the connections between these generations. Preparing new managerial behavior is becoming important. This explains why certain enterprises develop mentorial and tutorial practices so as to reconcile these generations and create a social bond between them; especially when baby boomers or Xs are called upon for this type of activity (Hulin, 2010).

2.2.New Management Tools to Favor

2.2.1.Tools for Attracting and Recruiting

The enterprise needs to rethink and renew its means of communication to be more attractive. The traditional tools have proved to be ineffective and the arrival of human resources platforms, blogs and employee forums are possible responses (speed-dating, etc.).

"All the macro-demographic data show a problem in recruiting engineers and business school students. Young people will have the whip hand tomorrow! I'm convinced this generation Y will give an unequaled performance level to the businesses that know how to make the most of their potential: optimism, resilience, international outlook, passion for communication, and the Internet are positive values these young people transmit. On the other hand it is difficult to force models on them we can't justify." François de Wazières, International Recruitment Department, L'Oréal [viii].

[viii] http://lagenerationy.com/2009/03/21/la-generation-y-vue-par-les-drh/.

Certain enterprises, currently, put their energy and communication action not into recruiting tools but into working on the image of their enterprise to make it more attractive and, sometimes, their employees more loyal. Let's take the example of FON. In this enterprise, the action taken is based on the relation generation Y has with the DSNs. Acting on the premise that this relation can be used to enhance the power and image of the enterprise, a double effect is expected:

- The first is internal to motivate and keep loyal the enterprise's internal customers – its employees;
- The second is external and acts on the attractive effect these types of actions can have on potential generation Y candidates and naturally on potential consumers of the enterprise's products and services.

This enterprise's concept is based on an approach that relies on sharing the network and not charging for it – two values intrinsically linked to Web2.0 that young people understand very well (Leroy, 2008). FON's aim is to make Wifi accessible all over the world and above all for free.

To do this, the company relies on experience pooling and co-creation. In fact, any cybernaut on the planet can become a “fonero” by subscribing and adding a FON router to his provider’s box. In this way, he offers free access via his line to all the other foneros who also undertake to share their connection. Many cybernauts have subscribed to this concept, thereby, creating the biggest free world web access network. It should be noted that the foneros are not paid for this service of sharing their connection; they pay their conventional subscription to their access provider with no reduction and have to buy the router to connect to their box at their own expense.

This co-creation of services is an unprecedented lever for the enterprise; its impact, however, on internal management must not be minimized. Co-creation marks a new stage in managing relations between the enterprise and consumers as much as between the enterprise and its employees. It requires the organization to be rethought as a whole; the consumer can intervene at any moment and in any way in the process of creating the offer. In the same way, Y employees can see in this experience the respect they seek: innovation and creativity, change, the will to become members of a community while individually contributing something to the system, the feeling they are useful to others, etc.

Furthermore, the case of Fon shows the importance of cybernauts’ adhesion to the values the company promotes, although the enterprise has no means of communicating its values formally to the participants. Still other, however, human resources problems present themselves to managers: how to ensure the enterprise’s values are adhered to; how to maintain the quality of service where the strength of the distribution network (in this case precisely, more than two million web accesses) depends uniquely on the goodwill of cybernauts who do not know one another; who must be deemed to be employees in such an enterprise with such open and enlarged frontiers? knowing the foneros are not really employees of Fon while being collaborators indispensable for the functioning of the network. Lastly, the extension of the network depends enormously on the co-optation of the foneros who become Fon’s emissaries. This example also shows the difficulty in understanding certain human resources policies such as training in this type of enterprise. The community of foneros proposes high-level tutorials and FAQ to help newcomers and this internal training – based on pooled experiences and transmission – is not the responsibility of the enterprise and depends on the goodwill of more or less external volunteers. This, therefore, begs the question of HRM and of what is the responsibility of a single enterprise or of several, or of a territory or of a sector.

2.2.2. Tools for loyalty and Motivation

A large majority of generation Y individuals do not foresee passing their whole career in a single enterprise. Paradoxically, for the Ys a career move generally means a change of position but not necessarily a change in responsibilities. In order to gain these employees' loyalty, giving them an idea of the positions they could obtain might limit how many actually leave.

Career management systems must take into account this generation's profiles, which are marked by a desire for balance between personal and professional life: "there is a real problem in making new recruits loyal to their employer. Among the classic and general HRM tools two levers have seemed most promising to me: giving real responsibilities and offering proper professional careers" (Rose, 2006: 14).

In organizational terms the members of this generation ask for flexible hours which corresponds to their wish for a balance between work and private life. They desire to benefit from a maximum of flexibility in the organization of their work: hours, in-house training, sabbaticals, family leave, solidarity leave, work place crèche. The contribution made by each can be observed outside the enterprise and the enterprises must take this into account in what they do. For example, possibilities will develop offering employees the chance to contribute to and participate in social or environmental activities for charities for instance. Pralong (2009) affirms that to succeed in integrating them and keeping them loyal "a new deal" is needed "between employees and enterprise". For this, he "first proposes to remember the relationship between employee and enterprise is dissymmetrical. The least influential (the employee) cannot be expected to be the most trusting party in the relationship. So it's up to the enterprises to make the first steps to restore trust. What could these steps be? [...] simply to make some commitments, albeit modest, and respect them. This should be possible.".

Thus, if generation X gave a greater place to its professional life, this is not the case of generation Y. This generation gives first place to its professional life but, for example, is not ready to do overtime. So from an HR point of view these data have to be born in mind. A human resources director must succeed in taking measures allowing his employees to reconcile their professional with their private lives. This finding is reinforced when it is realized that the individuals of generation Y, who already give great importance to their private life today, will give a still greater priority in 15 years. These perspectives must be taken into account in managing these people's careers. For example, enterprises offering their employees services such as crèches or dry-cleaning help stop them from being overcome by their personal life.

CONCLUSION

Research studies on juniors and seniors are more and more frequent but, on the other hand, the intergenerational aspect is little developed (Cartigny, 2006). That is why this article and study has endeavored to show not a systematic opposition between generations within the enterprise or to stigmatize different generations but rather some elements for adapting management systems that will facilitate links between the generations and improve the management of this generation Y.

Through mobilizing people from different generations and with tools better adapted for digital use or to these generations' values these systems will be more responsive to the needs and expectations generation Y expresses. Thus, the issues involved in recruiting and being attractive, in winning loyalty and motivation are at the heart of the concerns of enterprises and the paths envisaged today mark the renewal of practices in human resources.

In any case, this article cannot reject the idea of such an endeavor's relevance: does generation Y really exist? Some would answer in the negative such as Pralong (2009: 18) "Our results imply it doesn't. They show that the influence of belonging to a generation is less than that of belonging to the group of managers. The effect of socialization is stronger than that of being part of a generation". Others attempt to show that if the values sought are identical, how they are expressed is not, which makes a renewal of the systems necessary. It was in this latter perspective that this study was written.

REFERENCES

1. APEC (2009). "La Génération Y dans ses Relations au Travail et à l'Entreprise," Les Études de l'Emploi Cadre, décembre.
2. Bourhis, A. (2006). "Les Défis de la Gestion Intergénérationnelle," Conférence présentée dans le cadre du rendez vous technologique Montégérien.
3. Bourliataux-Lajoinie, S. (2007). "Le Web, le Consommateur et la Publicité ," Economie et Management, n°124, p. 4-14
4. Cardon, D. (2008). 'Réseaux Sociaux de l'Internet,' Réseaux, volume 26, n°152.
5. Cartigny, L. (2006). 'La Dynamique Intergénérationnelle au sein des Organizations,' XVIIème Congrès de l'AGRH, Reims.
6. Chaminade, B. (2007). 'Comprendre et Manager la Génération Y,' Journal du Net.
7. De Vaujany, F.-X. (2006). "Pour une Théorie de l'Appropriation des Outils de Gestion : vers un Dépassement de l'Opposition Conception-usage," Revue management et avenir, vol.3, n°9, p. 109-126.
8. Hulin, A. (2010). Les Pratiques de Transmission du Métier : de l'Individu au Collectif. Une Application au Compagnonnage, Doctorat de l'Université de Tours.
9. Jacob, R. & Harvey, S. (2005). 'La Gestion des Connaissances et le Transfert Intergénérationnel : une étude de Cas au Sein de la Fonction Publique Québécoise,' Télescope, revue d'analyse comparée en administration publique, 12 (2). p. 12-25.
10. Lacaze, D. (2009). "Pour une Gestion des âges Synergique : Décryptage d'un Conflit de Génération Chez Thalès," XXème congrès de l'AGRH, Toulouse.
11. Laize, C. & Pougnet, S. (2007). 'Un Modèle de Développement des Compétences Sociales et Relationnelles des Jeunes d'aujourd'hui et Managers de Demain,' XVIIIème congrès de l'AGRH, Fribourg.
12. Leroy, J. (2008). 'Gestion de la Relation avec une Communauté Virtuelle dans une Stratégie de Co-Création : les Leçons du cas Fon.com,' Décision Marketing, n°52.

13. Pralong, J. (2009). "La 'Génération Y' au Travail : un Péril Jeune ?," XXème congrès de l'AGRH, Toulouse.

14. Prensky, M. (2001). "Digital Natives, Digital Immigrants," On the Horizon, NCB University Press, vol. 9, n°5, octobre.

15. Rose, J. (2006). "Les Jeunes et l'Entreprise. Comment (re)construire la confiance ?," Personnel, n°474, p. 1 4.

16. Vincent, C. (2010). "L'avenir est aux Entreprises Y ," Enjeux Les Echos, p. 25-28.

12

CHAPTER

Knowledge Transfer within Strategic Partnerships: The Case of HRM in The Brazilian Motor Industry Supply Chain

Geoffrey Wooda , Pauline Dibbenb * and Juliana Meirab

a Essex Business School, University of Essex, Colchester, UK;

b Sheffield University Management School, University of Sheffield, Sheffield, UK

ABSTRACT

This paper investigates knowledge transfer (KT) of human resource management (HRM) across strategic partnerships in the Brazilian automotive industry, and the contextual factors impacting on KT within the supply chain. Case-study research in automotive companies and suppliers in Brazil is used to illustrate how in automotive industries, relationships with suppliers have traditionally been viewed as close, strategic partnerships, but over time, there has been a move towards more attenuated, supply chains, involving a shift towards more remote suppliers for basic components, and arms length relationships with them. In turn, this has impacted on how knowledge on HR has been transferred from manufacturers to suppliers. Both strategic partnerships and KT have been affected by internal drives towards cost cutting and talent retention, and external factors such as global competition through cheap imports, legislation, taxes, and unions. Evidence on the sometimes contradictory attitudes towards KT contributes towards the broader literatures on international HRM and KT in emerging economies, while the gradual unwinding of relationships has implications for policy and practice.

Keywords: automotive industry, Brazil, HRM, knowledge transfer, strategic partnerships, supply chains

This paper investigates how human resource management (HRM) is transferred within strategic partnerships in the Brazilian automotive industry, and the contextual factors that impact on knowledge transfer (KT) within the supply chain. It draws on case-study research in automotive companies and suppliers in Brazil to illustrate how in this sector, relationships have traditionally been viewed as close, strategic partnerships, but over time, there has been a move towards more attenuated supply chains. In turn, this has impacted on how knowledge has been transferred from manufacturers to suppliers. However, both inter-organizational relationships and KT have been affected by internal drives towards cost cutting and problems with talent retention, and external factors such as global competition through cheap imports and the employment relations system. The inherent, and intensifying, tensions and contradictions in these relationships shed light on how mature inter-firm supply relations and associated partnerships are being recon- figured, and dominant HR paradigms challenged and undermined, by structural changes in the global ecosystem, and the rise of new ultra-low-cost producers in the Far East. The paper focuses on the KT dimension: the sharing of information represents a pooling of knowledge, whilst transfer denotes a more focused passing on of knowledge, strategies and processes, with a view to encouraging the promotion and replication of best practices down the supply chain.

The paper moves knowledge forward in three main ways. First, it sheds additional light on the nature of relationships within automotive industry supply chains through revealing how inter-organizational relationships have changed over time between strategic partners within Brazil. Second, it adds to the literature on international human resource management (IHRM) through focusing on the relationship between context, the quality of relationships down supply chains and the implications for HRM. While recent studies of IHRM have considered the important issues of HR practices and knowledge exchange within multinational enterprises (MNEs) and KT between MNE headquarters and foreign subsidiaries (Bjorkman & Welch, 2015; Ozgo & Brewster, 2015; Pudelko, Reiche, & Carr, 2015), and reflected on the need for talent retention, training and communication (Weber & Tarba, 2010; Zhang et al., 2015), this paper highlights the complexities and contradictions of KT of HRM within supply chains. Increased global competitiveness has led to firms being more wary of engaging in KT, fearing a loss of talent. However, reduced KT across supply chains means exposure to greater uncertainty, which impacts in turn on future sustainability. Third, the paper extends the evidence base on KT. The international business literature considers the extent to which multinational firms transfer knowledge, either to their subsidiaries (Minbaeva, Pedersen, Bjorkman, & Fey, 2014; Minbaeva, Pedersen, Bjorkman, Fey, & Park, 2003) or during the process of undergoing mergers and acquisitions (M&As) (Sarala, Junni, Cooper, & Tarba, 2016). This study further highlights how the transfer of knowledge of HRM has been undermined by increased competitive pressures, even within Brazil, where there is a tradition of close networks of relationships between suppliers

The paper proceeds as follows. The next sections examine, in turn, the existing literature on: strategic partnerships within automotive supply chains; KT between firms and supply chain partners; and strategic partnerships, KT and HRM. These lead to the development of a conceptual framework. The following sections explain the methods used for case-study research in Brazil and then draw on the findings to illustrate how the conceptual framework might be applied in practice and further refined. The concluding discussion explains how this paper helps to move knowledge forward in relation to the automotive industry, KT and IHRM, and reflects more generally on the implications for the survival of the automotive industry in emerging economies that are experiencing economic crises.

Strategic partnerships within automotive supply chains

Strategic partnering is quite a diverse phenomenon, which may range from macroorganizational strategy to day-to-day operational issues (Mentzer, Min, & Zacharia, 2000). When purchasing is imparted with a strategic dimension, there is a focus on deepening relationships, communication and mutual gains with a limited panel of suppliers (Chen, Paulraj, & Lado, 2004); taken to its logical conclusion, this would lead to full strategic supplier partnerships or 'alliances' (Li, Ragu-Nathan, Ragu-Nathan, & Subba Rao, 2006), with the latter arguably implying more formalized relations and superior organizational outcomes. Strategic alliances may be undertaken by firms to gain competitive advantage in markets where there is turbulence, or where they need to broaden skills and resources without a major in-house investment (Cravens, Shipp, & Cravens, 1993). In this paper, the term strategic alliance is used interchangeably with strategic partnership, and the focus is on an informal relationship or alliance with a supply chain partner. How well they work, in turn, reflects the relative interdependence of the participating firms, planning, mutual collaboration and commitment.

External alliances may follow a strict logic of cost reduction (Eisenhard & Schoonhoven, 1996). This may involve outsourcing production to closely aligned lower cost producers to spread the risk of operating in an uncertain environment, and enable the firm to focus on core competencies whilst liquidating peripheral activities. However, such arguments centre on the nature of transaction costs, and routinized functions; firms may also form strategic alliances or partnerships in emerging industries, in highly competitive situations or to develop new technical solutions (Eisenhard & Schoonhoven, 1996). As Parkhe (1993) notes, strategic alliances require ongoing cooperation to work, and their relative efficacy may fluctuate over time; cost cutting may make it difficult to build trust and relationships. In the automotive industry, there has been a shift 'from a firm vs. firm' perspective to a 'supply chain vs. supply chain perspective' (Whipple & Frankel, 2000, p. 21), with firms basing their competitiveness on the depth and quality of their supply chain relationships. However, the maintenance and deepening of strategic alliances can be extremely challenging; a key dimension is to promote relative equity between partners, and, on behalf of suppliers, encourage a commitment to continuous improvement (Whipple & Frankel, 2000).

Narasimhan and Nair (2005, p. 301) argue that the 'architecture' of strategic alliances varies according to quality issues, with the latter ensuring close monitoring of quality and lean inventories. Whilst, in the motor industry, there have traditionally been long-term relations between the majors and their tier one suppliers, these relationships have tended to be less certain lower down the supply chain, and as this article will reveal, these tendencies have been accentuated. Supportive and stable institutional environments encourage firms to adopt long-term views towards their partners (Hitt, Ahlstrom, Dacin, Levitas, & Svobodina, 2004), and within the automotive industry, established Western and Japanese car majors and their principal suppliers are generally associated with work and employment relations with high levels of mutual interdependence (characterized by high investment in skills) and delegation (characterized by cooperative work and employment relations) (c.f. Whitley, 1999). However, as will become apparent, the rise of new component suppliers from East Asia has led to the globalization of production networks, and the weakening of strategic partnerships. Yet, the success of strategic alliances is dependent not only on financial and operational issues, but also on 'soft' issues, encompassing relationship capital which, in turn, encompasses commitment and trust (Cullen, Johnson, & Sakano, 2000, p. 223). Associational trust may be defined as a situation where it is assumed that, based on past experience and present contextual dynamics, one depends on another (Tomlinson, 2005, p. 1172). Such relationships are reconstituted and developed by individuals who monitor, collect and spread supportive information. Cooperation can be undermined by opportunism, which is more likely in situations of uncertainty and instability (Parkhe, 1993).

The Brazilian automotive industry is of particular interest. It has undergone a series of transformations since the 1950s. As part of an import substitution drive, the Brazilian Government heightened local content to between 90 and 95% in 1956, driving a change away from a production model centred on semi knock-down kits. To retain access to the large Brazilian market, automotive firms largely complied (Shapiro, 2006). However, this led to lower profit margins for the automotive majors, and contributed (along with an economic crisis in the mid-1960s) to the consolidation of the market, with dominance 2400 G. Wood et al. being secured by three firms, VW, GM and Fiat, but five other players retaining a presence (Shapiro, 2006). Whilst the automotive majors undeniably moved to a model of leaner staffing, this coincided with deepening capabilities of the core workforce, and more extensive alliances or partnerships with first tier suppliers located in close geographical proximity (see Crouch & Voelzkow, 2004; Crouch, Schroeder, & Voelzkow, 2009). Other dimensions included the transfer of production techniques and technologies, a spreading of risk, and the ability to specialize in and develop competencies around the manufacture of key components.

From the 1980s onwards, the Brazilian industry was transformed by large investments and gradual liberalization (Humphrey, 2003), leading to greater globalization in sourcing and design and deeper relationships with suppliers in the immediate proximity of car plants (c.f. Zilbovicius, Marx, & Salerno, 2002), and echoing more general trends in the worldwide automotive industry since the 1990s (Abreu, Beynon, & Ramalho, 2000; Pires, 1998). From the early 2000s, advanced supply chain management played a key role in binding firms together (Pires & Sacomano Neto, 2008). Linkages between foreign original equipment manufacturers (OEMs) and local suppliers helped to build the manufacturing base and contribute towards Brazil's reputation as a rising economy. But more recently, the country has had to cope with significant political instability, culminating in a 2016 constitutional coup and a return to rule by a small right-wing elite. Contributory economic factors to this instability have included volatile prices for primary commodities, and intensifying pressure from competition from ultralow-cost suppliers of basic components from China and South Korea. There have been frequent reports of halts in production and lay-offs, given fluctuations in demand and intensifying competition (Exame, 2015). This has challenged existing supply relationships and questioned the continued presence or scale of operations of a number of long-established players.

KT between firms and their supply chain partners

KT is widely acknowledged as an important source of competitive advantage (Sarala et al., 2016), and can be defined as 'the successful transmission of knowledge, including the sending or presenting of knowledge to a potential recipient and the absorption of knowledge by the recipient' (Sarala et al., 2016; see also Davenport & Prusak, 1998). This paper focuses on the first part of this definition, in other words, the sending or presenting of knowledge to a potential recipient, the inter-organizational and contextual factors that affect it and the transmission of information on HR practices within supply chains, given the relative lack of attention paid to this topic within an emerging economy context.

There is an extensive literature on KT, and more recently this has been extended to cover both advanced and emerging economies. There has been detailed discussion of the extent to which multinational firms transfer knowledge, either to their present subsidiaries (Minbaeva et al., 2003, 2014) or through mergers and acquisitions (M&As) (Sarala et al.,

2016). The literature on KT has highlighted the importance of strong and embedded linkages between firms (see Sarala et al., 2016). Sarala et al. (2016) provide an insightful analysis of KT within M&As, and in focusing on internal factors within firms, emphasize the need for sociocultural interfirm linkages, and complementary employee skills, trust, effective governance, cultural integration, knowledge-sharing routines and HR flexibility (defined as adaptation to changing conditions) to be present in order to promote effective KT. However, they acknowledge that whilst adding value,

internal flexibility may make employees more marketable to external organizations, with firms that invest in their people ending up providing training for competitors; this underscores the relevance of contextual circumstances, and the benefits of horizontal cooperation across an industry. In turn, the importance of context is confirmed by recent work on Japanese automotive supplier joint ventures and suppliers within Brazil, which highlights the importance of spatially specific socialization (Khan, Shenkar, & Lew, 2015). Further evidence from Chinese firms in Africa has highlighted the challenges of deepening and embedding inter-organizational relationships, particularly within emerging economies. When MNEs are involved, this may necessitate cross-cultural training and mutual learning; this should encompass an awareness of nationally specific macro-level factors, encompassing the wider employment relations system (Xing, Liu, Tarba, & Cooper, 2016).

Strategic partnerships, KT and HR practices

The HRM literature tended in the past to neglect what happens within and across supply chains (Fisher, Graham, Vachon, & Vereecke, 2010), although this has been partially remedied in recent years by a wide range of literature examining global supply chains, labour standards and regulation (see, for example, Riisegaard & Hammer, 2011; Reinecke, Manning, & von Hagen, 2012). Nevertheless, gaps remain in the area of KT of HR practices across supply chains, especially within areas where core firms and key suppliers have traditionally operated in close spatial proximity, which this paper helps to address. This paper also seeks to complement the burgeoning literature on HR practices and knowledge exchange within MNEs, and, more specifically, KT between MNE headquarters and foreign subsidiaries (Bjorkman & Welch, 2015; Ozgo & Brewster, 2015; Pudelko et al., 2015), and KT within M&As (Weber & Tarba, 2010; Zhang et al., 2015). For example, Weber and Tarba's

(2010) useful review of HR practices and M&As in Israel acknowledges the possibility of resistance to KT, and explains how internal factors necessary for integration include training on work processes, technologies and systems, in addition to communication (that may be affected by anxiety and trust). The review also covers institutional and associated factors such as sociocultural influences, labour relations, government policies and legislation. Meanwhile, in drawing on evidence from China, Zhang et al. (2015) indicates the need to consider how in times of uncertainty, talent retention may be improved by a combination of leadership styles and HR practices.

Conceptual framework

Drawing on the above literatures on IHRM and KT, Figure 1 presents a summarized conceptual framework. The figure highlights how KT of HR may lead to a range of outcomes, including increased competitiveness and talent retention. However, it also shows how KT is affected by inter-organizational relationships which are influenced, in turn, by both internal and external factors.

The case-study findings will next be used to illustrate the model and to suggest potential refinements to it.

METHODS

This paper draws primarily on the findings of seven case-study firms within the motor industry in three different regions of Brazil: the north-east (Pernambuco), south (Curitiba) and south-east (Sao Paulo). The case studies are used here for illustrative purposes, in order to draw out insights which help to develop the conceptual framework outlined above (Siggelkow, 2007). The case studies form part of a larger research project covering the automotive industries in Brazil and South Africa. The three regions indicated above were chosen due to the prevalence of automotive firms within these regions. In order to select firms, lists of companies were requested from the relevant state-initiated industrial associations (federações de indústrias), together with information on location, size of company (in terms of the number of employees), level (e.g. manufacturer, tier one or tier two suppliers) and contact details.

The case studies reported here include three international OEMs, each of which has a different country of origin (not named due to the need to preserve anonymity), and five first tier suppliers, again, each of which has direct relationships with different OEMs. The sample cannot be said to be representative of, nor generalizable to the whole population. However, given the relatively small number of OEMs operating in Brazil, and the diversity between them given different countries of ownership, the sample does give a useful picture of the current situation. Moreover, in order to improve validity there was a degree of triangulation between data sources (Johnson & Duberley, 2015) since the data include in-depth interviews with a range of participants including the following: CEOs, HR directors, supply chain directors and managers, accountants, Chief Financial Offi- cers, production managers, marketing specialists and trade unionists. In total, seven case-study organizations, involving 22 interviews, each of around three quarters of an hour's duration (but ranging from half an hour to over two hours), are drawn upon here, in addition to field notes undertaken during factory visits in three of the companies, where details regarding production and working practices were noted. Interview schedules were developed following a review of the literature, and then through a lengthy process of iteration between members of the project team and the larger External factors Government policy Legislation Trade unions Sociocultural influences Labour markets Internal (within firm) factors Socialization Training Communication Leadership styles HR flexibility Interorganizational relationships Strong linkages between firms Trust Knowledgesharing routines Outcomes include: Talent retention Competitiveness Knowledge transfer of HR practices Figure 1. Strategic partnerships and KT of HR practices. The International Journal of Human Resource Management 2403 advisory board that included academics and practitioners. Questions included those relating to the organizational context, relationships with suppliers and customers, communication and KT, and accounting and human resource management practices within the firm and its suppliers. In order to aim for authenticity of response, prompts and probes were used.

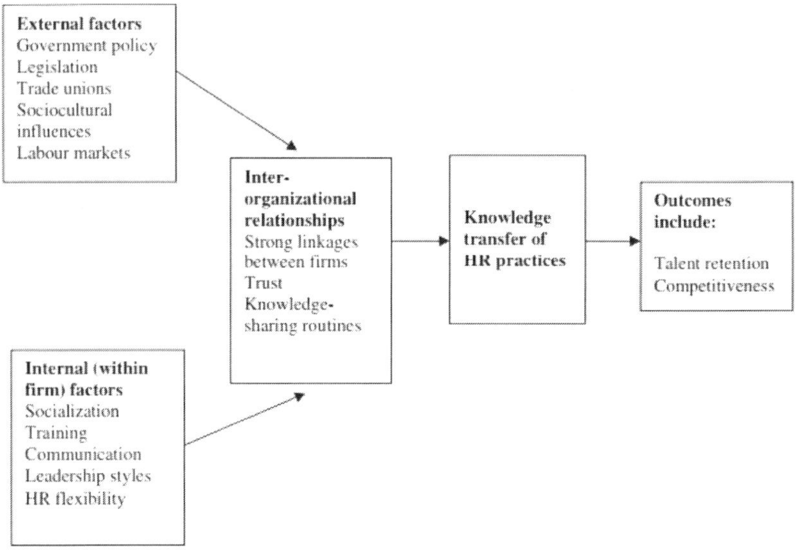

Figure 1. Strategic partnerships and KT of HR practices

All interviews were fully transcribed, and where necessary translated from Portuguese. Translators were carefully selected, and translation was checked by the researchers involved in the data collection process. Table 1 provides brief details about the companies and the participants within them

Data were coded using NVivo 8, a software package that facilitated the organization of data. The use of NVivo involved developing an initial coding frame that was informed by existent literature, followed by inductive coding of imported transcripts. Patterns were detected and organized into themes and subthemes. The analysis was primarily undertaken by one researcher (the project leader) and developed in consultation with co-investigators from the UK and Brazil. The major themes and subthemes are shown in Table 2 below

Each of the major themes and subthemes appeared across all of the case studies. This was since the interview schedules included set topic areas and suggestions for prompting and probing. However, the degree to which participants were able to comment on the particular topic varied depending on their role within the organization. Moreover, further down the hierarchy of nodes, subthemes emerged which did not necessarily contain data from other cases.

Table 1. Case-study companies and research participants

Case study code	OEM/First tier supplier	Car/ Motorbike	Participant code	Participant job role
BrOEM1	OEM	Car	Scm1	Supply chain director
			Scm2	Supply chain director
			Scm3	Supply chain director
			Mgr1	Production manager
BrOEM2	OEM	Car	HR1	HR director
			TU1	Trade union representative
BrOEM3	OEM	Car	Acct1	Accountant/Finance (Director)
			Acct2	Accountant/Finance (Director)
			Scm1	Supply chain director
BrSupplier1	First tier supplier	Car	CEO1	Director
			HR1	HR director
			PM1	Production manager
BrSupplier2	First tier supplier	Motorbike	Acct1	Accountant/Finance director
			HR1	HR Director
BrSupplier3	First tier supplier	Car	SCM1	Quality manager – supply chains
			Acct1	Accountant/Finance director
BrSupplier4	First tier supplier	Motorbike	HR1	HR director
			Mrkt	Marketing director
			Acct1	Accountant/Finance director
			Acct2	Accountant/Finance director
			Scm1	Supply chain/Quality director
BrSupplier5	First tier supplier	Car	HR1	HR manager

Findings

The findings cover, firstly, the way in which inter-organizational relationships have changed over time, revealing how they have moved from long-term relationships to those that are more attenuated. A willingness of players at various levels of the supply chain to adapt to suit the needs of other supply chain partners was accompanied by increasingly heated discussions, suggesting strain within relationships and even a breakdown in trust due to low-cost entrants further down the supply chain. Secondly, the findings show how changes in inter-organizational relationships have impacted on KT of HRM, including the ways in which knowledge was transferred, and what was shared, but also reveal reluctance to share knowledge, given fears around the cutting of costs, competition, poaching of staff and job loss

Table 2. Major themes and subthemes.

Major theme	Subthemes included:
Background-industry	Number of OEMs Competitiveness Growth or decline Legislation Labour relations
Background-company	Years in existence Products Plants in other regions Market share Country of ownership Internal relationships
Supply chain management	Which suppliers How choose suppliers Location of suppliers Company relationship with clients and suppliers Nature of contracts Influences on supply chain management
HR practices	Number and type of workers Performance management Recruitment Training Pay and reward Equal opportunities Redundancy and job loss Factors influencing HR practices
Information sharing	Strategic suppliers (or not) Sharing of HR information and HR costs Sustaining of relationships Trust Confidentiality Factors influencing sharing of information

Inter-organizational relationships within strategic partnerships and changes over time as the result of various contextual factors

In Brazil, the motor industry was traditionally characterized by enduring relationships between OEMs and established locally based suppliers. In referring to their relationship with a particular OEM, the CEO of one supplier commented, We ensure that relationships are at all times workable and good-natured. However, pricing discussions and occasional service failures or discussions relating to occasional service failures can obviously become quite warm ... Each major corporation has a style of its own. We adapt our approach to fit in with the company's, the client's style, and we ensure that good relations, good working relations, exist at all times to the fullest extent possible. (BrSupplier1, CEO1)

However, there appeared to be some variation in the depth and relative durability of these relationships. Some referred to the continuance of established relationships with suppliers. For example, one OEM had kept preferred suppliers on long-term contracts of 10 years or more, and had worked with one supplier for over 35 years. In that company, all of the production suppliers were on long-term contracts because they supplied a specific part solely for BrOEM3 (BrOEM3, scm1):

For over 20 years they've [name of company] been providing wires for us. Then, [name of another company] for some twelve years, more or less. There are people who have been providing us for centuries. (BrSupplier3, scm1)

Conversely, others referred to strain within previously strong relationships:

In the commercial area, [we have had] very close contact with the clients. And, with the OEMs, this is changing a lot here in Brazil. So, in a few companies, you could speak to the same person for two or three years ... It has changed a lot. (BrSupplier4, scm1)

Various reasons were given for these changes, including low volumes of production, new low-cost imports and the high costs of labour due to wage increases secured by unions (BrSupplier4, scm1). The marketing manager in the same company commented,

We cannot produce or manufacture in here anymore everything that we should, everything that we could and everything that we would like, because it's absolutely not competitive with China, for example, due to the cost – legally, the cost of the labour in Brazil. (BrSupplier4, mrkt1)

In another company wage increases had created the need to pass on costs:

Even in unfavourable situations, we have had real wage increases of around two to three percent a year. So when you do this over many years, this wage bill pressure, it affects the company's costs strongly. We cannot pass it on to the market because we have competition from China or Asia. And we find ourselves caught between the devil and the deep blue sea .... We have tried to change everything and there is nothing more to change. Then you go to your customer and say, 'Look, please, we don't have another alternative, we have to increase the price'.

And it will vary whether he passes the increased cost on to his product or not, or if he increases the order from Asia. (BrSupplier2, acct1)

Although they had worked in close partnership with a particular OEM for many years, this was not helping them to stave off competition from Asia. Thus, the emergence of new sources of basic components had placed new pressures on supply chains. Automotive majors placed renewed pressures on tier 1 suppliers to cut costs, and in turn, more closely scrutinized the costs of the components they themselves received. In practice, this meant that further down the supply chain, local suppliers were under renewed pressure. The end result was potentially a gradual unwinding of complex networks of alliances within and across Brazil. At the periphery of supply chains, and, in respect of lower cost, lower technology components, there was strong pressure to further globalize networks, discarding local suppliers in favour of even lower cost ones from abroad:

We have already sent professionals to visit Asia in order to get a part of that chain. Instead of acquiring certain supplies here, we tried to get them in Asia. (BrSupplier2, acct1)

At the same time, intensifying competition from other global sites of production, and the opening of a previously more protected home market, had forced the local affiliates of car majors to cut costs – and, above all, jobs – in order to make themselves better equipped to cope with changes in demand and to secure the production of new cycles of car models for global markets.

Our scenario, as much as we want to be optimistic, does not show signs of improvement. We did our first lay-off two years ago with [over a thousand employees] ... and now I know that there are many companies like [names of automotive companies], they have hundreds of employees in lay-off. (BrSupplier2, acct1)

Proposition 1: Strategic partnerships are under strain due to the need to adhere to labour standards, global competition and cost-cutting.

Inter-organizational relationships and KT of HR practices

In BrOEM3, there appeared to have been transfer of knowledge at a strategic level:

We have the manufacturer here ... for instance today we have purchasers inside [name of department]. We have business partners seated in each of these business areas following the day to day discussions, providing support, for instance. Just before our meeting we had our management meeting here with my boss who is the vice president for this operation here in [place] for the trucks operation, and one seated there was the business partner for HR. (BrOEM3, acct1)

KT appeared to be more restricted in the area of production. In BrOEM1, there was staff training of various suppliers in a range of areas, including specific manufacturing processes (BrOEM1, mgr1), and transferring information on 'linked techniques' in the assembly of vehicles (BrOEM1, scm2). However, there was limited KT around OEMs designed tools that were developed by the OEM then used by the first tier suppliers:

Normally our parts are made with tools. We purchase the tools, and the tools belong to us. And they are used only for supplying parts to us ... There's a philosophy behind some tools ... that we share with suppliers. Depending on the relationship, if it's a long-term relationship, if the supplier is one that we have a good interaction with, we share it. (BrOEM1, scm2)

It was also found that there appeared to have been an erosion of trust between strategic partners. Trust relationships depend on predictability (Dietz, 2004); any disruption of established ties and exchange relations will necessarily ripple within and between the different nested layers of relationships linking automotive majors and their various tiers of supplier. One interviewee explained that trust had diminished due to the actions undertaken because of fluctuations in demand. For example, he had needed to 'freeze scheduling' for two to three weeks,

... and the supplier asks us, what's happened? I can work, I cannot work, what's this forecast? Sometimes you need to ask us for one thousand, sometimes zero. (BrOEM1, scm3)

In this case, better KT on production and HR might potentially have enabled a better solution to be obtained.

In terms of HR practices, the transfer of knowledge to suppliers was, according to one OEM production manager, 'When we have some kind of problems or when we are discussing opportunities' (BrOEM1_mgr1). However, a supply chain director explained how additional information was given to suppliers on job roles, levels of responsibility and the type of skills that they needed for a particular aspect of production in order to reduce costs and to ensure health and safety (BrOEM1_scm1). Another reason was to ensure smooth production to 'control the pipeline' (BrOEM1_scm3). In another plant, knowledge of HR practices was transferred more often due to the physical closeness of their location to the suppliers (BrOEM1_scm2). Indeed, it was suggested that in the past, the transfer of HR information to suppliers was easier when suppliers were located closer to them (BrOEM1_scm3). In BrOEM3, the transfer of HR information took place when they were negotiating a price with a supplier. At that stage, they produced a 'simulation' of operations and included HR information such as absenteeism levels (BrOEM3_acct2).

The KT of HR practices by some suppliers did not seem to have been considered (BrSupplier6_ceo1; BrSupplier12_HR1; BrSupplier12_acct1). In contrast, BrSupplier9 shared information on certain HR practices, as long as it did not involve providing cost-related information (BrSupplier9_HR1):

Some practices that we have here it is possible that we can share, for example: the way we control absenteeism, the way we control ergonomics, right? There is not any problem in sharing ... we do not share numbers, but some practices without problems ... We share training practices, benefits. [This helps] us to understand how the market is positioned, because it helps us to retain our talents. (BrSupplier9_HR1)

In this case, the reason seemed to be because they expected information in return, and could then better retain talented members of the workforce.

Proposition 2: Reasons for KT of HR practices include damage limitation (health and safety), cost reduction, the need to guarantee supplies and talent retention

However, there were various factors that appeared to prevent the effective transfer of knowledge. In BrOEM3, resistance to KT was due to an anticipation that relationships may not endure. Consequently, it was regarded as 'common practice' for an OEM to let a supplier use their tools, but the (intellectual) property remained with the OEM:

... So when you need to change the supplier, you need to pick up your toolings, take your fixtures and bring it back to put it in another supplier. (BrOEM3, acct1)

In the same OEM, there had been a long history of providing intensive training for suppliers (BrOEM3_acct2), with the aim of making their suppliers more competitive by reducing costs. However, some suppliers were reluctant to be trained due to fear of revealing high costs, which might lead the OEM to try to lower the price for the product (BrOEM3, acct2). These tensions had led to a conflictual relationship rather than a collaborative partnership.

The OEMs seemed to rely on implicit understandings and trust with second tier suppliers, in areas ranging from quality control to labour standards:

We have our critical suppliers or key suppliers, that produce some complex parts, like big sets for suspension, big sets for wheel or some air conditioning and so on, and normally we have no contact with, but we have a close monitor with our first suppliers. Sometimes in between two or three months we make some short or informal survey about their suppliers, if everything is OK with the supply floor ... Because our focus is to know if theycould have any problems about capacity and buffers. So that is the normal process that you have. (BrOEM1, scm3)

On the one hand, this system worked quite well in cementing the type of trust relations that grow organically despite, or because of, the absence of close and direct monitoring. On the other hand, in other firms trust relations appeared to be at some risk, in the context of global concerns about survival, and with fears about job loss impacting on productivity (BrSupplier2, acct1). The intensity of competition had forced a closer and more instrumental scrutiny of costs down the supply chain, which had placed the greatest pressure on smaller local players further down the supply chain, and their workers. Another factor that impinged on KT was fear of the loss of talented staff to other firms:

We lost people to [name of OEM], which is our client, indirectly. We lost, right? And as we are a small company, I joke that I'm just training people for the larger companies. Free training. They say that those who are the 'sandwich' are the ones who suffer. (BrSupplier3, scm1)

It's something like this: partnership with these other companies, I think it's rather difficult. Each one is seeking what is best for them. What we try to do is some internal retention plan, but that is not an easy thing. (BrSupplier2, acct1)

For OEMs, the transfer of staff from suppliers was seen as a normal, and a positive move (BrOEM1). However, any erosion of trust will make meaningful delegation more difficult. And if jobs become scarcer, employees will have fewer options in terms of switching jobs within supply networks, making the grassroots dissemination of skills and capabilities within alliances more difficult.Although a trend within the global car industry has been a move towards greater delegation to employees and inter-dependence with them (Whitley, 1999), and the dissemination of the higher HR standards of the car majors to their allied suppliers, it can be argued that, above all in terms of job security, this model has become under threat, as, indeed, has the survival and continued Brazilian presence of suppliers. And, if jobs are insecure, it may become much more difficult to persuade employees to invest in developing their organization-specific skills, as adverse to those which are externally marketable.

Proposition 3: Factors impinging on KT of HR practices include fear of transitory relationships, competition, cost-cutting, and loss of talent.

Conceptual framework incorporating propositions

The findings presented above resulted in a series of propositions, leading, in turn, to the refinement of the conceptual model presented above. In summary, strategic partnerships are under strain due to global competition and cost-cutting and the need to adhere to labour standards; reasons for KT of HR practices include damage limitation (health and safety), cost reduction, the need to guarantee supplies and talent retention; and factors preventing KT include transitory relationships, and fear of competition, cost-cutting and loss of talent. The model is presented in Figure 2.

CONCLUDING DISCUSSION

In summary, it was revealed that relationships between strategic partners had changed over time from closer relationships, based on continuity and associated trust, to more transactional ones, based around costs. They had been placed under strain due to global competition and the need to adhere to labour standards. This had impacted on the predictability of inter-organizational KT; dominant players looking to cut costs and gain the flexibility afforded by greater use of arms length contracting were less inclined to invest in stable relationships characterized by close or 'thick' ties encompassing mutual learning, and the exchange of ideas, techniques and optimal HR practices. Companies still shared a range of types of information, including running supplier training events and supplier development workshops on manufacturing processes and shared tools (technological). However, there were signs that within the difficult economic climate, insecurity contributed to diminishing trust, with knock-on effects on HR knowledge flows; such insecurity encompassed more transitory relationships, and fear of competition, cost-cutting and loss of talent.

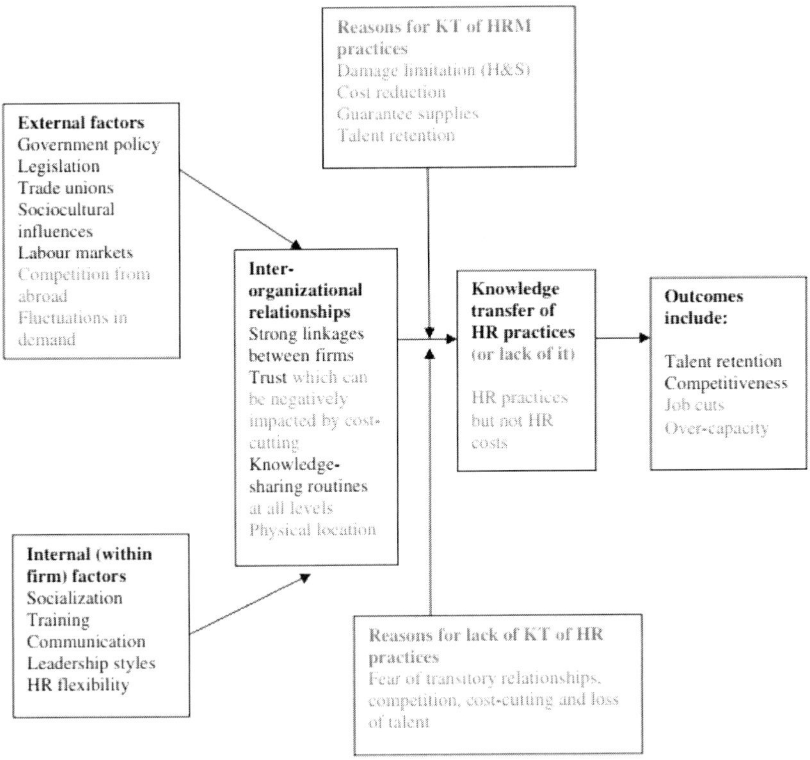

Figure 2. Strategic partnerships and KT of HR practices (refined).

This paper contributes towards knowledge on strategic partnerships in a range of ways. Firstly, it sheds additional light on the nature of relationships within automotive industry supply chains through revealing how inter-organizational relationships have changed over time. Second, it moves forward the literature on IHRM, through revealing the complexities and contradictions of KT of HRM within supply chains. Although the existing literature on KT highlights the importance of close ties and formalized relationships, this study highlights the extent to which mature and dense relationships are prone to disruption owing to intensified competition and the disjuncture between formal regulation and the needs of organizations and their stakeholders. Above all, it highlights the extent to which KT cannot be seen purely in terms of inter-organizational relations; regulation matters, be it in terms of national-specific institutional support that accords firms sufficient space to take a longer term view and/or the regulatory support that facilitates the rise of, and sustains new competitors. Central to this is the role of HRM, and the contradictions and dilemmas posed in seeking to reconcile the need to maintain and enhance skills and knowledge down supply chains with the challenges of reducing costs and securing flexibility in productive capability and numerical terms. The IHRM literature has tend to focus on the dissemination of HR practices and knowledge exchange within MNEs, and KT between MNE headquarters and foreign subsidiaries (Bjorkman & Welch, 2015; Minbaeva et al., 2003, 2014; Ozgo & Brewster, 2015; Pudelko et al., 2015), and/or during the process of undergoing mergers and acquisitions (Sarala et al., 2016), and highlights the central importance of talent retention, investment in people and communication, as a basis of competitiveness (Weber & Tarba, 2010; Zhang et al., 2015). This study extends this work through looking at the challenges of securing this within supply networks both within and across national boundaries, and with the need to retain proprietal knowledge, yet enhance the human capabilities of key partners. Without KT, firms expose themselves to greater uncertainty, and are increasingly forced along a path to competitiveness centring on low costs. This paper reveals how and why the transfer of knowledge of HR practices has been undermined, even within Brazil, where traditionally, there have been close relationships between strategic partners within supply chains.

The study has broader implications for HRM in automotive companies in Brazil, and in other countries. Although there has been a history of the dissemination of production models and associated HR standards across the interlinking automotive firms and various tiers of supplier, there appears to be a process of slow unwinding underway. At the same time, as KT and cooperation between automotive majors and their first tier suppliers has persisted, and, indeed, become increasingly sophisticated, heightened competition has forced a move to more tenuous relations further down supply networks. The entry of new low-cost suppliers of basic components has allowed the Brazilian branches of the automotive majors to cut costs, but the consequences have been offloaded further down the supply chain. Whilst the automotive majors and their suppliers have had to learn to make do with leaner workforces, suppliers further down are facing pressures to jettison established relations with their own suppliers, forcing more instrumental contracting.

As Whipple and Frankel (2000) note, the quality and durability of alliances is not only contingent on communication, effective performance evaluation, and good relations with core customers, but also a degree of evenness, if not equity, in terms of resources and benefits. The rise of ultra-low-cost suppliers of basic components from China and South Korea has challenged this balance of power, enabling the automotive majors to drive far harder bargains with first tier suppliers. Even if the majors remain in a mutually interdependent relationship with the latter, they are in a position – and indeed, are compelled by the intensification of competition in the global automotive industry – to insist on reductions in costs, that, beyond a certain stage, are only possible through first tier players abandoning or renegotiating their established relations with their own suppliers. This process has made for diminished job security for automotive workers in Brazil, discouraging industry-specific human capital development, with potential negative consequences for cognitive capabilities at the firm and local level, and for KT between organizations.

In turn, this presents specific challenges for HR managers. At the level of the majors and first tier suppliers, cooperation and the development of organizational-speci- fic skills and knowledge may be undermined by the reduction in employment security: employees may seek to develop what makes them externally marketable, rather than further developing their organization-specific skills. It is beyond the power of HR managers to control the rising internal competition model between the automotive majors, let alone structural changes in the industry and the global economy. The climate of insecurity therefore has to be offset through innovations in other areas, including a closer reflection on what internal individual and collective capabilities are unique, and can serve as a sustainable basis for production that reconciles cost with quality and innovation. Added to this, HR managers will need to work more closely with supply chain managers in order to ensure that KT takes place in a way which will forge closer relationships with suppliers and lead to the exchange of best practices. Supply chain managers' sourcing strategy and trust relations will affect KT, and relatedly, the degree of KT may affect the success of partnerships in the long term. This is of particular importance for emerging economy suppliers that appear to accept instructions, but not internalize them if they are not negotiated or carefully communicated to them (Khan et al., 2015).

The Brazilian motor industry has been able to survive a process of gradual liberalization, unlike countries such as Australia and New Zealand, not only on account of greater government interest in maintaining the industry, a larger home market and an associated knowledge of consumer taste, but also due to the well-developed nature of the strategic partnerships between various levels of supplier, which have been supported by relatively high volumes and also networks of implicit understandings and trust relations that have been constructed over many years. This approach faces great challenges, given intensified competition both at the level of final assembly and in the provision of the most basic of components, undermining established relationships down supply chains; this unwinding has implications for KT and capabilities development, and, hence, for the survival of the industry

ACKNOWLEDGEMENTS

The authors would like to acknowledge the support and contributions of the broader project team and Advisory Board, in addition to those interviewed for the purpose of this research. We would also like to thank Dr Shlomo Tarba and the anonymous reviewers for their feedback and encouragement regarding the development of this paper.

DISCLOSURE STATEMENT

No potential conflict of interest was reported by the authors.

REFERENCES

1. Abreu, A. R. D. P., Beynon, H., & Ramalho, J. R. (2000). The dream factory: VW's modular production system in Resende, Brazil. *Work, Employment & Society, 14*, 265–282.

2. Bjorkman, I., & Welch, D. (2015). Framing the field of international human resource management research. *The International Journal of Human Resource Management, 26*, 136–150

3. Chen, I. J., Paulraj, A., & Lado, A. A. (2004). Strategic purchasing, supply management, and firm performance. *Journal of Operations Management, 22*, 505–523.

4. Cravens, D. W., Shipp, S. H., & Cravens, K. S. (1993). Analysis of co-operative interorganizational relationships, strategic alliance formation, and strategic alliance effectiveness. *Journal of Strategic Marketing, 1*, 55–70.

5. Crouch, C., Schroeder, M., & Voelzkow, H. (2009). Regional and sectoral varieties of capitalism. *Economy and Society, 38*, 654–678.

6. Crouch, C., & Voelzkow, H. (2004). Introduction. In C. Crouch, P. Le Galès, C. Trigilia, & T. H. Voelzkow (Eds.), *Changing governance of local economies* (pp. 1–10). Oxford: Oxford University Press.

7. Cullen, J. B., Johnson, J. L., & Sakano, T. (2000). Success through commitment and trust: The soft side of strategic alliance management. *Journal of World Business, 35*, 223–240.

8. Davenport, T. H., & Prusak, L. (1998). *Working knowledge: How organisations manage what they know*. Boston: Harvard Business School Press.

9. Dietz, G. (2004). Partnership and the development of trust in British workplaces. *Human Resource Management Journal, 14*, 5–24.

10. Eisenhardt, K. M., & Schoonhoven, C. B. (1996). Resource-based view of strategic alliance formation: Strategic and social effects of entrepreneurial firms. *Organizational Science, 7*, 136–150.

11. Exame. (2015). *As indústrias não estão nem ai para pátios cheio de carros*. Retrieved from http://exame.abril.com.br/revista-exame/edicoes/106702/noticias

12. Fisher, S., Graham, M., Vachon, S., & Vereecke, A. (2010). Don't miss the boat: Research on HRM and supply chains. *Human Resource Management, 49*, 813–828.

13. Hitt, M. A., Ahlstrom, D., Dacin, M. T., Levitas, E., & Svobodina, L. (2004). The institutional effects on strategic alliance partner selection in transition economies: China vs. Russia. *Organization Science, 15*, 173–185.

14. Humphrey, J. (2003). Globalization and supply chain networks: The auto industry in Brazil and India. *Global Networks, 3*, 121–141.

15. Johnson, P., & Duberley, J. (2015). Inductive praxis and management research: Towards a reflexive framework. *British Journal of Management, 26*, 760–776.

16. Khan, Z., Shenkar, O., & Lew, Y. K. (2015). Knowledge transfer from international joint ventures to local suppliers in a developing economy. *Journal of International Business Studies, 46*, 656–675.

17. Li, S., Ragu-Nathan, B., Ragu-Nathan, T. S., & Subba Rao, S. S. (2006). The impact of supply chain management practices on competitive advantage and organizational performance. *Omega, 34*, 107–124.

18. Mentzer, J. T., Min, S., & Zacharia, Z. G. (2000). The nature of interfirm partnering in supply chain management. *Journal of Retailing, 76*, 549–568.

19. Minbaeva, D., Pedersen, T., Bjorkman, I., & Fey, C. (2014). A retrospective on: MNC knowledge transfer, subsidiary absorptive capacity, and HRM. *Journal of International Business Studies, 45*, 52–62.

20. Minbaeva, D., Pedersen, T., Bjorkman, I., Fey, C., & Park, H. J. (2003). MNC knowledge transfer, subsidiary absorptive capacity and HRM. *Journal of International Business Studies, 45*, 38–51.

21. Narasimhan, R., & Nair, A. (2005). The antecedent role of quality, information sharing and supply chain proximity on strategic alliance formation and performance. *International Journal of Production Economics, 96*, 301–313.

22. Ozgo, E., & Brewster, C. (2015). Knowledge flows in MNEs and the role of HRM. In C. Machado (Ed.). *International human resource management: Challenges and changes* (pp. 21–36). Switzerland: Springer International Publishing.

23. Parkhe, A. (1993). Strategic alliance structuring: A game theoretic and transaction cost examination of interfirm cooperation. *Academy of Management Journal, 36*, 794–829.

24. Pires, S. R. (1998). Managerial implications of the modular consortium model in a Brazilian automotive plant. *International Journal of Operations & Production Management, 18*, 221–232.

25. Pires, S. R., & Sacomano Neto, M. (2008). New configurations in supply chains: The case of a condominium in Brazil's automotive industry. *Supply Chain Management: An International Journal, 13*, 328–334.

26. Pudelko, M., Reiche, B. S., & Carr, C. (2015). Recent developments and emerging challenges in international human resource management. *The International Journal of Human Resource Management, 26*, 127–135.

27. Reinecke, J., Manning, S., & von Hagen, O. (2012). The emergence of a standards market: Multiplicity of sustainability standards in the global coffee industry. *Organization Studies, 33*, 791–814.

28. Riisegaard, L., & Hammer, N. (2011). Prospects for labour in global value chains: Labour standards in the cut flower and banana industries. *British Journal of Industrial Relations, 49*, 168–190.

29. Sarala, R. M., Junni, P., Cooper, C. L., & Tarba, S. Y. (2016). A sociocultural perspective on knowledge transfer in mergers and acquisitions. *Journal of Management, 42*, 1230–1249.

30. Shapiro, H. (2006). *Engines of growth: The state and transnational auto companies in Brazil*. Cambridge: Cambridge University Press.

31. Siggelkow, N. (2007). Persuasion with case studies. *Academy of Management Journal, 50*, 20–24.

32. Tomlinson, F. (2005). Idealist and pragmatic versions of the discourse of partnership. *Organization Studies, 26*, 1169–1188.

33. Weber, Y., & Tarba, S. (2010). Human resource practices and performance of mergers and acquisitions in Israel. *Human Resource Management Review, 20*, 203–211.

34. Whipple, J. M., & Frankel, R. (2000). Strategic alliance success factors. *The Journal of Supply Chain Management, 36*, 21–28.

35. Whitley, R. (1999). *Divergent capitalisms*. Oxford: Oxford University Press.

36. Xing, Y., Liu, Y., Tarba, S. Y., & Cooper, C. (2016). Intercultural influences on managing African employees of Chinese firms in Africa: Chinese managers' HRM practices. *International Business Review, 25*, 28–41.10.

37. Zhang, J., Ahammad, M. F., Tarba, S., Cooper, C., Glaister, K., & Wang, Jinmin (2015). The effect of leadership style on talent retention during Merger and Acquisition integration: Evidence from China. *The International Journal of Human Resource Management, 26*, 1021–1050.

38. Zilbovicius, M., Marx, R., & Salerno, M. S. (2002). A comprehensive study of the transformation of the Brazilian automotive industry. *International Journal of Automotive Technology and Management, 2*, 10–23.

13

CHAPTER

Research on Initiative Turnover Rate of the Post-90s Workforce—Taking Labor-Intensive Enterprises as an Example

Penglin Li, Hanglu Lu

School of Management, Xi'an University of Science and Technology, Xi'an, China

ABSTRACT

Based on the investigation of the traditional research on the factors which affect employee turnover rate, this paper aims at establishing a dynamic model of the post-90s workforce to explain the phenomenon of continuously high employee turnover rate of the post-90s workforce in labor-intensive enterprises. The model has explored the intervening factors of employee turnover and provided theoretical guidelines for companies to take actions against high turnover rate. The incentives for the post-90s employee initiative turnover have been probed thoroughly from the three aspects of employee, company and society and thus the managerial tactics have been proposed for companies to manage high turnover rate of employees. These tactics include mental health education, employee ethics education, improvement of working environments, rebuilding corporate culture, transforming employee management style, enhancing employee career planning management and setting up keep-to-the-point incentive mechanism, etc.

Keywords: The Post-90s Employees; Enterprise Turnover Intervention; Dynamic Turnover Model; Turnover Management Tactics

1. INTRODUCTION

People who were born after 1990 (hereinafter abbreviated as post-90s) are a group of labors with a distinctive trait and large scale, concentrating on labor-intensive enterprises. In the age of the late adolescence and early career, they are now facing the pressure of job, life, and marriage, which results in high turnover rate and large loss, not only a waste of corporate investment in human capital, but also a shortage of enterprise talents, which triggers the crisis of corporate human resources, and even endangers the enterprise survival and affects social stability. Therefore, study of initiative turnover of post-90s takes important theoretical value and practical significance.

2. THEORY ON EMPLOYEES' TURNOVER

2.1. Study of Employees' Turnover Intention

Turnover intention is the intention to leave the organization the employees show after they work for a period in a place and take into consideration the gap between their needs and reality of that in all aspects. Scholars in abroad have done a great deal of researches on factors affecting employee's turnover intention [1] and the main conclusions are as follows:

Zeffance attributes turnover intentions to four dimensions: external factors (labor market), the employees' individual characteristics (such as intelligence, ability, experience, gender, interests, age and tenure, etc.), institutional factors (such as working conditions, salary, participation in and supervision on organizational decisionmaking) and employees' reaction of their work (including job satisfaction, job involvement and job expectations, etc.) [2] . Quarles thinks factors influencing turnover intention can be attributed to five aspects: job-related factors, individual related factors, external factors, organizational commitment and job satisfaction [3] . Iverson divides it into four dimensions: individual factors (gender, full-time or part-time, work motivation and family relationship, etc.), work-related factors (such as self-control, support from partners and executives, risk of work, role ambiguity and conflict, distributive justice, etc.), external environmental factors (job opportunity) and factors related to employee themselves (job satisfaction and organizational commitment, etc.) [4] .

By studying the comprehensive model of the internal and external reasons affecting the employees' turnover in high-tech enterprises, Wang Yuqin and Ye Rensun proposed that the intention and external environment are the leading factors for employees' turnover [5] . Fu Yiqun Ling Wenqing, Fang Liluo attribute it into six dimensions: individual factors, work-related factors, organizational characteristics, personal adaptability in organizations, external factors, and other psychological factors like attitudes [6] . Liu Ying, Lin Qingdong, and Ling Wenqing put it into three dimensions: factors related to the staff, the organization and the society [7] .

From the above researches, it can be concluded that factors affecting the employees' turnover intention are mainly related to the social factors, organizational factors and staff factors. Social factors include the level of economic development, employment policy, social security policy, labor supply and demand conditions; organizational factors are like corporate culture, job characteristics, payroll system, management, training, support, and interpersonal relationship; and staff factors include intelligence, skills, experience, gender, interest, age, and expectation, etc.

2.2. Evolution of the Employees' Initiative Turnover Model

The turnover is the process an individual terminates his relationship with the organization from which he obtains the material benefits [8] . It can be either initiative or non-initiative. The present turnover research mainly concerns the former one. Construction of the employees' initiative turnover model has been the focus of theoretical study of turnover. The traditional influential turnover models are the causality model by Prire [9] and Mueller [10] , the intermediary chain model by Mobley [11] , and the "tip mutation" model by Sheridan and Abelson [12] . They concluded in this way: take the staff expected working conditions, environmental characteristics, as well as the individual characteristics as antecedent variables affecting the turnover intention, job satisfaction and organizational commitment as intermediate variables between the antecedent variables and turnover intention, and by constantly enriching mediating variable settings explain the employees' psychological change in the decision-making process of turnover.

Since there are constantly new theories applied to the model in the research, new theories are successively applied to the turnover study based on the traditional expected theory, such as the retreat cognitive theory by Hom and Griffcth [13] , and the image theory by Bcach [14] . Since 1990s, Lee and Mitchell have researched the turnover model from many ways, a significant breakthrough compared to the traditional model [15] . They introduced many concepts such as "system shock" and "job embeddedness" and explained from four aspects the motivation of the employees' retention or turnover decisions. Empirical studies have shown that the new model can better classify and interpret turnover [16] . Domestic researchers use this model to discuss employees' turnover problems in the science and technology enterprises, and have achieved a lot in digging the reasons for professional technical staffs.

2.3. Introduction of the Turnover Research

Overall, the present turnover studies mainly focus on cause analysis of the employees' turnover by use of the model, look for the decisive factors from the external environment of the organization, management of the organization and individual characteristics, and investigate employees' psychological change in the process from the initial turnover intention to the final turnover behavior. But the whole study ignores the corporate intervention on employees' turnover, as well as the positive effect of the intervention for blocking the formation of turnover intention and reducing employees' initiative turnover rate. As a result, the present theory can not well explain the differences of the turnover rate for post-90s employees in different enterprises in the same industry and same place. And it is difficult to theoretically provide effective means and measures to solve the initiative turnover problem of the post-90s employees for the enterprises.

3. WHOLE FEATURES OF POST-90S EMPLOYEES

3.1. Definition of "Post-90s Employees"

"Post-90s" refers to the generation of Chinese born among 1990-1999. "Post-90s employees" refers to post-90s workers directly or indirectly engaged in enterprises [17] . In accordance with the provisions that child labor is forbidden in China, by 2011, the maximum age of the post-90s employees are 21; the minimum age is 16; their birth time is among 1990-1995.

3.2. Quantity of "Post-90s Employees"

There were approximately 1296.6 million "post-90s" in 2011 in China, (see Table 1). 93.011 million students of 16 - 21 years old were receiving education in the school (see Table 2). Based on the above data, the number of post-90s employees in 2011 is approximately 36.649 million, accounting for 4.8% of national employment (764.2 million people) for the same period; in the future four years, 59.955 million college students are going to graduate and walk into the community as post-90s employees. With the continuous enlargement of the scale of post-90s employees, they increasingly play an important role in China's economic development.

Table 1. Statistical table of births from 1990-1995 unit: 10 thousand persons.

Year of birth	Age	Births
1990	21	2367
1991	20	2243
1992	19	2106
1993	18	2113
1994	17	2091
1995	16	2046
Total	/	12,966

Data sources: The main demographic data of China from 1949-2001.

Table 2. Statistical table of people receiving education in 2011 unit: 10 thousand persons.

Education category	Enrollment	Students enrollment	School attendance
College and university	681.5	2308.5	2990
Secondary vocational school	808.9	2196.6	3005.5
Senior high school	850.8	2454.8	3305.6
Total	2341.2	6959.9	9301.1

Data sources: The National Economic and Social Development Statistical Bulletin in 2011.

3.3. Structure of Post-90s Employees

Post-90s rural migrant worker is an important part of post-90s employee group. According to the 2011 China migrant workers survey and monitoring report released by National Bureau of Statistics, there were total 252.78 million rural migrant workers in 2011, including the migrant workers among the ages of 16 - 20 which account for 6.3% rural migrant workers reaches 15.925 million, and accounts for 43.45% of the total post-90s employees (36.649 million), which is an important part of the whole post-90 employees group.

3.4. Industry Distribution of Post-90s Employees

Post-90s employees generally received junior middle school, secondary technical school or equivalent education; however, comparing with urban workforce, their educational level and skill level is still at a lower level, lacking of professional knowledge and expertise. Therefore, their employment scope is mainly concentrated in laborintensive industries in the secondary and tertiary industries, including manufacturing, construction, catering, electronics, textiles, clothing, footwear, plastics, and toys industries, among which manufacturing industry accumulates the most post-90s employees.

3.5. Occupational Qualities of Post-90s Employees

1) Cultural education situation. With the development of the nine-year compulsory education and vocational education, more post-90s employees have the opportunity to access into schools to receive education and improve cultural knowledge level. According to our current education system and post-90s employees' age structure, post-

90s employees' qualifications are mainly concentrated in junior middle school, secondary technical school or equivalent education level, and they had not received higher education.

2) Vocational education situation. Post-90s employees with elementary school, junior middle school education level have not yet received the systemic vocational education, lack of expertise, and their vocational skills level is low. Post-90s employees with secondary technical school or equivalent education although have received secondary vocational education, but they are restricted by the level of China's vocational education, that is, moral education is lacked, mental health education is weak, skill cultivation level is low, their professional ethics is weak, they are lack of mental health knowledge and their skill level are low and uneven.

3.6. Social Relations of Post-90s Employees

Post-90s employees are in the early stage of their career; their job is unstable; they have a high turnover rate; their liquidity is frequent; they have no fixed abode, it is difficult to develop and maintain a stable relationship among colleagues, friends, and leaderships for them. Since they are away from family and friends, their original social relations support are gradually weakened. Therefore, social relation of post-90s employees is in a temporary shortage state; they lack of social support channel of talk, exchange thought and being cared.

3.7. Living Environment of Post-90s Employees

As for Labor-intensive industries, workers are intensive and living environment is poor. The majority of post- 90s employees live in dormitories, rental, and living conditions are relatively poor; living space is crowded and repressed. Take industry as example, workplace manufacturing, construction, mining industry is relatively fixed, some enterprises provide dormitories for employees, with water, electricity, warm .etc basic living conditions in them, however, the accommodation arrangements are compact and crowded and living space is cramped. As for services industry, due to the broad scope of practice, unfixed working hours, employees choose to live in urban fringe and share living with others which has convenient transportation, cheap rent, but living space is repressed.

3.8. Physiological, Psychological and Behavioral Characteristics of Post-90s Employees

1) Physiological characteristics of post-90s employees. Post-90s employees are in the late adolescence, which is a period of a child to early adulthood, rapid transition, physical growth towards mature and sexually mature. The development of the brain causes the significant progress in cognitive ability. Adolescent brain development behavior are: excessive gray substance of the brain in adolescence stage will be trimmed in the rate of 1% - 2% per year and growing neurons (nervous system cells) and the connection among them becomes increasingly complex and rich make thinking more and more complex; increasing of myelin—the process that neuron cell is surrounded by fat cell—makes neural information transmission more efficient; significant development of regions is the prefrontal which enables people to think, evaluate and make complex decisions in a unique way, its development may lead to the progressive development of fine intelligence. Trimming of gray substance and continues increasing of neurons and myelin and significant development of prefrontal play an important role in development of adolescent cognition and thinking ability [18] .

2) Psychological characteristics of post-90s employees. Post-90s employees are psychological sensitive, their mood changes rapidly; they are easy to be anger and impulses, which has a close relationship with adolescent physical development. With the rapid growth of height and weight, the pituitary signals stimulate other glands in the body, secreting adult levels of sex hormone and growth hormone and these growth hormone and sex hormone promote rapid growth and development, while higher hormone level may lead to emotional fast change and extremely sensitive psychological reactions. At the same time, responsible for the impulse control, brain areas of forehead leaf develops completely, the ability to control impulses is also not formed, this immature brain development likely to lead to dangerous and impulsive behavior which has adolescent characteristics, and even more extreme behavior may appear [18] .

3) Behavioral characteristics of the post-90 employees. Post-90s employees are self-centered, critical to others and publicize themselves, which are notable feature of adolescent egocentrism. With the development of complex meta-cognitive, youth can have a deeper introspection and self-awareness and these two characteristics will lead to high degree of self-centeredness. Adolescent egocentrism is the status of self-absorption; they think that the whole world is paying

attention to them; being self-centered and adolescent at the same time, they are full of the spirit of criticism to authority, are not willing to accept the criticism, and easy to point out others' errors in behavior [18] .

4) Demanding characteristics of post-90s employees. A large part of post-90s employees are born in one-child families, they have a favorable life conditions, and they are at the intersection of late puberty and early career stage; their demanding characteristics are complex in structure and level. From demanding structure point of view, on the one hand, they are in the early days of his career and have special demanding of friendship, care, attention, recognition, affirmation, growth, respect, independence, autonomy, self-expression, self-play. On the other hand, they are in a stage of loving and marriage, they need to communicate with the opposite sex, to be accepted, loved, and intimate contacted; their demanding have the characteristics of times, such as the electronic entertainment products (MP3, game consoles, digital cameras etc.), brand-name clothing, internet access and other significant consuming propensity.

5) Value characteristics of post-90s employees. a) With the development of China's market economy, competitive pressures and interest relationship are complex and changeable, so post-90 employees pay more attention to the real interests, pursue quality of life and like to live according to their own interest and way. b) With the development of Internet, the widespread use of mobile phones, especially popularity of mobile internet taking phone as the terminal, a massive information resources and autonomy creation network are provided for post-90 employees, which makes them vision-widened, well-informed, mentally-alerted, and pursue equal participation, freedom of expression and self-creation. c) With the continuous development of globalization, the western values continually clash with China traditional value, traditional moral values are weakened gradually, which makes post-90s pursue enjoyment, stimulation, and brand-name, evade struggle and ridicule simple. Because of the weak belief education in school and family, they are often in a confused spirit state and generally lack ideals and beliefs.

3.9. Working Characteristics of Post-90s Employees

1) Unclear career goals. Post-90 employees lack a clear career direction and goals, on one hand, they do not know what they can do, and they can not determine and identify their target positions in accordance with

their expectations, interests, and hobbies. They are unable to determine vocational learning and development plans. On the other hand they don't know economic and industrial structure and social position structure, moreover, they do not know the specific requirements of the knowledge skills, experience, toward different positions, there is no clear industry whereabouts and job goals of employment, their employment are full of contingency and blindness.

2) High working expectations. Post-90 employees were born in one-child families; their life conditions are favorable and live a free and happy life. They have high expectations towards their work and hope have professional skill to earn more money through working and want to have more time to rest, entertainment and learn. They want opportunities to self-express and self-shots and to be endorsed by the managers, and want excellent accommodation and living condition.

3) Unbalanced capacity development. Physical and mental development of post-90s employees is basically mature; they are energetic and agile; have flexible thinking, good memory, and strong ability to imitate. After the systematic skills training, they are able to quickly grasp the business knowledge and skills to meet the position needs in a short term, and being qualified to the task. They relatively lack of interpersonal communication skills, emotional management capacity, pressure regulating ability, conflict resolution capacity, wages disposable capacity and self-care ability, which results in their interpersonal relationships and mental health problems.

4) Un-strong working responsibility. Post-90s employees are self-centered, pursue their own comfort and freedom, lack of responsibility and professionalism to work, lack of love to work, especially lack of rigorous work attitude. In the course of their work, due to lack of concentration, negligence and un-strict implementation of operating procedures, operational errors, wrong materials using, quality issues, safety accidents frequently occur, many of which are major security incidents and quality accident.

5) Belonging sense missing. Post-90s employees engage in operation working in the grass-roots level of labor-intensive enterprises, they experience boring job content, long working hours, monotonous work, poor working conditions, lack cultural and recreational life, and they are under heavy work pressure; they experience mental and physical exhaustion, lack of care, recognition and praise from the enterprise support; they are difficult to approve and rely on corporate and corporate culture; they are full of the sense of loss to their enterprises; it

is difficult to produce a sense of dependence and a sense of belonging to enterprise for them.

6) Low enterprise loyalty. Workforce became a commodity; it has the nature of pursuing benefits and can maximize the own value through free exchange in the market, which has become a widely accepted talent concept. Workface market mechanisms, however, have a serious impact on the traditional concept of "Take plant as house; my honor prospers with plant" so that employees become more and more indifferent with enterprise loyalty. Post-90s employees change their jobs frequently, which seems to be a normal and natural thing; they generally lack the love to enterprise, ideology of enterprise loyalty; their feelings towards enterprise is weak; their corporate loyalty is very low; their first thought is to leave when encountering something goes wrong.

7) Extremely low job satisfaction. Post-90s employees pursue comfort, freedom, equality, love, performance and self-express, and they have a very high expectations towards their work, but in reality they do the dirtiest, most tired, most suffering and most monotonous work, what they earned has a big disparity with urban labor, coupling with lack of entertainment and cultural life, brutal and simple management of managers, they are full of loss and disgust towards work and their job satisfaction is low.

4. CHARACTERISTICS AND HARMS OF POST-90S EMPLOYEE'S INITIATIVE TURNOVER

4.1. Characteristics of Post-90s Employee's Initiative Turnover

4.1.1. High Initiative Turnover Rate

1) Post-90s rural migrant workers have a very high liquidity which seriously affects the employee turnover rate of post-90s employees. According to China's rural migrant workers survey and monitoring report in 2011 released by National Bureau of Statistics: the total rural migrant workers reached 25.278 million people in 2011; about 22.7% rural migrant workers engage in present work less than 1 year, 43.1% less than 1 - 2 years, 20.9% less than 3 - 5 years, the rural migrant workers among 16 - 20 years old engaged in present work more than five years accounted for 1.3%, which is far less than post-80s and post-

70s rural migrant workers' proportion: 7.6%, 22.3%, which fully explains that post-90s rural migrant workers have a very low stability, a high turnover rate and strong liquidity. According to a new generation migrant workers survey data by the studies ministry of the East China Normal University shows that [19] : the average turnover rate is 0.11 years of those who change their job most frequently. They change their job almost every month; the lowest turnover rate is average of 2 years who change their job least frequently, that is, their longest working time in the same enterprise is no more than 2 years. Average flow time interval within three months accounted for 17.6%; the interval among 3 months to 6 months accounts for 47.3%; the interval among 6 months to 9 months accounts for 18.6%; the interval among 9 months to 12 accounts for 13.8%; above data adequately shows that the new generation of migrant workers flows very frequently.

2) The author tracks company A in long-term, which is an electronic product manufacturing enterprises. Production workers account for 72.5% in company A, and more than 90% operating positions rely on manual labor with boring job content, a single working manner, average 6.5 days weekly work time, more than 10 hours work time a day. 65 hours weekly working time or more is more than the national statutory working time standard and it is a typical labor-intensive enterprises. Post-90s employees' initiative turnover rate is much higher than post-70' and post-90s' initiative turnover rate of Company A. Company A recruited 113 workers of post-90s in 2011, 89 resign initiatively, and initiative turnover rate reaches 78.76% , far higher than post-80s and post-70s' proportion of 21.67% and 17.14%, see Table 3. (Because of involving corporate trade secrets, company A's real name is hidden, if necessary, it can be obtained from the author.)

4.1.2. Initiative Turnover Fluctuates with Time

Post-90s employees' initiative turnover peak generally appears within three months after recruiting. Take A company as example, 89 person choose initiative turnover in 2011, of which 68 resigned within the first three months, accounting for 76.40% of the number of post-90s employees' turnover (see Table 4). Two peaks of initiative separation within 3 months after recruitment appear; the first peak appears in 2 - 3 weeks after recruitment; the other appears in 4 - 8 weeks after recruitment.

4.1.3. Initiative Turnover Manner Is in Group

Post-90s employees' initiative turnover manner is in group, generally they are leaded by one or a few employees with influence or inciting force and then their classmates, fellow and roommates begin to leave one after another, giving rise to mass initiative turnover, however, individual initiative turn is less.

4.2. Initiative Turnover Damage of Post-90s Employees

4.2.1. Increase Enterprise Operation Cost Greatly

Employees' initiative turnover will inevitably result in direct costs and indirect costs loss; the direct costs loss includes turnover costs, vacancy costs, replacement costs and training costs; the indirect costs loss includes the productivity cost losses, human resources productivity losses and the cost of new employee productivity loss [20] . The loss of indirect costs caused by an ordinary worker' initiative turnover is not very serious, but the mass turnover of post-90s employees in a short

Table 3. Statistical table of turnover of enterprise A in 2011.

Sequence	Staff category	Position	Recruiting numbers	Initiative turnover number	Initiative turnover rate
1	Post-90s	ordinary worker	113	89	78.76%
2	Post-80s	ordinary worker	120	26	21.67%
3	Post-70s	ordinary worker	35	6	17.14%

Table 4. Turnover table of post-90s employees in 2011 of enterprise A.

Sequence	Turnover number of whole year	Turnover time	Turnover number	Proportion
1	89	Within 30 days	35	39.33%
2	89	31 - 60 days	21	23.60%
3	89	61 - 90 days	12	13.48%
4	89	91 - 1230 days	9	10.11%
5	89	121 - 150 days	6	6.74%
6	89	151 - 180 days	2	2.25%
7	89	181 - 360 days	4	4.49%
Total	/	/	89	100.00%

term will result in an insufficiency of workers, machine halting to wait for workers and other serious problems, which has direct impact on the normal operations of enterprises, so the mass turnover of post-90s will caused enormous loss of indirect costs.

4.2.2. Cause Employees' Psychological Fluctuations and Impact Enterprise Operation Order

Post-90s employees' turnover is in mass, leading to rapid quantity reduction of workers in a short time, which not only causes employees' mass psychological fluctuations, disrupts production schedule, procurement plan, the materials plan, sales plan, personnel plan, and destructs the normal operation order of enterprises.

4.2.3. Cause Talents Fault and Human Resource Crises

Under the situation of "labor shortage" in China; labor supply is a serious problem; the shortage of production workers in labor-intensive enterprises is very serious, recruitment is very difficult; post-90s employees resign in mass quantity, which makes the worker shortage even worse, fault enterprise workers, triggers the crisis of corporate human resources and even endangers enterprise survival.

5. INITIATIVE TURNOVER ANALYSIS OF POST-90S EMPLOYEES

5.1. Initiative Turnover Dynamic Model of Post-90s Employees

The factors affecting employee turnover intention mainly include social factors, organizational factors and employee factors. Social factors include economic development level, employment policy, social security policy, workforce supply and demanding condition; organizational factors include enterprise culture, job characteristics, wage system, management manner, training support, interpersonal relationship; employee factors include intelligence, skills, experience, gender, interests, age, and expectations. Based on management practices, the writer proposes the turnover intervention factors, including improving and optimizing work environment, increasing wages, and reshaping the corporate culture, enhancing the quality of cadres, changing management mode, providing mental health help, introduction of career management, improvement of the incentive mechanism; based on this, the traditional turnover model is improved; post-90s employees initiative turnover dynamic model is constructed (Figure 1); and post-90s initiative turnover process is divided into four stages: working stage, working comprehensive evaluation stage, initiative turnover intention formation stage and initiative turnover behavior stage, this division provides operating space for the enterprises' implementation of turnover intervention. If enterprise obtain information of employees towards work in time, and evaluate, determine turnover intervention target, take targeted turnover interventions measures and block initiative turnover intention formation, they can effectively reduce the initiative turnover rate of post-90s.

5.2. Strategy of Staff Level

As mentioned before, post-90s employees are born in one-child family, along with the dramatic social transformation of China, grew up with the development and popularization of high-speed internet and globalization, they are now in the intersection point of late adolescence and career exploring stage, and they have distinct groups characteristics and brand of the times. Their psychological quality, ability level, view of value, the structure of demand, job expectations, sense of responsibility, a sense of belonging, corporate loyalty and work satisfaction, etc. are significantly different from what of the 80 employees and 90 employees, this significant group characteristics (Table 5) have an important impact on employees' initiative turnover.

Post-90s employees' career development goals are not clear, development of the working ability is uneven, work expectations are too high, their psychology is fragile, their social relations are lacked, sense of corporate belonging is missing, corporate loyalty is low, which all lead post-90s' initiative turnover.

5.3. Strategy of Enterprise Level

Although post-90 employees have received junior high school, technical school or equivalent education, but their educational level and the skill level are still low, the scope of their employment is mainly concentrated in labor-intensive industries of the secondary and tertiary industries; and manufacturing accumulate the most.

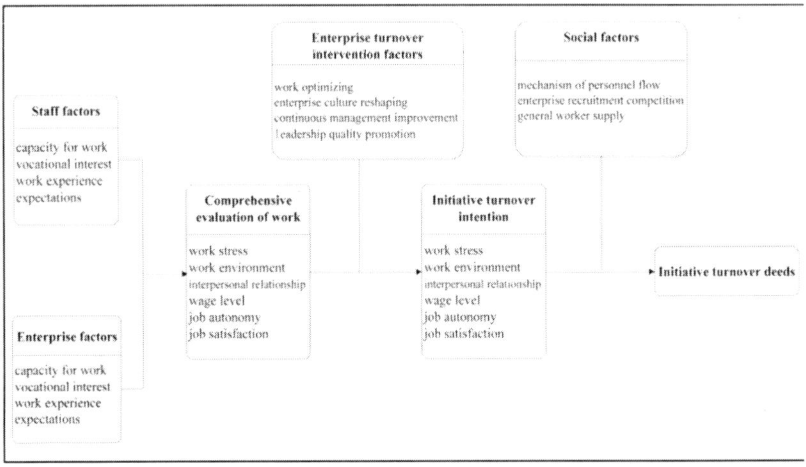

Figure 1. Dynamic model of post-90s initiative turnover.

5.3.1. Work and Working Conditions

Post-90s employees work on the grassroots operation jobs in labor-intensive enterprises, mainly manual labor, with a poor working conditions, long working hours, monotonous work content, and high labor intensity. a) Working conditions are poor. Labor-intensive enterprises have many problems in the work environment, such as noise, radiation, toxic substances, glass fiber, grinding dust, heat and humidity etc. which not only endanger the health of employees, but also are the major obstacle for employees to adapt to enterprise. b) Working time is long. They work five days a week, eight hours a day, working 40 hours a week, which is our current legal system of working hours. But the working hours of the most labor-intensive enterprises are far more than the statutory working time, which seriously consume the physical fitness of the employees, causing extreme physiological and psychological fatigue. c) Working content is dull. Positions of labor-intensive enterprises operating mainly manual labor work, employees repeat the same work in the same environment for a long time; they can not feel the fun and freedom of life, which easily lead to psychological attrition and aggravate frustration and disgust. d) Labor intensity is high. Many grassroots jobs in labor-intensive enterprises have physical requirements, plus the daily working time of about 10 hours and high working intensive, which may overdraft employees' energy.

Table 5. Comparison table of characteristics of post-90s, post-80s and post-70s.

Comparison item	Employee style	Post-70s	Post-80s	Post-90s
Basic situation	Date of birth	1970-1979 year	1980-1989 year	1990-1995 year
	Age level	32 - 41 years old	22 - 31 years old	16 - 21 years old
	Career Stage	Middle stage of career	Early stage of career	Exploration stage of career
	Family role	Main strength of family	Most are married and have baby	Most are single
	Family burden	Burden is heavy	Burden is relatively heavy	Burden is not heavy
Mental characteristics	Emotional state	Mature, stable, rational	Relatively mature, stable, emotion	Quick mood change
	Pressure adjustment	Self-adjustment, patience, acceptance	Can self-adjust and release pressure	Don't know how to release pressure
	Interpersonal communication	Experienced and good at communication	Can communicate smoothly	Lack of experience and have many hinders
	Characteristics of demand	Emphasize wage and resection	High salary and in a good mood	Emphasize mental feelings and high salary
	Values	Diligence, frugality, patience	emphasize interest, eager to be respected	Equality, freedom, and be comfort
Working characteristics	Working expectation	Safe, stable and high income	Higher wages, pleasant atmosphere	Easy, free, have the development
	Career goal	Clear goal	Clear goal, but have some confusion	Unclear goal, confusion
	Job responsibility	Professional, responsible and conscientious	Responsible and relative conscientious	Weak sense of responsibility, drifts along
	Job involvement	Devoted and initiative	Enthusiastic and relatively initiative	Lack of entrepreneur spirit and devotion
	Job satisfaction	Mostly satisfied	Relative satisfied and helpless	Low degree of satisfaction and full of disappointment
	Enterprise belonging	Have feeling and strong sense of belonging	Position and relatively strong sense of belonging	Lack of position and sense of belonging
	Enterprise loyalty	High loyalty	Relative high loyalty and quit sometimes	Lack of loyalty
	Occupational stability	High stability	Relative stability and quit sometime	Poor stability and quit at any time

5.3.2. Enterprise Culture Analysis

1) Lack of humanistic care. Labor-intensive enterprises' competitive advantage is cheap workforce; employees in the enterprises play a role of the "working tools"; tool features dominates; subjectivity of person has been ignored to a large extent; the interests of enterprises over-encroach the interests of employees and extrude life time of staff; corporate culture is cold and ruthless and lacks of care, resection, cherishing and support for employees.

2) Lack of cultural life. Restricted by characterizes and management levels of manual labor, main approach of labor-intensive enterprises to complete production tasks is working overtime; under the guidance of the core values, pursuing corporate profit maximization, close working arrangements, high-speed pace of work and endless overtime all encroaches the staff cultural life time, which leads to the shortage of employee culture life.

3) Lack of fairness. Most labor-intensive enterprises are not standardized in management; many enterprises adopt "rule of man" mode; bosses are the masters, and promotion of employees and wage adjustments are casual and often decouple with contribution responsibilities and skill level. Internal corporate lacks of fair and equity.

5.3.3. Human Resource Management Analysis

1) Personnel management is not standardized. There are many illegal problems in the area of personnel management in Labor-intensive enterprises, such as, working hours excesses of the statutory standards, overtime pay is not in accordance with the statutory standard, payment is defaulted, social insurance is unpaid, there is no system of annual vacation, labor contracts are ignored, labor protection products are insufficient and occupational disease examination is lacked.

2) Employee management mode is simple. Grass roots supervisor of labor-intensive enterprises are charged by senior staff, and they are experienced, proficient, have a strong sense of responsibility, but they are lack of the education and management knowledge, their management mode is simple, and mainly in requesting and commanding. Some supervisors even publicly abusive employees, which is easy to dampen the enthusiasm of the staff, resulting in employee psychological conflict and leading to strained relations between managers and employees.

3) Lack of psychological health education. Employees' psychological health education in China started relatively late. After the Foxconn employees' jumping events, several labor-intensive enterprises begun to introduce employees assistance of psychology (EAP) to provide psychological healthy education and psychological assistance, but generally, labor-intensive enterprises employees' psychological health education are missing.

4) Lack of career development and planning. Human resource management level of labor-intensive enterprises is generally low, employee career development and management is simply limited to knowledge and skills training; enterprises are lack of systematic employee career planning and management; employees training system is not sufficient to support the career development demand and it lacks of personnel incentives mechanism and career development channels.

5) Employee incentive mechanism is not perfect. Labor-intensive enterprises generally take wage as the main incentive; incentive mode is single, employee incentive is not combined with acknowledgement demand, honor demand, achievement demand, and career development demand effectively; they can incentive employees for a long time and in diversified style.

5.4. Social Environment Factors Analysis

5.4.1. The Impact of Supply and Demand of Workforce in Market on

As a commodity in the talent market, workforce is bound to be affected by the impact of supply and demand in market. Under the situation of nationwide "workforce shortage", a large number of employment opportunities appear in the market, but ordinary workers supply is in serious shortage, which accelerates post-90s employees' initiative turnover.

5.4.2. The Impact of Enterprise Competition on Initiative Turnover

Labor-intensive enterprises' core competitiveness is cheap workforce, that is, the ordinary worker. Under the situation of a serious shortage of ordinary workers, the enterprises continue to increase wages to attract more ordinary workers to meet their production needs; which objectively facilitated post-90s initiative turnover.

6. POST-90S EMPLOYEES' INITIATIVE TURNOVER MANAGEMENT STRATEGY

6.1. Strategy of Staff Level

6.1.1. Carry out Psychological Health Education

Proceed from the mental characters and real mental problem, hold mental healthy knowledge lecture, help staff realize these problems such as work pressure, international relationship, career development, Internet dependency and job burnout etc., guide staff how to cope with stress, manage mood, resolve interpersonal conflict, communicate effectively, face Accident Work Injury, help staff to improve coping capacity of mental quality and mental problem, foster and improve staff's mental capital. If condition allows, enterprises can buy EAP (employee assistance plan) service to provide professional mental welfare.

6.1.2. Enforce Professional Ethics Education of Staff

In the process of staff management and education, Set model or lead by outstanding staff, enforce to foster staff' professional ethics, love spirit of staff to enterprise and responsible attitude toward work, enforce their acknowledgement and independency to enterprise culture, foster staff's Enterprise belonging and loyalty.

6.1.3. Make the Best Use of the Circumstances So As to Develop Informal Organization

Establish informal organization such as "woodpecker group", "golden idea group", "film group", "basketball team", "Wei Chi group" and so on to provide platform for employees' autonomy and creativity. Informal organization takes autonomous management mode which is good for employee to participate in enterprises' management activities, develop good interpersonal relationship, and experience a strong sense of belonging and achievement, which plays an important role in guaranteeing staff's mental health.

6.2. Strategies in Enterprise Level

6.2.1. Improve the Working Environment

1) Improve the hard working environment.

The hard environmental improvement, such as lighting, ventilation, dust removal facilities, security facilities, can reduce the work pressure, improve the working comfort, and reduce employee initiative turnover rate; it has great significance. Working environment design of labor-intensive enterprise is easy to fall into the mistaken region: task-centered environment, that is, environmental design pursuits of clean and order, but lost the human caring and interactive elements, therefore, enterprises should pay attention to hard environmental improvement, create a comfortable, safe, sanitary, and clean work environment through the optimization of light, temperature, humidity, noise, color, items placement through the research on the nature of work, job content and psychology and physiological features.

2) Optimize the soft working environment.

Working design optimization can make employees get encouragement and a sense of achievement, thereby reducing the initiative turnover rate. Following three measures can be accepted for working design: job rotation, job enrichment and job enlargement. Job rotation, employees can feel the freshness of the work through job rotation, so they can acquire more skills, and get more understanding of different work and improve collaboration capabilities. Job enrichment, diversification of job content and responsibility level changes can enhance the participation of the employees into work, which is the longitudinal expansion of job. Job enlargement, job expansion can make employees to take on more tasks, which is the horizontal expansion of the job, and it will give employees a greater sense of accomplishment.

6.2.2. Remodel Enterprise Culture

1) Remodel a people-oriented enterprise culture. Enterprises have to attach importance on fundamental role of people in the process of management, adequately consider the employee's personality and individuality, respect, concern and care every employee; build a culture atmosphere of equality, friend, mutual assistance in the enterprise; pay attention to foster employee's professional ethics quality; improve employees' vocational ability and foster a people-oriented enterprise culture.

2) Improve leaders' management quality. Strengthen the leadership cadres; train leading cadres to take virtues as first, treat workers as people, respect, care for, train each employee, closely combine the enterprise development with employee training; train a large number of management and technical personnel with good ethics and innovation awareness, and promote the sustained and healthy development of the enterprise.

3) Actively carry out cultural activities. a) Hold enterprise culture activities, such as employee sports meeting, karaoke ok contest, photography contest, staff birthday party etc.; create a environment of self-expression, actively participation and help with each other, allowing employees to enjoy the entertainment and to be respected. b) Organize all kinds of knowledge contest, skill contest, experience exchange meeting, book reports meeting, case seminars and other activities to accelerate the cross-sector spreading, integration and innovation of knowledge; improve employees' knowledge attainment; foster a organizational culture of love learning. c) Start outstanding deeds report, model figures learning activities, seminars and other activities in organizations; train staff to have professional ethics of dedication, honesty and trustworthiness.

6.2.3. Change Employees' Management Manner

Strengthen the training of grassroots management quality; help them to properly understand the psychological characteristics of the post-90s employees, reflect the shortcomings of the previous command-style management, guide them to change the management style; focus on training employees' moral character and professional competence; give employees opportunity to involve in the management; give employee the space self-management; defuse employees' resentment to management and greater exert their initiative and creativity.

6.2.4. Build Occupation Career Development System

Concerning post-90s' low vocational ability, fragile psychology, communication skills, set a step-by-step career development goal and clarify their career development promotion channel and criteria; develop a set of training courses; provide vocational mentoring system; finish career development plan through on-the-job training and combine with full-time training; build employees' career development files; records and track the various stages of the employees' level of skills, psychological quality and development of professional qualities.

6.2.5. Build Targeted Incentive Mechanism

Concerning post-90s employees, from their demand characteristics and career development stage goal, based on refining enterprises' existing payment incentive mode, design incentive mechanism; increase emotional motivation, respect motivation, example motivation, honor motivation and achievement motivation; actively explore the enterprise culture incentive mode; constantly improve the incentive system; combine long-term incentives with short-term incentive; in the incentive process fully consider the personality characteristics of incentives target; maximize avoid random incentive for leaders.

7. CONCLUSIONS

Post-90 employee is a special labor group; the quantity is large; and they are widely distributed among all walks of life due to the industry characteristics and difference of enterprise management mode. Post-90s employees have characteristics of complexity and diversity; this paper takes labor-intensive enterprises as an example to study the post-90s employee initiative turnover, proposes turnover intervening variables which affect initiative turnover of employees, constructs dynamic model of post-90s employees initiative turnover, provides theoretical guidance for enterprises, deep analyzes the reason of post-90s employees' initiative turnover from the staff level, the corporate level, the social level, and proposes enterprises turnover management strategy.

The drawback of this paper is that it is difficult to fully reflect a picture of post-90s employees' turnover, and the turnover intervention strategies mentioned has certain industry limitations. At the same time post-90s employees are growing and new joined employees have higher education level; their employment scopes are broader and the occupation is not limited to the operation, so the initiative turnover of post-90s employee is becoming increasingly complex, which needs continuing research by managers and researchers to put forward a more effective response.

REFERENCES

1. Mobley, W.H. (1977) Intermediate Linkages in the Relationship between Job Satisfaction and Employee Turnover. Journal of Applied Psychology, 62, 237-240.
2. Zeffane, R.M. (1994) Understanding Employee Turnover: The Need for a Contingency Approach. International Journal of Manpower, 15, 22-38.
3. Quarles, R. (1994) An Empirical Examination of a Model of the Turnover Intentions of Information Systems Auditors. Journal of Applied Business Research, 10, 73-86.
4. Iverson, R.D. (1999) An Event History Analysis of Employee Turnover: The Case of Hospital Employees in Australia. Human Resource Management Review, 4, 397-418.
5. Wang, Y.Q. and Ye, R.S. (2000) An Analysis with Game Model on the Turnover of Enterprises' Employees. System Engineering Press, Beijing.
6. Fu, Y.Q., Ling, W.Q. and Fang, L.L. (2002) An Analysis with Game Model on the Turnover of Enterprises' Employees. China Labor, 7, 23.
7. Liu, Y., Lin, Q.D. and Ling, W.Q. (2006) Analyses and Suggestions of the Influencing Factor of the State-Owned Enterprise Employee Turnover Tendency. Jiangsu Commercial Forum, 4, 129.
8. Mobley, W.H. (1982) Employee Turnover: Causes, Consequences, and Control. Addision Wesley Publishing Company, New York.
9. Price, J.L. and Mueller, C.W. (1981) A Causal Model of Turnover for Nurses. Academy of Manatement Journal, 24, 543-565.
10. Price, J.L. (1977) The Study of Turnover. Iowa State University Press, Ames.
11. Mobley, W.H. (1977) Intermediate Linkages in the Relationship between Job Satisfaction and Employee Turnover. Journal of Applied Psychology, 62, 238.

12. Sheridan, J.E. and Ahelson, M.A. (1983) Cusp Catastrophe Model of Employee Turnover. Academy of Management Journal, 26, 418-436.

13. Hom, P.W. and Griffeth, R.W. (1991) Structural Equations Modeling Test of a Turnover Theory: Cross Seletional and Longitudinal Analyses. Journal of Applied Psychology, 76, 350-366.

14. Beach, L.R. (1990) Image Theory: Decision Making, in Personal and Organizational Contexts. Wiley, New York.

15. Lee, T.W. and Mitchell, T.R. (1994) An Alternative Approach: The Unfolding Model of Turnover. Academy of Management Review, 19, 51-89.

16. Donnelly, D.P. and Quirin, J.J. (2006) An Extension of Lee and Mitchell's Unfolding Model of Voluntary Turnover. Journal of Organizational Behavior, 27, 59-77.

17. Zheng, X.Y. (2010) Research on the Incentives of Post-90s Employees in China Labor-intensive Enterprise. Wuhan University of Science and Technology, Wu Han.

18. Feldman, R.S. (2011) Developmental Psychology: Explore the Life Development Track. China Machine Press, Beijing.

19. Fu, P. and Tang, Y.C. (2009) Inverted "U" Type Trajectory and New Generation of Rural Workers' Social Mobility. Zhejiang Social Sciences, 12, 43.

20. Zhou, Y. (2009) Enterprise Human Resources Turnover Cost and Control Strategy. Human Resource Management, 11, 128.

14

CHAPTER

Empirical Research on the Relationship among Sense of Control, Control Demand and Job Burnout

Caihong Zhang, Chunlan Li, Fengshuo Feng

Management School, Jinan University, Guangzhou, China

ABSTRACT

Based on the literature research, the paper proposes a relational model of sense of control, control demand and job burnout. A questionnaire survey is conducted on the enterprise employees, and 362 valid questionnaires are collected, finally using the SPSS19.0 software to analyze the collected data. The results show that 1) sense of control and control demand are correlated; 2) sense of control has a significant negative impact on the three dimensions of job burnout (exhaustion, cynicism and inefficacy); 3) control demand has significant effects on job burnout.

Keywords: Sense of Control, Control Demand, Job Burnout

1. INTRODUCTION

"Job burnout" was first proposed by USA clinical psychologist Frudenberger [1] in 1974. This word is used to describe the negative psychological symptoms of individual experience in the service industry and medical field. Job burnout phenomenon not only exists in the field of emotional work such as medical service, but also becomes a universal social phenomenon. With the development of society and economy, people's life and work pressure are increasing, when employees lack of organizational support, and can't be timely distracted from their own negative emotions, job burnout may occur.

Maslach & Jackson definite the job burnout as a physiological, psychological multi dimension comprehensive symptom, which is composed of exhaustion, cynicism and inefficacy [2] . The three dimensions of job burnout have interaction relationship: inefficacy is the pre-influence factor of cynicism and exhaustion, and the cynicism and exhaustion influence each other (Zhang Yongwang [3] , 2012). Burnout has a negative influence on the employee's work efficiency, interpersonal relationship and health of body.

There are many factors leading to job burnout. Maslach, Schaufeli and Leiter (2001) proposed job matching theory that employees matched the lower degree of mismatch between the person and six domains (workload, control, remuneration, social activities, fairness and values), the more easily they prone to job burnout [4] . The existing researches mainly focus on the following aspects: workload, remuneration, social activities, fairness and values; however, there are a few researches on the relationship between control and job burnout.

Job control is the ability of staff to better handle the work environment. Research shows that sense of control is higher, the environment is more beneficial for employees (Ngo [5] , 2005). At the same time, control demand also affects employees' perceptions of job control, and the extent of employees' control demand is different. This paper is based on an empirical research to explore the relationship among sense of control, control demand and job burnout.

2. LITERATURE REVIEW AND HYPOTHESIS

Schaubroeck (1997) argues that job control refers to a job can give their employees the degree of sufficient autonomy, let employees feel the work under their control [6] . The sense of control as an important psychological resource to maintain a balanced state of mind, its strength decides whether the individual can actively improve their situation (Manne & Glassman [7] , 1998). Research shows that, lack of autonomy and loss of control sense will make the job pressure increase, especially in collectivistic culture, low sense of control and high sense of pressure are particularly obvious. Furthermore, overwhelming job pressure will lead to job burnout and even turnover. Siu & Cooper (1998) also find that when the job control falls, the employees will get lower job satisfaction, and show a higher turnover intention, also prone to anxiety, depression and other psychological symptoms [8] . Schaubroeck finds that in high demand environment, lack of control sense is especially harmful to the high self-efficacy people, because of uncontrollable situation may change the individual agent cognitive [6] . Jia Tao (2007) investigates the clinical nurses find that, when job control sense is in the low level, the nurse's job satisfaction is low neither, and it isn't beneficial to the realization of high quality of nursing service [9] . Liu Liquan's (2007) research on the teachers' burnout shows that job control is psychological intermediary variable between teachers' work pressure sources and job burnout, high work pressure and low job control are the psychological mechanism of job burnout [10] .

Based on the analysis above, this paper puts forward the following hypothesis:

H1. Sense of control has a negative correlation with job burnout;

H1a. Sense of control has a negative correlation with exhaustion;

H1b. Sense of control has a negative correlation with cynicism;

H1c. Sense of control has a negative correlation with inefficacy.

Maslow defines that demand is the person's feeling of some basic survival state be denied [11] . And control demand is the psychological desire and psychological tendency on controlling external things development. Karasek's (1979) "job demand-control model" points out that working scene demand and the decision freedom of facing these demand have directly effect on staffs' body tension [12] . Deci et al. (1989) study the influence factors of employees' psychological needs, and find that employees self-psychological needs significantly affected by managers' leadership style, the support worker autonomy style of leadership is conducive to enhance the employees' intrinsic motivation, and make employees produce lasting performance and good mental state, on the contrary, the employees' autonomy demand can't be met, their work motivation and work enthusiasm will be significantly reduced, and there's a negative impact on employee work efficiency sense [13] . Klaus & Helmut (2007) research on the relationship of self-control demand, cognitive control disorders and burnout, and discover that cognitive control disorders act as a regulatory role in the relationship between self-control demand and burnout, at the same time, self-control demand and cognitive control disorders have significant correlation with exhaustion and cynicism [14] .

Based on the analysis above, this paper puts forward the following hypothesis:

H2. Control demand has a correlation with job burnout;

H2a. Control demand has a correlation with exhaustion;

H2b. Control demand has a correlation with cynicism;

H2c. Control demand has a correlation with inefficacy.

Current researches about control focus on the sense of control, but pay a little attention to control demand in the process. Liu Liquan (2007) researches on teachers' job burnout and finds that teachers describe their sense of control related of their control demand in the initial interview. Then sense of control and control demand are the two dimensions of the job control experience [10] . Ma Jianhong and Zhang Tingwen (1999) define the job control experience as the process of influencing and deciding the external things development in the work, the psychological cognition and evaluation process on the control requirement of working environment and individual behaviors, and their own conditions either meet the control demand [15] . Employee control demand influences on sense of control degree, and on the other hand, the sense of control degree will boost the control demand extent. Since the lack of research on the control demand, this paper puts forward the following hypothesis and will prove it by empirical research:

H3. Sense of control has a significant correlation with control demand.

Through the above analysis, this paper puts forward the theoretical model, as shown in Figure 1.

3. RESEARCH METHODOLOGIES

3.1. Research Sample

This research data mainly acquired through two ways: the mail and on-site questionnaire. In this survey, 450 questionnaires are distributed, 395 are recovered, and the recovery rate is 87.8%. Remove the duplicate and incomplete questionnaire, there are 362 valid questionnaires, and effective rate is 91.7%. The survey sample comes from different industry employee, including education, consulting, manufacturing, computer, financial industry and so on. The staff level distribution is as follows, 279 general staff, accounting for 77.1%, 47 first- line managers, accounting for 13%, 29 middle managers, accounting for 8%, and top managers is 7, accounting for 1.9%. The ratio of male and female is 163:199. The sample education contains high school diploma and below 156, college diploma 38, bachelor degree 114, master degree or above 54.

3.2. Measurement Tools

In this study, the job burnout scale used is revised by Li Chao according to MBI-GS scale, the scale includes 3 subscales, namely exhaustion, cynicism and inefficacy, respectively contain 5, 4 and 6 items, job burnout with 7 grade Likert scale, 1 represents never, 2 represents several times a year or less, 3 represents one time a month or less, 4 represents several times a month, 5 represents one time a week, 6 represents several times a week, 7 represents everyday. Sense of control and control demand questionnaire use control experience scale which compiled by Ma Jianhong, with 5 levels Likert scale: 1 totally inconsistent to 5 fully consistent.

Job burnout and control experience scale's reliability and validity in the existing studies are validated. In this paper, after using z-score standardization method to handle the collected data, the internal consistency coefficient of job burnout scale is 0.847 and internal consistency coefficients of each dimension (exhaustion, cynicism and inefficacy) are 0.860, 0.880 and 0.906. The internal consistency coefficient of control experience scale is 0.874, sense of control and control demand's internal consistency coefficient respectively are 0.852 and 0.744. The reliability of each scale is larger than 0.7, which means that the research data obtained has good reliability.

3.3. Procedure

This paper tests the reliability of the questionnaire through reliability analysis, and uses correlation analysis method to analyze the correlation between sense of control, control demand and job burnout, finally explores the linear relationship between variables by linear regression analysis.

4. DATA ANALYSIS AND RESULTS

4.1. Correlation analysis of variables

Using SPSS19.0 to analyze the correlation, as table 1 shows, we can see that the correlation coefficient between sense of control and three dimensions of job burnout (exhaustion, cynicism and inefficacy) are −0.256, −0.278 and −0.447, namely there are a significantly negative correlation in $P < 0.01$ level. Likewise, control demand has a significantly negative correlation with three dimensions of job burnout at the level of $P < 0.01$, the correlation coefficient respectively are −0.135, −0.152, −0.332. Sense of control and control demand exist a significantly positive correlation in the level of $P < 0.01$, and the correlation coefficients 0.598.

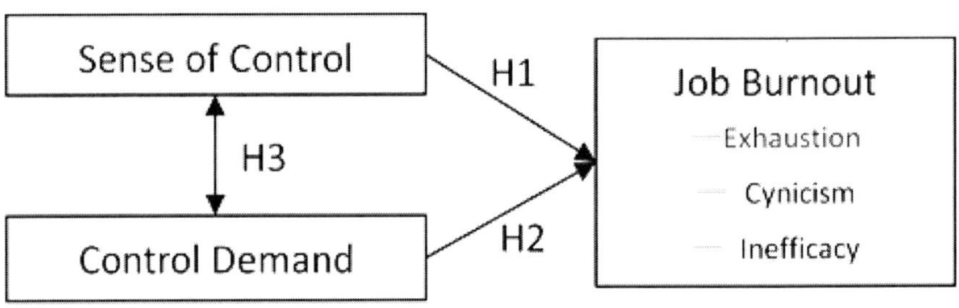

Figure 1. Theoretical model.

Table 1. Correlations.

	Exhaustion	Cynicism	Inefficacy	Sense of control	Control demand
Exhaustion	1				
Cynicism	0.627**	1			
Inefficacy	−0.023	0.090	1		
Sense of control	−0.256**	−0.278**	−0.447**	1	
Control demand	−0.135**	−0.152**	−0.332**	0.598**	1

**P < 0.01.

4.2. Regression Analysis

In order to better explore the effect of control experience on job burnout, so this study investigates the main effect of control sense and control demand on job burnout by linear regression. In regression analysis, respectively using the three dimensions of job burnout (exhaustion, cynicism and inefficacy) as the dependent variable, the two dimension control experience (sense of control and control demand) as independent variables. Form table 2, we know that sense of control and three dimensions of job burnout both exist significant negative correlation in $P < 0.01$ level, and the regression coefficients are −0.312, −0.357 and −0.456. Namely the sense of control is higher, the exhaustion, cynicism and inefficacy are lower, therefore assume that H1a, H1b and H1c set up. However, the results of regression analysis between control demand and three dimensions of burnout are not significant, and indicate that the control demand has no significant linear relationship with exhaustion, cynicism and inefficacy.

5. CONCLUSION AND SUGGESTION

5.1. Conclusion

Through empirical research, this paper examines the relationship among sense of control, control demand and job burnout. And we get the following main conclusions. First, sense of control has a negative correlation with three dimensions (exhaustion, cynicism and inefficacy) of job burnout, and shows that when the employees have higher sense of control, they are less prone to work fatigue. Second, control demand significantly correlates with exhaustion, cynicism and inefficacy, but there's no significant linear relationship among them; then it suggests that there's no direct relationship between the control demand and job burnout. Probably it has indirect effects on job burnout through other factors. Third, there is a significant relationship between sense of control and control demand, namely the employees' perception degree of control affected by their control demand.

5.2. Suggestion

In order to prevent and reduce enterprise employees' job burnout, the enterprises need to provide a good working environment for staffs, and give them the appropriate work autonomy. When employees' sense of control is in a high level, they will feel the work more meaningful, and the perception of pressure is smaller, so as to enhance the employees' sense of self-efficacy and efficiency. Therefore, the organization authorization is necessary to prevent employee burnout and achievement decline, and improve the efficiency of the staff and organization.

Table 2. Regression analysis result.

Model	Exhaustion		Cynicism		Inefficacy	
	β	Sig	β	Sig	β	Sig
Sense of control	−0.312	0.000	−0.357	0.000	−0.456	0.000
Control demand	0.031	0.665	0.027	0.772	−0.118	0.086

Caihong Zhang, Chunlan Li, Fengshuo Feng (16,17)">16] . Therefore, giving employees necessary organizational support is the effective way to increase employees' sense of control.

REFERENCES

1. Frudenberger, H.J. (1974) Staff Burnout. Journal of Social Issue, 30, 59-65.
2. Maslach, C., Jackson, S.E. and Leiter, M.P. (1996) The Maslach Burnout Inventory: Manual. Consulting Psychologist Press, Palo Alto.

3. Zhang, Y.W. (2012) Research on Model Construction of Job Burnout Development Process. Journal of Hubei University of Economics: Humanities and Social Sciences, 8, 73-75.
4. Maslach, C., Schaufeli, W.B. and Leiter, M.P. (2001) Job Burnout. Annual Review of Psychology, 52, 397-422.
5. Ngo, A. and Murphy, S. (2005) A Theory Based Intervention to Improve Nurses' Knowledge, Self-Efficacy, and Skills to Reduce PICC Occlusion. Journal of Infusion Nursing, 28, 173-181.
6. Manne, S. and Glassman, M. (1998) Perceived Control, Coping Efficacy, and Avoidance Coping as Mediators between Spouses' Unsupportive Behaviors and Cancer Patients, Psychological Distress. Health Psychology, 19, 155-164.
7. Siu, O.L. and Cooper, C.L. (1998) A Study of Occupational Stress, Job Satisfaction and Quitting Intention in Hong Kong Firms: The Role of Locus of Control and Organizational Commitment. Stress Medicine, 14, 55-66.
8. Schaubroeck, J. and Merritt, D.E. (1997) Divergent Effects of Job Control on Coping with Work Stressors: The Key Role of Self-Efficacy. Academy of Management Journal, 40, 738-754.
9. Jia, T. (2007) Analysis of Work Empowerment Effected on Clinical Nurses' Self-Efficacy and Job Control. Sichuan University School of Medicine, Sichuan.
10. Liu, L.Q. (2007) Study on the Relationship between Preschool Teachers Work Stress, Job Control Experience and Work Exhaustion. Shanxi University, Shanxi.
11. Maslow, A.H. (1943) A Theory of Human Motivation. Psychological Review, 50, 370-396.
12. Karaske, R.A. (1979) Job Demand, Job Decision Latitude and Metal Strain: Implications for Job Redesign. Administrative Science Quarterly, 24, 285-308.
13. Deci, E.L., Connell, J.P. and Ryan, R.M. (1989) Self-Determination in a Work Organization. Journal of Applied Psychology, 74, 580-590.
14. Schmidt, K.-H., et al. (2007) Self-Control Demands, Cognitive Control Deficits, and Burnout. Work & Stress, 21, 142- 154.

15. Ma, J.H. and Zhang, T.W. (1999) Analysis of the Relationship between the Role Perception, Sense of Control and Working Pressure. Ergonomics, 5, 15-19.

16. Li, J.B., Xu, B.H. and Zuo, W.H. (2006) Analysis of Organizational Contextual Factors Affect Job Burnout Formation. China Journal of Clinical Psychology, 14, 146-149.

15

CHAPTER

A Review of Researches on Sleepiness at Workplace

Xiang Jiao, Maolin Ye

School of Management, Jinan University, Guangzhou, China

ABSTRACT

Sleepiness at workplace, the biological drive to sleep, has a highly negative impact on employees' working behavior in organizations. Recently, this phenomenon has attached more and more attention in the management filed; and it has attracted much attention of researchers from other fields, such as management and psychology. By reviewing and analyzing the previous studies, this paper clarifies the concepts of sleepiness in the workplace, and then delineates the causes and effects of sleepiness in the workplace. Through the organizational understanding of the relevant causes of sleepiness, some intervention measures which can mitigate companies' sleepiness situation will be put forward. Finally, the paper has an outlook about the future researches of sleepiness at workplace.

Keywords: Sleepiness at Workplace, Job Performance, Accident Rate, Job Rotation

1. INTRODUCTION

Nowadays, management and psychology have expanded its focus on the impact of non-work variables on job performance, and especially on the relationship of sleep and job performance. As we all know, adults spend most of their time on work and sleep, but there is little exploration of the relationship between these two. In recent years, scholars in the field of management and applied psychology have gradually focused on the relationship between sleep and work, and conducted some empirical researches. These studies show that the most common sleep problem is the phenomenon of sleepiness. That is, whenever and wherever, it is accompanied by a desperate desire to sleep. Sleepiness seems to be a simple concept, but if it occurs in the workplace, then it will lead to lots of negative effects. For example, when driving, the driver will cause a serious traffic accident due to sleepiness; in the steel industry, workers can also cause serious accidents because of sleepiness. However, in China, scholars only explored the effects of sleep restriction and sleep deprivation on the body from the perspective of clinical medicine, such as, their impact on the human nervous system, immune system, and biochemical indicators [1] . And few scholars discuss the influence of sleep problems in workplace on work results. Therefore, it is necessary to comprehensively outline the domestic and international researches on sleepiness at workplace, which is of great practical and theoretical significance. By reviewing and analyzing the previous studies, this paper will clarify the concepts of sleepiness in the workplace, and then delineate the causes and effects of sleepiness in the workplace. Through the organizational understanding of the relevant causes of sleepiness, some intervention measures which mitigate companies' sleepiness situation will be put forward. Finally, the paper has an outlook about the future researches of sleepiness at workplace.

2. SLEEPINESS DEFINED

Throughout the research history of sleepiness, the concept has not yet formed a unified conclusion. In the most basic sense, researchers adopted Dement and Carskadon perspectives that sleepiness can be defined as "a craving or desire for sleep" [2] . Recently, the meta-analysis of sleep issue showed that the sleepiness included difficulties to wake up, problems to stay awake and falling asleep during daytime [3] . For the working people, the occurrence of sleepiness depends on sleep quality, sleep duration, the circadian rhythms, and substances and CNS disorders. Therefore, Sleepiness can be defined as a phenomenon of desperate desire to sleep resulted from poor sleep quality, shortened sleep duration, the disordered circadian rhythm and the factors that act on the central nervous system [4] .

This paper will combine the previous researches about the definitions of sleepiness with the unique field of workplace, and then come to the concept of sleepiness at workplace. That is, sleepiness at workplace is a phenomenon of desperate desire to sleep resulted from sleep lacking, poor sleep quality. And this paper will review and analysis the previous studies about sleepiness based on the above concepts.

2.1. Sleepiness and Narcolepsy

Narcolepsy and sleepiness at workplace have the essential differences in terms of definition, and so can't be confused. Narcolepsy is a neurological disorder, neither caused by sleep lacking, drugs, alcohol, somatic diseases, or it is a mental disorder symptoms. The peak of its incidence is at the age of 10, its characteristic symptoms include excessive daytime sleepiness, cataplexy and skeletal muscle paralysis [5] . At present, the medical profession generally believe that the narcolepsy maybe caused by genetic and environmental factors, including pressure. But the specific mechanism is not clear, and there is no cure method. The workplace sleepiness is simply the increase of sleep tendency at work, and it is not very serious compared with narcolepsy. In addition, the reasons of sleepiness are more specific, such as: sleep duration, the circadian rhythms, and substances and CNS disorders. Finally, a good sleep habit and regular nap can slow down the condition of sleepiness.

2.2. Sleepiness and Fatigue

The meanings of fatigue and sleepiness are very confusing, and the research time about fatigue is earlier than sleepiness. Some articles made clear distinctions about the relationship between sleepiness and fatigue. First, Fatigue is an overwhelming sense of tiredness, lacking of energy and a feeling of exhaustion, associated with impaired physical and/or cognitive functioning [6] . Sleepiness is that of one's tendency to fall asleep, also referred to as sleep propensity. Secondly, their antecedents are also different, fatigue is caused by time on task and cognitive load and is influenced by emotional state and immune state.

And the occurrence of sleepiness depends on sleep quality, sleep duration, the circadian rhythms, and substances and CNS disorders. Finally, fatigue can be reversed by rest (e.g., time off task), while sleepiness can only be naturally (e.g., without the use of stimulants) reversed by sleep [7] . Thus, fatigue and sleepiness differ from each other in concepts, antecedents, and in the way that they are reduced. Furthermore, both of them have the same negative effects on production efficiency.

3. CONSEQUENCE OF SLEEPINESS

3.1. Information Processing

Decreases in activation of the brain regions which responsible for higher order cognitive abilities result in substantial deficits in information processing, particularly in the areas of processing speed, attention, learning and memory [8] . For this part, some scholars focus on sleepiness itself, while others focus on one of its immediate antecedents: sleep deprivation. Sleep deprivation results in deficits in information processing speed, which is evidenced by slower response times, increases in errors, and decreases the ability to correct errors. Moreover, the selective attention of individuals with sleep deprivation may also get worse, and compared to the later stage of information processing (e.g., response selection), the earlier stages of information processing (e.g., visual processing) will get a greater damage. In addition, sleep deprivation can decrease the level of activation in the hippocampus, which can affect the memory ability. In summary, sleepiness leads to poorer information process- ing through impacting on attention, processing speed, and memory. Sleepiness can interfere with the process of information processing by affecting the individual's attention, processing speed and memory. Information processing can be a mediator, and it will mediate the relationship between sleepiness at workplace and other variables. For example, sleepiness affects job performance through interference with information processing; it also affects individual attention, and eventually causing work accidents. However, the specific mediated interference process needs further empirical research.

3.2. Affect

Affect is a central construct in workplace psychology. Research has shown that sleepiness impacts individual affect. For instance, sleepy individuals have poor emotion regulation ability, and they can't deal with the negative emotions so that they fall into depression easily; sleepy individuals have more difficulties to moderate expression of happy and angry emotions; sleepy individuals are more easily distracted by negative emotional stimuli [9] . In addition, the antecedent of sleepiness has a direct impact on the affect. For example, poor sleep quality and sleep deprivation are related to a decrease in positive affect and an increase in negative affect [10] . So far, emotional variability (such as the decrease of positive affect and the increase of negative affect) has been studied by many scholars as the mediator between sleepiness and job satisfaction. Survey research showed that sleepy individuals are more likely to get angry, depressed, and have a low sense of accomplishment. Although the negative affect come from outside field of work, and they also have a negative evaluation of their work and lower job satisfaction [11] . Individuals with good sleep habits (e.g., sleep 6 hours or more a night on average) experience fewer depressive symptoms and experience a positive sense of purpose in life [12] . Therefore, affect is an important consequence of workplace sleepiness.

3.3. Job Performance

Job performance is a variable which is highly susceptible to individual sleepiness, and it is composed of task performance, adaptive performance and contextual performance. Task performance refers to the behavior and performance of individuals that can control and contribute to the achievement of organizational goals. Sleepiness impairs aspects of task performance related to reaction times, response accuracy, errors of omission, and lapses [13] . Adaptive performance refers to the behavior and performance of units within the organization (such as individual, group) that can effectively respond to the work demands in a dynamic environment [14] . Adaptive performance requires the capability to learn work tasks, technologies, and procedures, but sleepiness caused by sleep lacking may lead to decrements in learning or memory consolidation and to decrements in the ability to clear the old information, so that individuals are more difficult to adapt to the changing workforce [15] . Contextual performance refers to the support that individual provide to their colleagues and organizations as well as positive attitude towards work [16] . Because sleepy individuals are more likely to incorrectly recognize emotions such as anger or happiness, and social interactions rely on the accurate recognition of emotion, and individuals who are sleepy due to sleep loss may be more likely to incorrectly interpret social situations [17] . Therefore, the components of contextual performance that are dependent on affect and interpersonal skills are most likely to be affected by sleepiness.

3.4. Accidents

A workplace accident is a safety-related incident resulting in property damage, injury, or death [18] . When working, in order to avoid accidents, individuals must not be sleepy and keep vigilant at all times. Being sleepy will weaken the perception of visual stimuli, and delay the reaction time to increase the error prone, and ultimately lead to dangerous accidents [19] . Objective measurement of sleepiness resulting from common causes in the general population, such as insufficient sleep, has been found to predict police-verified automotive accidents [20] . In addition, the impact of sleepiness on the medical accident can't be ignored, and excessive work and lack of sleep will directly lead to medical accidents. Therefore, getting adequate sleep and proper rest is essential for doctors to reduce the medical accidents. Previous studies have investigated the sleep status of employees at night by self-report, and it reveals that sleep disorder at night will make employees have more serious sleepiness next day, and this kind of sleepiness can induce accidents [21] .

4. ANTECEDENTS OF SLEEPINESS

Now that we have discussed the negative effects that sleepiness brings to individuals and organizations. In this section, we will discuss the job demands (e.g., work schedules, time pressure, workload, and perceived control) that can impact a worker's experienced sleepiness. Through an understanding of the organizationally relevant antecedents of sleepiness, we can begin to develop interventions that will reduce the sleepiness of individuals within an organization.

4.1. Time Pressure, Workload, and Perceived Control

If the company demands individual to finish the excessive workload in a short time, then they will have a sense of pressure and anxiety, and further affect the quality of sleep, reducing sleep time, and ultimately increase the frequency of sleepiness at work. Åkerstedt, Knutsson, et al. (2002) found that keeping on thinking about work while after work predicted both disordered sleep and feeling tired once awakening [22] . De Lange et al. (2009) found that over time, cumulative exposure to high job demands and low perceived control was related to an increase in sleep-related problems (e.g., trouble falling asleep, waking up early in the morning) and that cumulative exposure to low job demands with high perceived control was related to the highest levels of sleep quality [23] . When exploring these relationships at the within-person level, it is found that employees were accompanied by a significant improvement sleep quality when they change from the higher job demands to the lower job demands. All in all, making the proper job demands will make employees develop good sleep habits, and have adequate sleep time, ultimately reducing the frequency of sleepiness at work.

4.2. Work Schedules

A large number of studies have indicated that there is a connection between the work length and work rotation to sleepiness. As we all know, non-traditional or flexible work arrangements are of great help to achieve employee performance and organizational benefits. But due to the changing of working time, these schedules often require individuals to work outside the traditional nine-to-five workday, which will certainly influence individual sleeping status [24] . Besides, Staff often have to work overtime in the evening or late night or on the weekends when they facing with emergency situations. For example, factory manager must come back to the factory to deal with the emergence; a heart disease specialist may be called up for emergency surgery in the late night. When the length of the workday is increased or the number of hours in the workweek is increased, which tends to reduce sleep hours that an individual needs per night. These schedules must shorten sleep duration and worsen sleep quality, and day by day it will cause serious sleepiness at work.

4.3. Job Rotation

Job rotation refers to the arrangement for staff to complete their workload in the day, evening or late night [25] , and some researches have shown that job rotation is the main reason of sleepiness [26] . Job rotation consists of two types. One is fixed shifts, in which an individual only works a single assigned shift of days, evenings, or nights; another kind is rotating shifts, in which an individual rotates among day, evening, or night shifts. Scholars found that rotating shifts will lead to greatest impact on sleepiness, especially end-of-day shifts and begin- of-night shifts [27] . Rotation work is bound to cause the disorder of the circadian rhythm, because it requires employees to work in normal sleep time [28] . Shift workers are awaking and working at their circadian nadir in alertness, but usually this time is suitable for sleeping. Shift workers have not sufficient time to recover from the severe sleep restriction due to excessive workload. Therefore, more job rotation is associated with more sleepiness at work.

5. INTERVENTION

So far, the construct of sleepiness at workplace is quite original. The research of the concept, the occurrence mechanism and the factor about sleepiness are still in the embryonic stage, and then there are still fewer studies on sleepiness at workplace. From existing researches, intervention for sleepiness at workplace can be divided into individual intervention and organization intervention. In the long run, the combination of the two will become the mainstream in the future.

5.1. Individual Intervention

On the individual level, previous studies have found that individuals often reduce their sleep time to engage in private activities, such as watching TV, playing games and playing mobile phone [29] . Full-time workers have no extra time to schedule their private activities, because they spend much time on work, so that they often reduce their sleep time to engage in private activities. Based on above, employees can reduce the arrangement of private activities, for example less time for watching TV, less time for playing games, less time for playing mobile phones, and go to sleep on time and keep enough sleep duration. That is, developing good sleep habits can contribute to reduce sleepiness. In addition, emotional regulation will also affect the individual sleep quality. Compared to the people in a bad mood, people in a good mood will have a higher sleep quality. Therefore, the individual must learn the appropriate skills to adjust their emotion, and positive emotion can contribute to the high quality of sleep. As is known to all, coffee is good for refreshing, a cup of delicious coffee can ease the sleepiness at work.

5.2. Organization Intervention

The potential of organizational intervention is great, but it is difficult to implement, because it's hard to get enough cooperation, time, money, and effort. As previously discussed, the important organizational factors that affect the sleepiness at work have overtime work, overload work, low control sense and job rotation. According to these, we can put four intervention measures. As follows, first of all, it is necessary to arrange moderate work time. The extra hours about work must be limited, and organizations can't blindly pursue the performance and ignore the potential drawbacks. Secondly, it is a key to arrange moderate workload. On the condition that staff completes their task with high quality on time, they won't be required to pay extra labor. Thirdly, giving more rights to employees is also very significant. Leaders can guide employees to work effectively and organization can provide the chance of train about working skills to them. Finally, arrangement rotation work according to personal preference. Because some people prefer to work at night while some others like to work during the day, and it is worth noting that employees must have adequate recovery time during the rotation. One possible intervention is that of providing the opportunity for napping. Although fewer than 5% of organizations currently have onsite nap rooms [30] . Napping may be able to reduce the effects of sleepiness and keep employees working hard.

6. DEVELOPMENT

At present, there are few researches on the sleepiness at work, and there are still many aspects not developed very well. This paper suggests that the current studies of the sleepiness can be strengthened in the following aspects.

6.1. Diversification of Research Methods

From the research methods, there has not been an empirical study about the sleepiness at workplace. In the field of sleep study, scholars have developed the sleep scale of various subjective rating, such as Epworth sleepiness scale, Stanford sleepiness scale, Pittsburgh sleep quality scale. Besides, they measure sleepiness by combining objective measurement of multiple sleep diagrams with multiple sleep latency tests. However, the scale of sleepiness at work has been not made up. Therefore, it's very urgent to develop the scale of sleepiness at work and create the study methods. Such as interview, case study, field survey and laboratory study; and we also can do a survey with the qualitative and quantitative method.

6.2. Developing the Moderate Variables

In the future, the moderate variables affecting sleeping need to be further explored. Individual differences may influence the relationship sleepiness with the work-relate variables. Physiology study shows that the sleep state will change with the age, and that personality traits (such as outgoing personality) can affect the outcome of sleep deprivation [31] . In addition, the different preferences for time types also affect the sleepiness at work. For example, night types may not perform at their peak during the day job assignments, and job design may be used to structure the workday to minimize sleepiness. But the moderated effect of preferences time types need the empirical study to verify.

6.3. The Influence of Cultural Factors and Studying in China

For the researchers and practitioners, the conclusion of the study in the west only has reference value, because different cultural backgrounds can bring different influential factors and intervention mechanism to sleepiness. Domestic theoretical and empirical researches on sleepiness at workplace are rare. With the development of economic globalization, developing domestic economy and the heavy working pressure, the sleepiness at work needs to explore in depth. In the future, we should face with the sleepiness challenges positively.

7. CONCLUSION

In summary, in order to avoid subsequent researchers confusing the similar concept with sleepiness, this paper clarified the concept of sleepiness at workplace, and respectively distinguished sleepiness at work with fatigue and narcolepsy. I believe that the following researchers will more accurately understand the concept of sleepiness at workplace. By reviewing and analyzing the previous studies, this paper delineated the causes and effects of sleepiness in the workplace. Among these studies, which main causes can mostly make employees fall asleep are time pressure, workload, perceived control, work schedules, and job rotation. It will lead to some negative results when employees being sleepiness at work, for example, poor information processing, more negative emotions, lower job performance, and increase in accidents. In a word, it is very important to study the sleepiness at workplace, especially for the manager. In order to maximize the interests of the company, managers must pay attention to the staff's sleepiness at work. In this article, we put forward some intervention measures from the level of individual and organization, and managers can learn from this article to deal with the problem of sleepiness at work. Because there are few researches on the sleepiness at work and still many aspects not developed very well, we put forward several research directions about the sleepiness at work, such as the diversification of research methods, developing the moderate variables. We hope that more researchers can keep on enrich- ing the theoretical and empirical research about sleepiness at workplace in the future.

CITE THIS PAPER

Xiang Jiao, Maolin Ye (2016) A Review of Researches on Sleepiness at Workplace. *Journal of Human Resource and Sustainability Studies*,**04**,155-161.

REFERENCES

1. Dou, W., Zhao, Z.X. and Huang, L.Q. (2005) Physical Effects of Sleep Restriction. Chinese Journal of Neuromedicine, 4, 748-751.

2. Dement, W.C. and Carskadon, M.A. (1982) Current Perspectives on Daytime Sleepiness: The Issues. Sleep: Journal of Sleep Research & Sleep Medicine, 5, S55-S56.

3. Uehli, K., Mehta, A.J., Miedinger, D., Hug, K., Schindler, C., Holsboer-Trachsler, E., Leuppi, J.D. and Künzli, N. (2014) Sleep Problems and Work Injuries: A Systematic Review and Meta-Analysis. Sleep Medicine Reviews, 18, 61- 73.

4. Mullins, H.M., Cortina, J.M., Drake, C.L. and Dalal, R.S. (2014) Sleepiness at Work: A Review and Framework of How the Physiology of Sleepiness Impacts the Workplace. Journal of Applied Psychology, 99, 1096.

5. Xiong, J.D. and Liu, W. (2009) Sleep Disorder. The People's Medical Publishing House.

6. Shen, J., Barbera, J. and Shapiro, C.M. (2006) Distinguishing Sleepiness and Fatigue: Focus on Definition and Measurement. Sleep Medicine Reviews, 10, 63-76.

7. Balkin, T.J. and Wesensten, N.J. (2011) Differentiation of Sleepiness and Mental Fatigue Effects.

8. Barnes, C.M. (2012) Working in Our Sleep: Sleep and Self-Regulation in Organizations. Organizational Psychology Review, 2, 234-257.

9. Bayard, S., Abril, B., Yu, H., Scholz, S., Carlander, B. and Dauvilliers, Y. (2011) Decision Making in Narcolepsy with Cataplexy. Sleep, 34, 99-104.

10. Bower, B., Bylsma, L.M., Morris, B.H. and Rottenberg, J. (2010) Poor Reported Sleep Quality Predicts Low Positive Affect in Daily Life among Healthy and Mood-Disordered Persons. Journal of Sleep Research, 19, 323-332.

11. Barnes, C.M., Ghumman, S. and Scott, B.A. (2013) Sleep and Organizational Citizenship Behavior: The Mediating Role of Job Satisfaction. Journal of Occupational Health Psychology, 18, 16.

12. Hamilton, N.A., Nelson, C.A., Stevens, N. and Kitzman, H. (2007) Sleep and Psychological Well-Being. Social Indicators Research, 82, 147-163.

13. Tucker, A.M., Whitney, P., Belenky, G., Hinson, J.M. and Van Dongen, H.P. (2010) Effects of Sleep Deprivation on Dissociated Components of Executive Functioning. Sleep, 33, 47-57.

14. Wu, X.H. and Yuan, D.H. (2010) Adaptive Performance: A Domain Remains to Be Further Studied. Advances in Psychological Science, 2, 339-347.

15. Hagewoud, R., Havekes, R., Tiba, P.A., Novati, A., Hogenelst, K., Weinreder, P., Van der Zee, E.A. and Meerlo, P. (2010) Coping with Sleep Deprivation: Shifts in Regional Brain Activity and Learning Strategy. Sleep, 33, 1465-1473.

16. Zhou, H. (2011) Effect of Psychological Capital on Task Performance and Contextual Performance. Forum on Science and Technology in China, No. 7, 122-128.

17. Van Der Helm, E., Gujar, N. and Walker, M.P. (2010) Sleep Deprivation Impairs the Accurate Recognition of Human Emotions. Sleep, 33, 335-342.

18. Smith, M.J., Karsh, B.T., Carayon, P. and Conway, F.T. (2003) Controlling Occupational Safety and Health Hazards.

19. Dinges, D.F. (1995) An Overview of Sleepiness and Accidents. Journal of Sleep Research, 4, 4-14.

20. Drake, C., Roehrs, T., Breslau, N., Johnson, E., Jefferson, C., Scofield, H. and Roth, T. (2010) The 10-Year Risk of Verified Motor Vehicle Crashes in Relation to Physiologic Sleepiness. Sleep, 33, 745-752.

21. Kling, R.N., McLeod, C.B. and Koehoorn, M. (2010) Sleep Problems and Workplace Injuries in Canada. Sleep, 33, 611-618.

22. Demerouti, E., Bakker, A.B., Nachreiner, F. and Schaufeli, W.B. (2001) The Job Demands-Resources Model of Burnout. Journal of Applied Psychology, 86, 499-512.

23. ?kerstedt, T., Knutsson, A., Westerholm, P., Theorell, T., Alfredsson, L. and Kecklund, G. (2002) Sleep Disturbances, Work Stress and Work Hours: A Cross-Sectional Study. Journal of Psychosomatic Research, 53, 741-748.

24. De Lange, A.H., Kompier, M.A., Taris, T.W., Geurts, S.A., Beckers, D.G., Houtman, I.L. and Bongers, P.M. (2009) A Hard Day's Night: A Longitudinal Study on the Relationships among Job Demands and Job Control, Sleep Quality and Fatigue. Journal of Sleep Research, 18, 374-383.

25. Kossek, E.E. and Michel, J. (2010) Flexible Work Schedules. Handbook of Industrial-Organizational Psychology, 1, 535-572.

26. Drake, C.L. and Wright, K.P. (2011) Shift Work, Shift-Work Disorder, and Jet Lag. Principles and Practice of Sleep Medicine, 784-798.

27. Tucker, P., Smith, L., Macdonald, I. and Folkard, S. (2000) Effects of Direction of Rotation in Continuous and Discontinuous 8 Hour Shift Systems. Occupational and Environmental Medicine, 57, 678-684.

28. Gumenyuk, V., Roth, T. and Drake, C.L. (2012) Circadian Phase, Sleepiness, and Light Exposure Assessment in Night Workers with and without Shift Work Disorder. Chronobiology International: The Journal of Biological and Medical Rhythm Research, 29, 928-936.

29. Basner, M. and Dinges, D.F. (2009) Dubious Bargain: Trading Sleep for Leno and Letterman. Sleep, 32, 747-752.

30. Fegley, S., Esen, E. and Schramm, J. (2010) Employee Benefits: Examining Employee Benefits in the Midst of a Recovering Economy.

31. Killgore, W.D., Richards, J.M., Killgore, D.B., Kamimori, G.H. and Balkin, T.J. (2007) The Trait of Introversion- Extraversion Predicts Vulnerability to Sleep Deprivation. Journal of Sleep Research, 16, 354-363.

16

CHAPTER

Research on Tendency and Behavior of the New Generation Employees Turnover

Ruifeng Yang

School of Business Administration, South China University of Technology, Guangzhou, China

ABSTRACT

In recent years, a large number of new generation employees entered the enterprise and gradually became the mainstay of enterprises, but the turnover rate is high and it brought heavy pressure and burdens to employers. Therefore, considerable importance has been attached to the research on the behavior of the new generation employees by the academic researchers and business managers. Unfortunately, so far, there is little theoretical research on the behavior of the new generation employees from the perspective of talent environment. This paper makes a theoretical review of the environmental factors that affect the turnover behavior of new generation employees and then designs an effective intervention mechanism to reduce the turnover rate of new generation employees and provides the reference for the enterprise managers to make policies of keeping employees.

Keywords: Talent Environment, The New Generation Employees, Mechanism for Turnover Intervention

1. INTRODUCTION

In recent years, Chinese leaders such as president Xi Jinping and Premier Li Keqiang have made a series of important speeches about the work of talents. Among them, the President Xi repeatedly emphasized the need to make good use of talents. He stressed that China should establish a much more flexible talent management mechanism in order to eliminate obstacles of the flow and the use of talent, to maximize support and help for scientific and technological personnel to innovate enterprises and strive to create a favorable environment for the growth of innovative talents. With the continuous improvement of China's market economic system and the accelerating pace of economic globalization, competition among enterprises has become increasingly fierce and corporate human resources have become the core competitiveness and important factor in sustainable development of enterprises.

After entering the 21st century, the new generation gradually transferred from the campus into the workplace and become the main force of enterprise development and competition. "The new generation employee" is a new vocabulary of management academia. In enterprise it mainly refers to those who were born in the 1990s and their age are in accordance with the "labor law" provisions of the staff [1] . They are a generation of witnessing Chinese higher education transfer from elite education to mass education and also they are the most creative and productive talents in the future. But they have great differences in the growth environment, ways of thinking and behavior characteristics from the employees in the past. The new generation employees' loyalty to the organization is weak, and so the problem of the new generation employee turnover has become the difficult point and the focus of human resource management. Of course, it also brings a lot of troubles to the organization and management. As the saying goes, "good birds choose wood and habitat". Therefore, enterprises must be combined with talent environment to retain talent. Based on this paper, from the perspective of talent environment, it is very important to find out the law of regional talent flow and new generation employee turnover and then put forward effective methods, which can not only help reduce the turnover of the new generation employees, but also improve the efficiency of leadership and management.

2. THEORY REVIEW

1) Employee turnover

Since the birth of modern enterprise management system, employee turnover has been a hot research topic. There are two main types of employee turnover: one is the employee's voluntary resignation, that is, the circumstance of active abdication, and the other is that the employee is disqualified or severely violates the company's rules and regulations, so the enterprise proposes to terminate the labor relationship between the two parties (Dessler, 2010) [2] . Historical experience shows that most of the turnover of enterprise core staffs is the initiative to leave, and they are often the key elements of the survival and development of enterprises. The employee turnover in this paper is mainly aimed at the situation of voluntary turnover. Voluntary turnover refers to the process that employees choose to take the initiative to leave the enterprise according to the enterprise and their own situation. The subject of employee turnover has already developed some research bases in the United States, Japan, Britain and some other industrialized countries. Price (1977) put forward the first influential model of employee turnover [3] , and then on the basis of previous studies, researchers put forward many different models from different sides to study the mechanism of voluntary turnover. There are three main turnover models in the history of turnover research, including Intermediary Chain Model (Mobley, 1979) [4] , Psychological Reason Model (Steers and Mowday, 1981) and the model of Price-Mueller (2000) [5] .

Intermediary Chain Model (Mobley, 1979) focused on the employee turnover intention, and then set up a model of employee turnover selection. Mobley stressed that leaving is a process of choosing, that employees intend to resign from the organization depend on four factors: job satisfaction, expected return of new job, expected return of original job, non-work values and occasional factors. Steers and Mowday (1981) proposed the model which depends on the basis of the models of Price and Mobley, seek to identify key variables that affect employees turnover and examine their relationship in the turnover process, and then expressed them in a conceptual model and block diagram. The model states that the following variables determine the leave or stay of employees in the organization. Firstly, job expectations and values affect the subjective attitude of employees to work. Secondly, subjective attitudes affect the intention to leave or remain, and also need to consider the influence of a number of non-working factors such as spouse work and family time. Moreover, the intention of leaving the organization leads to the actual separation behavior (Liu Shuzhen & Li Yougen, 2008). The Price-Mueller (2000) model is based on an overall theory of turnover. The core of this theory consists of a series of assumptions. The model points out that employee turnover is mainly determined by four variables such as environment variables, individual variables, structured variables and intermediate variables. In this model, the expected external environment condition of the employee is called "environment variables", and the expected working conditions of the employee are referred to "structured variables". Individual variables (including general training, participating decision-making, positive or negative emotions) and intermediate variables (including job satisfaction, organizational commitment and turnover intention) are the other two variables.

In terms of model of employee turnover, the researches of Chinese scholars are less than that of the western countries. Chinese scholars mostly focus on the review of foreign models, or imitate, optimize, revise and test the established models of foreign scholars. Ma Shujie and Chen Jingqiu (2003) divided the factors of staff turnover into social level (labor market and economic factors), organizational level (organizational factors and work factors) and individual level (demographic factors, psychological factors and family factors) [6] . Ma Jingui and Zhang Changyuan (2005) constructed the "offbeat" employee turnover model which named "push-pull model". He believes that the negative factors in the organization are the thrust of employee turnover, and social factors are the force of employees to stay in the enterprise [7] . Qian Shiru (2014) discussed the relationship between psychological contract and turnover intention by using empirical data [8] . Linghu Ke Rui (2013) argued that turnover behavior of the new generation migrant workers is mainly affected by environment variables, individual variables, structural variables and process variables. Wang Zhenyuan and Sun Shanshan (2014) pointed out that the external attribution of colleague turnover events and the strength of the relationship among colleagues have a positive effect on the negative emotions and turnover intention of employees, which have a negative impact on job satisfaction and organizational commitment. Therefore, the turnover of individual employees could lead to "dominos", which enterprises must pay great attention to [9] .

To summarize, first of all, domestic and foreign previous research on staff turnover still mainly focus on the individual and organizational factors. And thus less attention be paid to the macro factors of community, region and society, especially lacks the mechanism of interaction among individual employees, business organizations and social factors. Secondly, under different culture backgrounds, the employee's turnover thinking and behavior will be different. Therefore, the study on the departure behavior of Chinese employees needs to not only refer to the usefulness of foreign researches, but also to combine it with the actual situation in their own country.

2) The turnover of the new generation employees

In China, the new generation is more popularly known as the "post-80s and post-90s". According to the "labor law" adopted by China in 1994, in addition to the arts, sports and special processing units, the legal working age of working population is 16 years old. Thus, for now, the age of the new generation employees is between 16 and 36. According to the data from "Chinese statistical yearbook", the number of the new generation employees is about 248 million, which is huge and cannot be ignored (Fu Hong, Duan Wanchun, 2013) [10] .

Due to different historical backgrounds was born, the new generation workers have shown some new features compared with the older generation workers, including strong desire to learn, good sense of innovation, strong need for respect and self-actu- alization, high self-awareness, disregard workplace unspoken rules, loss of sense of responsibility, high turnover rate, and so on. In the face of complex social and economic environment, the new generation employees are better than the older staff at mastering knowledge, skills, accepting new things, and learning ability, but the new generation employees are often more anxious at the pursuit of faster self-realization and are more dissatisfied with the status quo. All this resulted into the turnover rate staying at a high level. According to a Chinese enterprises survey about employee turnover in 2007, the average turnover rate of the modern service industry, traditional manufacturing industry and high-tech industry is 20.4%, most of them are new generation employees. The turnover rate of employees with less than 2 years of work experience is 28% [1] . In 2015, the public data center conducted a comprehensive survey for the turnover rate of 2014. The result showed that graduates are lack of career planning, and the turnover rate at the first year of work is as high as 35.4%. And what is worse, the turnover rate of employees with less than 3 years of work experience remained above 30%. It could be argued that frequent job-hopping has become the occupational characteristics of post-90 generation employees. In addition, survey data also shows that the rate of voluntary employee turnover is much higher than the passive one.

The high turnover rate easily brings heavy financial and human capital loss to the enterprise, and the research on employee turnover intention is the focus of experts and scholars in recent years. Saporta and Farjoun (2003) argued that there is less chance of separation when employees have had better promotion opportunities within the organization. Duan Xingmin and Wang Yazhou (2005) summed up the seven factors that affect the turnover of knowledge workers by factor analysis, the first one is the employee's self development [11] . Wu Xiaoyi (2007) held that the new generation of employees have different characteristics and needs from older employees. Therefore, human resources management must adapt to the needs of the new generation of employees, and make a positive and forward-looking response and decision-making, so as to better attract, motivate and retain the talents of the new generation. Luo Exiang (2012) pointed out that the key reasons for the employee turnover are the family, salary, benefits, career development opportunities and training, working conditions, and so on. He proposed to proceed from the recruitment process, to establish a sound training and development system, and improve the salary and welfare system. Through the further improvement of staff working and living conditions, to meet the real needs of employees, improve the communication mechanism and so on to solve the problem of employee turnover [12] . In addition, there are a lot of scholars believed that the differences in leadership style will have a greater impact on the new generation employees [8] .

3) Talent environment

Marx holds that people create an environment, the same environment also creates the people. It can be seen that the growth and development of talents are closely related to the environment. This close relationship makes the talent environment a very important part in the study of talent management. Guan Peilan and Zhou Xinjun (2009) argued that talent environment refers to the organizational environment, social environment and natural environment for human's survival and development. It includes all kinds of external factors that influence the growth of talents [13] .

Peng Jianfeng (2004) pointed out that the competition of talent attraction, in essence, is the competition of talent ecological environment, and then he put forward that a good talent environment should have a series of indicators [14] . Talent environment has many unique properties. Luo Hongtie (2007) pointed out that the talent environment has the characteristics of systematicness and complexity, dynamism and stability, correlation and independence, humanity and nature [15] . There are many ways to divide the talent environment. According to the scope of the environment, the talent environment can be divided into small environment and macro environment. According to the boundary of the environment, it can be divided into the internal and external environment of talent. According to the nature of the environment, it can be divided into natural environment and social environment. According to the close degree of environment and material condition, it can be divided into hard environment and soft environment, or physical environment and spiritual environment. According to Maslow's hierarchy of needs, it can be divided into basic environment, dominant environment and driven environment. According to the nature of the environment on the role of talent, it can be divided into favorableness, adversity and normal. According to different talent subject system, it can be divided into micro talent environment, middle talent environment, and macro environment, and so on [13] [15] .

At present, there are many researches on urban talent environment at home and abroad, and at the same time there are many mature scales. However, the researches on the talent environment of enterprises are relatively few. Therefore, this paper comprehensively analyzes the internal and external factors that affect the turnover of employees. And then from the perspective of talent environmental intervention, to further study the turnover behavior of the new generation employees.

3. INTERVENTION MECHANISM

Talent environment has a great impact on turnover behavior, especially in the era of information, science, technology and mobile network. Li Wenyong (2004) suspected that the role of talent is always inseparable from the specific environment. Environmental attraction and exclusion mechanisms play an important role. Talent environment has multiple effects and functions on talent's decision about whether to leave or stay, such as the function of environmental contrast effect and decision making, the function of environmental guidance and value added, the function of conditional control and interactional effect, as well as global and local effects [16] . Hu Yang (2007) pointed out that the battle for talent developed from the initial policy of war, price war to the current environmental warfare [17] . Throughout the history of all time, when the environment is good, people will get together, and the enterprise will flourish. On the contrary, when the environment is bad, the talent will be discrete, the cause will decline. As the saying goes, "man struggles upwards, water flows downwards". For most of the employees, they hope that their own enterprise has a good talent environment in order to have a suitable living space and growth opportunities. As the deterioration of the environment will lead to soil and water loss, the deterioration of the enterprise talent environment will lead to the loss of talent. Job hopping, although it seems to be personal behavior, in fact, more often is the refraction of corporate behavior. Therefore, when the enterprise employee turnover, what managers need to do is not only to try to retain a person, but also to reflect on whether the deterioration of enterprise talent environment has happened. According to Levin's field theory, there is a field strength function relationship among individual performance, ability and environment. If a person works in a bad environment, it is difficult for him to develop his talents, and it is difficult to achieve good performance. In this case, individuals are often difficult to change the impact of the environment, and only choose to leave the environment and go to a suitable environment for themselves [18] . David (2015) drew the conclusion with the social synergy theory and founded that three factors such as society, organizations and individual are acting synergistically on the flow of talent [19] .

In fact, for the change of enterprise talent environment, it needs to pass the employee's perception and identity, and then to generate the intention of leaving, it may eventually lead to separations. The antecedents of organizational identification include three factors, individual factors, organizational factors and external environmental factors. An organization may have a lot of responses and interventions to the talent environment. Executives often also think that these policies have been implemented, but only when employees perceive the importance of these measures for them, these policies and measures will become meaningful (Amabile et al., 1996) [20] . That is to say, only by the staff perceived, can the talent environment intervention mechanism play a real role. Wright and Nishii (2006) proposed a link relation between employee turnover and the environment. This relationship includes the external social environment and the natural environment (the change is passive, but the organization can take the initiative to adapt), the internal environment of the organization (what can be controlled to the extent by organization) and perceived talent environment (perceived by the staff) [21] . Subsequently, they pointed out that the employee's turnover intention and behavior is the feedback of the perception of the talent environment and intervention measures. Identity or not can cause psychological changes, leading to changes in attitude and behavior. When employees perceive the current talent environment is not able to meet their individual goals and needs, they always tend to find and choose the better one to meet their needs, and thus generate turnover intention. Currently, in the context of the mobile Internet, the new generation employees have become more convenient, efficient, and low perceived cost for the perception of the talent environment. As a result, the information asymmetry between enterprise talent environment and employees' perception will become weaker and weaker. There is no doubt that this will bring great challenges and threats to the enterprise.

As for the relationship between organizational identity and turnover intention, a large number of literatures have shown that organizational identity has negative predictive effect on turnover intention, including direct effect and indirect effect. Abrams (1998) argues that organizational identity is significantly negatively correlated with turnover intention and has a direct impact [22] . The survey of Bamber and Iyer (2002) also shows that organizational identity will significantly reduce the tendency of employee turnover [23] . Xiong Mingliang (2008) pointed out that employees' organizational identification will make him stand by a common fate with the organization. As a result, employees are more likely to be more closely associated with the organization, thereby weaken turnover intentions [24] . Organizational identity has a moderating effect on the relationship between employee's job satisfaction and turnover intention. In other words, under the premise of the same degree of satisfaction, the turnover intention is low when employees have high organizational identification, and the turnover intention is high when employees have low organizational identification [25] . Edwards and Peccei (2010) constructed the structural equation model of organizational support, employee organizational identification, employee participation and turnover intention. The result showed that employee organizational identification has a negative predictive effect on turnover intention, and then has a direct and indirect impact on employee involvement and turnover intention through organizational identification and organizational support [26] .

Combined with the above analysis, this paper proposes a multi-path combinational intervention mechanism of talent environment. 1) The talent environment mainly refers to the organization environment, social environment and natural environment for the survival and development of talent, and the talent environment has a great impact on turnover behavior. 2) The new generation employees have special characters., and they pay more attention to the needs of high-level self-realization. Career attitudes of these employees vary widely and change rapidly. Especially in the context of mobile internet, they can more quickly and fully grasp the external information, which has a significant impact on employees' perception, identity and turnover intention. 3) According to the theory of social synergy, the synergy of social, organizational and personal factors leads to the flow of talents. The synergy of the talent environment and the characteristics of the new generation have led to the flow of the new generation employees. 4) The change of the talent environment needs to be perceived by the employees, and then to generate the intention of leaving, ultimately resulting in turnover behavior. 5) A large number of previous literatures show that the organizational identity of employees has a negative predictive effect on turnover intention. Based on the perspective of talent environment, this paper tries to find a preventive mechanism to solve the problem of the high turnover rate of the new generation employees (as Figure 1).

4. CONCLUSIONS AND IMPLICATIONS

Talent is the foundation of the enterprise development. Recently, with the disappearance of Chinese demographic dividend, an increasing number of enterprises begin to be trapped in recruiting and retaining talent. According to the data from multiple recruitment sites, the turnover rate of the new generation employees in China is more than 60%. Among them, nearly 30% of the staff quit frequently in a year with more than 5 times. How to reduce the turnover rate of the new generation employees, and improve their organizational loyalty and work enthusiasm, has become an urgent matter at the moment.

The talent environment of an enterprise is the basis for the survival and continuous improvement of talents. It can be said that a good talent environment is conducive to attract talents and beneficial to promote the sustained and stable development of enterprises, and finally achieve the scale effect of talent agglomeration. Therefore, if the enterprise wants to cultivate and retain the core employees of the new generation, and improve the enterprise loyalty of talents, reduce their turnover rate as well, enterprises should create an environment for the growth of talents, to meet the needs of their own development. That is to create the talent environment that enhances employee loyalty.

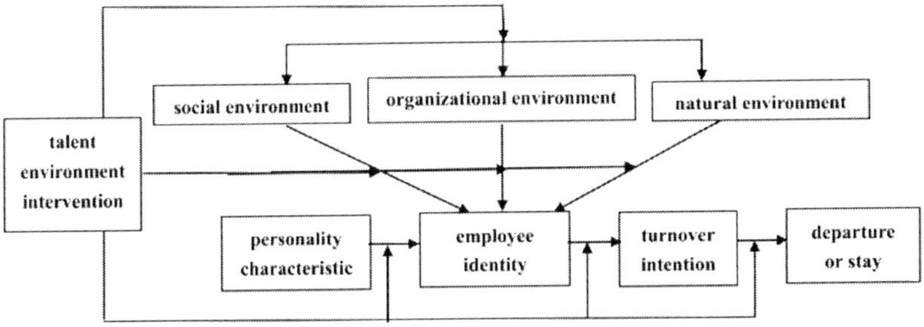

Figure 1. Intervention model of talent environment on the new generation employee turnover.

From the perspective of the intervention mechanism of talent environment to employee turnover, under the background of the new generation employees with special characters, we can start from the point of view of talent environment, and then conduct multi-stage and all-round response and intervention to employees from their adapting to the environment to their implementing behavior of leaving. To be more specific, only organizational environmental factors can be controlled by enterprises, but companies still have the influence on the individual factors and external environmental factors by taking a variety of matching measures.

1) Establish a rapid response mechanism for environmental factors that are not controlled by the organization, including natural environment and social environment

For enterprises, in terms of uncontrollable environmental factors, Li Xiangmin and Ren Yushi (2007) emphasized that uncontrollable factors include alternative employment opportunities, market environment, economic conditions, scientific and technological environment, social environment, political environment, and so on. Because these environmental factors are mainly caused by external factors, it is difficult for enterprises to control them. Especially the development of the science and technology in the field of communication and internet provides more convenient access to the acquisition and utility of information [27] . From a macro point of view, regional government and society create a good environment for talent, and provide a good public resource and service (for example, library, internet, university, convenient transportation and living facilities), which will significantly improve the organizational commitment of talent, and thus reduce their turnover intention and behavior. Because the government and the social services have a great impact on cross-regional mobility of talent, enterprises in the region not only cannot passively allow employees to perceive the inferior position of enterprise talent environment, but also cannot passively respond to the reduction of employee organizational identification and the formation of turnover intention. Therefore, the enterprise should not only increase its business income, increase government revenue, increase employee income, and effectively fulfill their social responsibilities, but also actively promote the sharing of information resources within and outside the organization. At the same time, enterprises should grasp the latest developments of the external market environment, establish effective early warning systems and fast response mechanism for the changes of the external environment, and then make timely readjustment. In addition, enterprises can establish a harmonious relationship with the government, enterprises and institutions. In this way, the enterprise can get more involved in the decision-making process of government affairs, timely feedback related problems, and give advices and suggestions in order to create a good social environment and natural environment.

2) Strengthen intervene mechanism of the environmental factors controlled by the organization

In terms of controlled environment, it mainly includes job satisfaction, organizational commitment, organizational justice, organizational culture and so on. Many researchers show that employees are more likely to leave their jobs when they are dissatisfied, low commitment, lack of organizational justice, and in the case of weak organizational culture. Growth environment, sustainable surroundings, professional environment, personal environment, and recreational environment have a significant effect on the turnover intention and behavior. In fact, for the construction of the talent environment, it is not enough for enterprises to formulate relevant rules and regulations. The most important thing is to make employees perceive and identify the company's concern of their growth and the praise for their efforts. In order to achieve a better effect, companies should try to change the ways of employee's perception, evaluation and identification. For example, organizational culture in the organization's internal environment is a symbol of enterprise development ability and core competitiveness, which is beneficial for companies to create a strong centripetal force, appeal and cohesion. Through mutual selection, competition, organizational culture, professional career design and the improvement of incentive mechanism, the enterprises will gradually create an environment that will be beneficial to the growth of human resources. In addition, job satisfaction, organizational commitment, organizational justice, and colleague relationship are also closely related to employee turnover. Therefore, the enterprise should combine its own resources with the characteristics of the new generation employees, use innovative and flexible management methods to achieve interaction with them to increase the recognition of new employees to the company, reduce turnover intention and accumulate a wealth of human resources for the enterprise.

Mobley (1979) points out that turnover intention is the most predictive variable of turnover behavior. As long as we take a test for turnover intention, we can predict the possible factors which affect the future turnover. And then we can improve the intervention measures, so as to reduce the occurrence of turnover behavior [4] . According to the mechanism of talent environment intervention, the enterprise should not give up easily at this time because the enterprise can also take many intervention measures. Enterprises can identify and eliminate unfavorable environmental factors, so as to determine the key factors that influence the employee turnover behavior. If the enterprise takes effective measures, it can be successful to retain the core talents. In fact, even the employee had made a turnover decision, as long as it has not been put into action, the talent environment intervention can still play a role. In the end, enterprises can use the exit interview to implement the intervention measures. On the one hand, try to keep the employees you want. On the other hand, former employee can also be an important resource for the enterprise, such as supporter of the enterprise, customer or business partner. To make it more important, by founding out the reasons of the employee's leaving the company, to identify problems and provide a basis for solving the problem.

3) Comprehensive and multi-stage interventions

Combined with the intervention model, we can draw the conclusion that leaders and managers should take a variety of measures to deal with the problem of employee turnover, no matter it happened before and after turnover. Based on the internal and external environment of enterprise, on the one hand, the managers should pay attention to the external environment, and be able to timely and accurately understand the needs of the new generation employees by the way of connecting social advanced enterprise and fashion trend. On this foundation, enterprises adopt targeted measures to retain key employees. On the other hand, enterprise managers should pay more attention to the internal environment of the enterprise, and use various methods of leadership and management measures to prevent and intervene the employee turnover that impenetrate the whole consider and decide process. Detailed measures can be: a) cultivate talents with the guidance of ability cultivation and career development; b) use scientific and reasonable performance evaluation and rewards and punishment system; c) customized incentive policy; d) excellent service for talent, including humanized management, flexible working hours, career planning and employee assistance program; e) create a distinctive corporate culture and a good working atmosphere; f) carry on the psychological management to the new generation employees.

CITE THIS PAPER

Yang, R.F. (2016) Research on Tendency and Behavior of the New Generation Employees Turnover. Journal of Human Resource and Sustainability Studies, 4, 325-336.

REFERENCES

1. Lin, L.P. and Wang, H.B. (2012) AHP Analysis on the Turnover Reasons of the New Generation Employees. Jiangsu Commercial Forum, No. 3, 132-134.
2. Dessler, G. (2010) Human Resource Management. Prentice Hall, Upper Saddle River, 612-650.
3. Price, J.L. (1977) The Study of Turnover. Iowa State University Press, Ames, 45-60.
4. Mobley, W., Griffeth, R., Hand, H. and Meglino, B. (1979) A Review and Concep-Tual Analysis of the Employee Turnover Process. Psychological Bulletin, 86, 517-532.
5. Price, J.L. (2001) Reflections of Determinants of Voluntary Turnover. Journal of International Manpower, 22, 600-624.
6. Ma, S.J., Chen, J.Q. and Wang, L. (2003) Research on the Reason of Employee Turnover. Human Resource Development of China, No. 9, 18-20.

7. Ma, J.G. and Zhang, C.Y. (2005) Cause Analysis and Countermeasures of Core Staff Turnover in Enterprises. Journal of Hunan Business College, No. 4, 42-44.

8. Qian, S.R., Xu, Z.Q. and Wang, L.Q. (2015) Study on the Relationship between Psychological Contact Breach and Turnover Intention among the New Generation Employees. Modern Finance and Economics-Journal of Tianjin University of Finance and Economics, No. 2, 102-113.

9. Wang, Z.Y., Sun, S.S. and Dai, R.L. (2014) Research of the Impact of Colleague Turnover on Stayer's Turnover Intention—A Mediated Moderating Model. Management Review, No. 4, 82-92.

10. Fu, H. and Duan, W.C. (2013) The Characteristics and Motivations of the New Generation Employees in China—Reflections from the New Generation Hot Events. Social Scientist, No. 1, 88-91.

11. Duan, X.M. and Wang, Y.Z. (2005) An Empirical Analysis on the Influencing Factors of Knowledge Workers' Turnover Intention. Human Resource Development of China, No. 5, 18-22.

12. Luo, E-X., Wang, J.Y. and Wu, X.Y. (2012) Analysis on Causes and Solutions of Employee Turnover in SMEs: Based on the Study of S Company. Science-Technology and Management, No. 1, 116-119.

13. Guan, P.L. and Zhou, X.J. (2009) Current Situation of Talent Environment in Wuhan and Its Countermeasures. To Promote the Rise of the Central China Expert Forum and the Fifth Hubei Science and Technology Forum in 2009, No. 1, 470-475.

14. Peng, J.F. and Zhu, X.D. (2004) On the Scientific Connotation of Talent Powerful Country and Its System Promotion. Chinese Talents Magazine, No. 1, 39-42.

15. Luo, H.T. (2007) Rediscussing the Principle System of Talents Studies. Journal of Southwest University (Humanities and Social Sciences Edition), No. 1, 107-110.

16. Li, W. (2004) Study on the Optimization of Talent Environment in Shandong Province Based on the Analysis of Talent Flow. Master's Degree Thesis, Tianjin University, Tianjin.

17. Hu, Y., Liu, G. and Li, L. (2007) Talent Environment Situation and Countermeasure State-Owned Enterprise under TBC. Journal of Hubei Correspondence University, 20, 16-19.

18. Lewin, K. (1951) Field Theory in Social Science. Harper & Brother Publishers, New York, 11-150.

19. David, G. (2015) Talent Management: Progress and Prospects. Human Resource Management Review, 4, 233-235.

20. Amabile, T.M., Conti, R., Coon, H., Lazenby, J. and Herron, M. (1996) Assessing the Work Environment for Creativity. Academy of Management Journal, 39, 1154-1184.

21. Wright, P.M. and Nishii, L.H. (2006) Strategic HRM and Organizational Behavior: Integrating Multiple Levels of Analysis. Cahrs Working Paper, Center for Advanced Human Resource Studies, Cornell University, Cornell, 43-66.

22. Abrams, D., Ando, K. and Hinkle, S. (1998) Psychological Attachment to the Group: Cross-Cultural Difference in Organizational Identification and Subjective Norms as Predictors of Worker Turnover Intentions. Personality and Social Psychological Bulletin, 24, 1027-1039.

23. Bamber, E.M. and Iyer, V.M. (2002) Big 5 Auditors' Professional and Organizational Identification. Auditing: A Journal of Practice & Theory, 21, 21-38.

24. Xiong, M., Sun, J. and Gu, L. (2008) A Study on the Correlation between Job Satisfaction, Organizational Identification and Turnover Intention. Journal of Business Economics, 6, 34-40.

25. Sun, J., Li, X. and Lin, C. (2016) Conceptual Evolution and Dimensional Measurement of Work Wellbeing. Human Resource Development of China, 38-47.

26. Edwards, M.R. and Peccei, R. (2010) Perceived Organizational Support, Organizational Identification, and Employee Outcomes: Testing a Simultaneous Multifoci Model. Journal of Personnel Psychology, 9, 17-26.

27. Li, X. and Ren, Y. (2007) Analyse on Employee's Turnover and Contributing Factor in Enterprise. Journal of Central University of Finance & Economics, 65-70.

Index